A Practical English Grammar
Exercises 2

Third edition

A Practical English Grammar
Exercises 2

A. J. Thomson
A. V. Martinet

Oxford University Press

Oxford University Press
Walton Street, Oxford OX2 6DP

Oxford   New York   Toronto
Delhi   Bombay   Calcutta   Madras   Karachi
Petaling Jaya   Singapore   Hong Kong   Tokyo
Nairobi   Dar es Salaam   Cape Town
Melbourne   Auckland

and associated companies in
Berlin   Ibadan

Oxford and *Oxford English* are trade marks of
Oxford University Press

ISBN 0 19 431344 1

© Oxford University Press 1961, 1962, 1964,
1972, 1975, 1980, 1986

Exercises 1 and *2* were originally published between 1961 and
1972 as ten individual books of exercises.

Exercises 2 first published as *Combined Exercises Volume II* 1975
Second edition 1980 (reprinted seven times)
Third edition 1986
Eighth impression 1990

Typeset in Great Britain by
VAP Group, Kidlington, Oxford.
Printed in Hong Kong

Preface to the third edition

This is one of two books of exercises designed to accompany
A Practical English Grammar.

To coincide with the publication of the fourth edition of the
Grammar the books have been altered in the following ways:

1 Some exercises have been transferred from Book 1 to Book 2
  and some from Book 2 to Book 1. Where exercises on similar
  structures appear in both books, those in Book 2 are slightly
  more difficult than those in Book 1.

2 The sequence of the exercises in both books has been
  rearranged to conform to the order of chapters in the *Grammar*.

3 Four exercises have been added to Book 1, bringing the total to
  100, and one to Book 2, bringing the total to 90.

4 Changes have been made to the text of some of the exercises,
  chiefly in Book 1.

5 The grading of the exercises has now been extended to both
  books. ■ means difficult, ◪ means moderately difficult and
  □ means easy. The gradings are printed at the head of each
  exercise.

6 The numbers printed after 'PEG' at the head of each exercise
  now refer to paragraphs in the fourth edition of the *Grammar*.

Answers have been supplied to most of the exercises. They are to
be found in the key at the end of each book.

Some of the exercises are in the form of a dialogue between two
people. Where the speakers are not named, a change of speaker is
shown by the symbol ' ~ '.

Preface to the third edition

Contents

Contents

14 Present, past and perfect tenses
PEG chapters 17–18

15 Future forms
PEG chapter 19

16 Conditionals
PEG chapter 21

17 Gerund, infinitive and present participle
PEG chapters 23–6

18 Unreal pasts and subjunctives
PEG chapters 28–29

19 The passive
PEG chapter 30

20 Indirect speech
PEG chapter 31

Contents

21 Time clauses
PEG chapters 32, 34

22 Phrasal verbs
PEG chapter 38

Key

11 **some, any** etc. and relatives

101 **some, any** and compounds, e.g. **somebody, anything, somehow**

☑ PEG 50-1

Insert **some** or **any**, making the appropriate compounds if necessary.

1 There's . . . milk in that jug.
2 She wanted . . . stamps but there weren't . . . in the machine.
3 I'm afraid there isn't . . . coffee left; will you grind . . . ?
4 Is there . . . one here who speaks Italian?
5 I'd like to buy . . . new clothes but I haven't . . . money.
6 There's . . . gin in the cupboard but there aren't . . . glasses.
7 They can't have . . . more strawberries; I want . . . to make jam.
8 . . . one I know told me . . . of the details.
9 Have you . . . idea who could have borrowed your bicycle?
10 I saw hardly . . . one I knew at the party, and I didn't get . . . thing to drink.
11 When would you like to come? ~
. . . day would suit me.
12 Are there . . . letters for me?
13 Don't let . . . one in. I'm too busy to see . . . body.
14 . . . thing tells me you've got . . . bad news for me.
15 I can't see my glasses . . . where.
16 We didn't think he'd succeed but he managed . . . how.
17 You're looking very miserable; has . . . thing upset you?
18 If you had . . . sense you wouldn't leave your car unlocked.
19 Scarcely . . . one was wearing a dinner jacket.
20 . . . one who believes what Jack says is a fool.
21 She put her handbag down . . . where and now she can't find it.
22 Will you have . . . pudding or . . . fruit?
23 Haven't you got . . . friends in Rome? I feel sure you mentioned them once.
24 Haven't you got . . . friends here? You should join a club and get to know people.
25 I see you haven't . . . maps. Would you like to borrow . . . of mine?
26 . . . one can tell you how to get there. (*Everyone knows the way.*)
27 Come and have supper with us if you aren't doing . . . thing tonight.
28 I . . . how imagined the house would be much larger.
29 All the salaries are being paid much later now; it's . . . thing to do with the computer.

30 He lives . . . where in France now.
31 You can't expect just . . . student to solve the problem. It requires a mathematician.
32 He's not very well known here but he's . . . one (*an important person*) in his own country.
33 Where shall we sit? ~
    Oh, . . . where will do.
34 Is there . . . one moving about downstairs? I heard . . . thing falling.
35 Is there . . . one living in that house? It looks deserted.
36 Would you like . . . thing to drink? There's . . . very good beer in the fridge.

102 Relatives: defining, non-defining and connective

◢ PEG 72–84

Read the following passage and then do the exercises on it. In answers to questions, use a relative clause.

Example:
Lucy was shaking the mat out of the window of the flat. Tom happened to be passing underneath. Suddenly Lucy's baby gave a cry and she dropped the mat. It fell on Tom and knocked his hat off.

    (a) What mat are we talking about?
    The mat that/which Lucy dropped or
    The mat that Lucy dropped or
    The mat that fell on Tom's head.

    (b) Who was Tom?
    The man who was passing underneath or
    The man (that/whom) the mat fell on or
    The man whose hat was knocked off.

1 Mr Black usually catches the 8.10 train. This is a fast train. Today he missed it. This annoyed him very much. He caught the 8.40. This is a slow train and doesn't reach London till 9.40. Mr White usually travels up with Mr Black. Today he caught the 8.10 as usual.
Mr White normally borrows Mr Black's paper to read on the train. As Mr Black was not there today he borrowed a paper from another passenger, Mr Brown.
(a) What is the 8.10?
(b) What is the 8.40?
(c) Who is Mr White?
(d) Who is Mr Brown? (*Connect him with Mr White.*)

Combine the following pairs of sentences into one sentence (one for each pair) using relative pronouns:
(e) Mr Black usually catches the 8.10. This is a fast train.
(f) Today he missed the 8.10. This annoyed him very much.
(g) He caught the 8.40. This doesn't get in till 9.40.

2 Mr Penn has two umbrellas, a brown one and a black one. Today he took the black one but left it in the bus on his way to work. When he was putting on his coat after his day's work, he saw a dark blue umbrella hanging on the next hook and took it, thinking it was his. Actually it belonged to Mr Count.
(a) What was the brown umbrella?
(b) What was the black umbrella?
(c) What was the blue umbrella?
(d) Who was Mr Count? (*Relate all your answers to Mr Penn.*)

3 Jack and Tom both wanted to go to Malta for their holidays. Tom liked flying so he went to the Blue Skies Agency. They booked him a seat on a tourist flight. Jack hated flying. He went to the Blue Seas Agency. They booked him a berth on the MS Banana. Jack enjoyed his voyage on the MS Banana, especially as he met a very pretty girl on board. She was called Julia.
(a) What is Malta? (*from the point of view of Jack and Tom*)
(b) What is the Blue Skies Agency?
(c) What is the Blue Seas Agency?
(d) What is the MS Banana?
(e) Who is Julia? (*Relate all your answers to Jack or Tom or both.*)
(f) Combine the second and third sentences in the passage into one sentence (*Tom . . . flight*).
(g) Combine the next three sentences into one sentence.

4 George and Paul were working on Mr Jones's roof. When they stopped work at 6.00 they left their ladder leaning against the house. At 7.00 Bill, a burglar, passed and saw the ladder. The house was now empty as Mr and Mrs Jones were out playing cards with Mr and Mrs Smith. Bill climbed up the ladder, got in through a first-floor window and went straight to the main bedroom, where he opened a locked drawer with the help of a screwdriver and pocketed Mrs Jones's jewellery.
   Just then Tom returned. Tom was a student. He lodged with Mr and Mrs Jones. Bill heard him coming. He climbed quickly out of the window, leaving his screwdriver on the floor.
(a) Who were George and Paul?
(b) Who was Bill?
(c) Who was Tom?
(d) Who was Mrs Jones? (*Mention jewellery.*)
(e) Who were Mr and Mrs Smith?
(f) What ladder are we talking about?
(g) What window are we talking about?

(h) What was the screwdriver found on the floor? (*Connect it with Bill.*)
(i) Combine into one sentence:
George and Paul were working on the roof. They left the ladder leaning against the house.
(j) Combine: Mr and Mrs Jones were out playing cards. They knew nothing of the burglary till they arrived home at 11.30.
(k) Combine: Bill's fingerprints were on the screwdriver. He was later caught by the police.

5 Ann is an au pair girl. She works for Mr and Mrs Green, in Tunbridge Wells. One day Mrs Green unexpectedly gave Ann the day off. (She thought that Ann was looking rather tired.) So Ann rang up her boyfriend, Tom, and said 'I'm coming up to London by the 12.10 from Tunbridge Wells. It gets into Charing Cross at 13.10. Could you meet me for lunch?'

'Yes, of course,' said Tom, 'I'll meet you at the station under the clock. We'll have lunch at the Intrepid Fox.' Tom usually goes to the Intrepid Fox for lunch.

On the 12.10 Ann met a boy called Peter. Peter was attracted by Ann and asked her to have lunch with him. Ann explained that she was having lunch with Tom. 'Well, I'll wait till he turns up,' said Peter. So Peter and Ann waited under a clock, with another passenger, Mary, who had come up to meet a boy called Paul.

Meanwhile Tom was waiting under another clock. When Ann didn't turn up he thought she'd missed the train, and asked a porter about the next train from Tunbridge Wells. 'The next train leaves Tunbridge Wells at 12.30,' he said, 'and gets in at 13.40. The next one gets in at 14.30.' Tom met the 12.30 but Ann wasn't on it. He couldn't meet the next train because he had to be back at work by 14.00. So he walked slowly towards the exit, wondering what had happened. Luckily the exit was almost directly under the other clock so he met Ann after all.

(a) Who are the Greens?
(b) What was the 12.10 from Tunbridge Wells?
(c) What was the 12.30? (*Connect it with Tom.*)
(d) Who was Peter? (*Connect him with Ann.*)
(e) Who was Paul?
(f) What is the Intrepid Fox? (*Connect it with Tom.*)
(g) Combine: Mrs Green thought Ann looked tired. She gave her the day off.
(h) Combine: Peter hated eating by himself. He hoped to have lunch with Ann.
(i) Combine: Tom had only an hour for lunch. He couldn't wait any longer.
(j) Combine: Mary's boyfriend didn't turn up. She ended by having lunch with Peter.

(k) Combine: Tom and Ann wasted half an hour at the station. This meant that they hadn't time for a proper lunch.

(l) Combine: Tom and Ann very nearly missed one another. This shows that you should never arrange to meet under a clock.

103 Relatives: defining, non-defining and connective

◼ PEG 72–84

Combine the following pairs or groups of sentences by means of relative pronouns, making any changes necessary.

1 You sent me a present. Thank you very much for it. (*Thank you very much for . . .*)
2 She was dancing with a student. He had a slight limp. (*two ways*)
3 I am looking after some children. They are terribly spoilt. (*two ways*)
4 The bed has no mattress. I sleep on this bed. (*The bed I . . .*)
5 Romeo and Juliet were lovers. Their parents hated each other.
6 There wasn't any directory in the telephone box. I was phoning from this box.
7 This is Mrs Jones. Her son won the championship last year.
8 I was sitting in a chair. It suddenly collapsed. (*The chair . . .*)
9 Mr Smith said he was too busy to speak to me. I had come specially to see him.
10 The man was sitting at the desk. I had come to see this man.
11 I missed the train. I usually catch this train. *And* I had to travel on the next. This was a slow train. (*Make into one sentence.*)
12 His girl friend turned out to be an enemy spy. He trusted her absolutely.
13 The car had bad brakes. We were in this car. *And* The man didn't know the way. This man was driving. (*Make into one sentence.*)
14 This is the story of a man. His wife suddenly loses her memory.
15 We'll have to get across the frontier. This will be difficult.
16 A man brought in a small girl. Her hand had been cut by flying glass.
17 The car crashed into a queue of people. Four of them were killed.
18 The roads were crowded with refugees. Many of them were wounded.
19 I was waiting for a man. He didn't turn up. (*The man . . .*)
20 Tom came to the party in patched jeans. This surprised the other guests. Most of the other guests were wearing evening dress.
21 The firm is sending me to York. I work for this firm. (*The firm . . .*)
22 The Smiths were given rooms in the hotel. Their house had been destroyed in the explosion.
23 I saw several houses. Most of them were quite unsuitable.
24 He wanted to come at 2 a.m. This didn't suit me at all.

25 This is a story of a group of boys. Their plane crashed on an uninhabited island.
26 They tie up parcels with string. This is so weak that the parcel usually comes to pieces before you get it home. (*The string . . .*)
27 He introduced me to his students. Most of them were from abroad.
28 He expected me to pay £2 for 12 eggs. Four of the eggs were broken.
29 He spoke in French. But the people didn't know French. He was speaking to these people. (*Combine these last two sentences only.*)
30 The boy was a philosophy student and wanted to sit up half the night discussing philosophy. Peter shared a flat with this boy. (*two ways*)
31 They gave me four very bad tyres. One of them burst before I had driven four miles.
32 She climbed to the top of the Monument to see the wonderful view. She had been told about this view.
33 I was given this address by a man. I met this man on a train.
34 The bar was so noisy that I couldn't hear the person at the other end of the line. I was telephoning from this bar.
35 A man answered the phone. He said Tom was out.
36 The horse kept stopping to eat grass. I was on the horse. This (*his continual stopping*) annoyed the riding instructor.

104 Relatives: non-defining and connective

◢ PEG 78–84

Combine the following pairs or groups of sentences, using relative pronouns.

1 Tom had been driving all day. He was tired and wanted to stop.
2 Ann had been sleeping in the back of the car. She felt quite fresh and wanted to go on.
3 Paul wanted to take the mountain road. His tyres were nearly new.
4 Jack's tyres were very old. He wanted to stick to the tarred road.
5 Mary didn't know anything about mountains. She thought it would be quite safe to climb alone.
6 He gave orders to the manager. The manager passed them on to the foreman.
7 She said that the men were thieves. This turned out to be true.
8 The matter was reported to the Chief of Police. He ordered us all to be arrested.
9 In prison they fed us on dry bread. Most of it was mouldy.
10 We slept in the same room as a handcuffed prisoner. His handcuffs rattled every time he moved.
11 We lit a fire. It soon dried out our clothes.
12 They rowed across the Atlantic. This had never been done before.

13 The lorry crashed into a bus-load of schoolchildren. Six of them were slightly injured.

14 She refuses to use machines. This makes her work more arduous.

15 I met Mary. She asked me to give you this.

16 The women prayed aloud all night. This kept us awake.

17 The river bed is uneven and you may be in shallow water one moment and in deep water the next. This makes it unsafe for non-swimmers.

18 Mary said that there should be a notice up warning people. Mary's children couldn't swim.

19 Ann said that there were far too many notices. Ann's children could swim very well.

20 He paid me £5 for cleaning ten windows. Most of them hadn't been cleaned for at least a year.

21 Jack, the goalkeeper, and Tom, one of the backs, were injured in last Saturday's match. Jack's injuries were very slight. He is being allowed to play in today's match. This is a good thing because the team hasn't got another goalkeeper. (*Combine the last three sentences only.*)

22 But Tom's leg is still in bandages. He will have to watch the match from the stand.

23 Mr White didn't get a seat on his train this morning. This put him in a bad temper, and caused him to be very rude to his junior partner. The junior partner in turn was rude to the chief clerk; and so on all the way down to the office boy.

24 On Monday Tom's boss suddenly asked for a report on the previous week's figures. Tom had a hangover. He felt too sick to work fast. (*Combine the last two sentences only.*)

25 His boss didn't drink. He saw what was the matter and wasn't sympathetic.

26 In the afternoon he rang Tom and asked why the report still hadn't arrived. The report should have been on his desk by 2 o'clock.

27 Tom's headache was now much worse. He just put the receiver down without answering. This was just as well, as if he'd said anything he would have been very rude.

28 Fortunately Ann, the typist, came to Tom's assistance. Ann rather liked Tom.

29 Even so the report took three hours. It should have taken an hour and a half.

30 I went to Munich. I had always wanted to visit Munich.

31 'Hello, Paul,' said Mr Jones to the headwaiter. The headwaiter's name was Tom. He said 'Good evening, sir,' without any sign of recognition. This disappointed Mr Jones. Mr Jones liked to be recognized by headwaiters. (*Omit the first sentence.*)

32 And this time he was with Lucy. He was particularly anxious to impress Lucy.

105 what and which

☑ PEG 81-3

Fill the gaps in the following sentences by using either **what** or
which. (When **which** is used it should be preceded by a comma
which the student must insert for himself.)

1 He didn't believe . . . I said . . . annoyed me very much.
2 In detective stories the murderer is always caught . . . doesn't
happen in real life.
3 He wasn't surprised at . . . he saw because I told him . . . to expect.
4 In hospitals they wake patients at 6 a.m. . . . is much too early.
5 There was no directory in the first telephone box . . . meant that I
had to go to another one.
6 I did . . . I could . . . wasn't much.
7 The clock struck thirteen . . . made everyone laugh.
8 I am sure that . . . you say is true.
9 We travelled second class . . . is cheaper than first class but more
crowded.
10 He didn't know the language . . . made it difficult for him to get a
job.
11 People whose names begin with A always get taken first . . . is most
unfair.
12 He played the violin all night . . . annoyed the neighbours.
13 When the mechanic opened the bonnet he saw at once . . . was
wrong with the car.
14 I didn't buy anything because I didn't see . . . I wanted.
15 They sang as they marched . . . helped them to forget how tired they
were.
16 I saw a coat marked down to £10 . . . was just . . . I was prepared to
pay.
17 He was very rude to the customs officer . . . of course made things
worse.
18 Show me . . . you've got in your hand.
19 Tell me . . . you want me to do.
20 The frogs croaked all night . . . kept us awake.
21 All the roads were blocked by snow . . . meant that help could not
reach us till the following spring.
22 You needn't think you were unobserved! I saw . . . you did!
23 She was once bitten by a monkey . . . made her dislike monkeys for
the rest of her life.
24 Some dairies have given up electric milk floats and gone back to
horsedrawn vehicles . . . shows that the horse still has a place in
modern transport.
25 She expects me to clean the house in half an hour . . . is impossible.
26 He poured water on the burning oil stove . . . was a crazy thing to
do.
27 Would you know . . . to do if you were bitten by a snake?

28 They turned on the street lights . . . made it suddenly seem much darker than it really was.

29 I don't know . . . delayed the train, but it went much slower than usual . . . made me late for my appointment.

30 He asked a question . . . I answered, and then he asked exactly the same question again . . . showed me that he hadn't been listening.

31 The crime was not discovered till 48 hours later . . . gave the criminals plenty of time to get away.

32 My neighbours on either side of me have painted their houses . . . of course only makes my house look shabbier than it really is.

33 The headmaster believed that children should do . . . they liked . . . meant, of course, that they didn't learn much.

34 I couldn't remember the number of my own car . . . made the police suspicious.

34 He said that . . . frightened him was the appalling silence of the place.

36 You will be punished for . . . you have done.

106 whatever, whenever, whoever etc.

☑ PEG 85

Fill each of the gaps in the following sentences with one of the following words: **however, whatever, whenever, wherever, whichever, whoever.**

1 . . . you do, don't mention my name. (*I particularly don't want you to.*)

2 He lives in Wick, . . . that is (*I don't know and don't much care.*)

3 Ann (looking out of the window): Bill's van—
Tom: It isn't a van, it's a station wagon.
Ann: Well, . . . it is, it's just been given a parking ticket!

4 You'll never escape. He'll find you, . . . you hide yourself. (*no matter where*)

5 . . . of you broke this window will have to pay for it.

6 . . . broke this window will have to pay for it.

7 The lift works perfectly for Tom, but . . . I use it, the doors stick. (*every time*)

8 I'd rather have a room of my own, . . . small, than share with someone.

9 . . . told you I'd lend you £500 was pulling your leg.

10 Shall I type it or send it like this? ~ . . . you like.

11 You're wanted on the phone! ~ I can't come now. Ask . . . it is to leave his number and I'll ring him back in half an hour.

12 . . . rich you are you can't buy happiness.

13 He's a phrenologist, . . . that is. (*I don't know.*)

14 We must finish tonight, . . . long it takes us. (*no matter how long*)

15 . . . it rains, my roof leaks.

16 Announcement: A box of dangerous drugs has been removed from the hospital dispensary. Will . . . took it please return it immediately?

17 Mothers in this district are not letting their children out alone till . . . committed these murders has been arrested.

18 He started half an hour ago and his car is faster than yours. . . . fast you drive, you won't catch him up.

19 Married man (to bachelor friend): You can do . . . you like in the evenings but I have to go home to my wife.

20 . . . my neighbour is cooking there is a smell of burning. (*every time*)

21 I hope that . . . left this rubbish here is going to clear it away.

22 We each draw a card and . . . of us has the lowest card does the washing up.
Or . . . has the lowest card.

23 If I say, 'Heads, I win; tails, you lose,' I will win . . . happens.
Or I will win . . . way the coin falls.

24 . . . used the bathroom last forgot to clean the bath.

107 Relative clauses replaced by infinitives

☐ PEG 77

Part 1   Replace the clauses in bold type by an infinitive or infinitive phrase.
> I have books **that I must read**.
> *I have books to read.*
> a peg **on which I can hang my coat**
> *a peg to hang my coat on*
> a form **that you must fill in**
> *a form for you to fill in*

1 We had a river **in which we could swim**.

2 The child is lonely; he would be happier if he had someone **that he could play with**.

3 I don't much care for cooking for myself; if I had a family **that I had to cook for** I'd be more interested.

4 Here are some accounts **that you must check**.

5 I've got a bottle of wine but I haven't got anything **that I could open it with**.

6 I have some letters **that I must write**.

7 I don't want to go alone and I haven't anyone **that I can go with**.

8 I don't like him playing in the streets; I wish we had a garden **that he could play in**.

9 We had to eat standing up because we hadn't anything **that we could sit on**, and the grass was too wet.

10 The floor is dusty but I haven't got a brush **that I can sweep it with**.

11 My files are all over the place. I wish I had a box **that I could keep them in**.

12 She said that she wasn't going to buy any cards; she hadn't anyone **to whom she could send cards**.

Part 2 Replace the clauses in bold type by infinitives.
He was the first man **who reached** the top.
He was the first man to reach the top.

13 He was the first man **who left** the burning building.

14 You are the last person **who saw** her alive.

15 My brother was the only one **who realized** the danger.

16 The pilot was the only man **who survived** the crash.

17 He simply loves parties. He is always the first **who comes** and the last **who goes**.

18 The Queen Elizabeth is the largest ship **which has been built** on the Clyde.

19 The last person **who leaves** the room must turn out the lights.

20 I was the only person **who saw** the difficulty.

21 He was the second man **who was killed** in this way.

22 Neil Armstrong was the first man **who walked** on the moon.

23 Lady Astor was the first woman **who took** her seat in Parliament.

24 The fifth man **who was interviewed** was entirely unsuitable.

12 Prepositions

108 Prepositions: **at, to**; preposition/adverb: **in**

☐ PEG 90, 93

Insert suitable prepositions in the following.

1 Could I speak . . . Tom, please? ~
  I'm afraid Tom's . . . work. But Jack's . . . . Would you like to
  speak . . . him?
2 How do I get . . . the air terminal? ~
  Turn right . . . the end of this street and you'll see it . . . front of
  you.
3 He started going . . . school . . . the age of five. So now he's been
  . . . school for ten years. He's leaving . . . the end of this year.
4 He goes . . . his office every day except Sunday. On Sundays he
  stays . . . home and works . . . the garden.
5 I think I left my umbrella . . . the bus. I'd better write . . . the Lost
  Property Office.
6 We arrived . . . the airport . . . good time for the plane.
7 Can I look up a word . . . your dictionary? I left mine . . . home.
8 Our train arrived . . . York . . . 6.30. Paul met us . . . the station.
9 Have you been . . . the theatre recently? ~
  Yes, I was . . . the Old Vic last night.
10 I'm returning . . . France . . . the end of this term. ~
  Are you coming back . . . England after the holidays?
11 He isn't living . . . home now, but if you write . . . his home they'll
  forward the letter . . . his new address.
12 I went . . . bed early but I couldn't get . . . sleep because the people
  . . . the next room were talking so loudly.
13 . . . first I found the work very tiring, but . . . a few weeks I got used
  . . . it.
14 There was an accident . . . the crossroads . . . midnight last night.
  Two men were taken . . . hospital. I believe one of them is still . . .
  hospital.
15 . . . the daytime the streets are crowded but . . . night they are quite
  deserted.
16 . . . first her father refused to allow her to go back . . . work; but . . .
  the end he agreed.
17 . . . the beginning of a textbook there is a preface, and . . . the end
  there is an index.
18 He went . . . sea . . . 18, and spent all his working life . . . sea. He
  retired . . . 56 and went to live . . . the country.

19 I saw Tom . . . the bus stop this morning but couldn't speak . . . him because we were standing . . . a queue and he was . . . the front of it and I was . . . the back.

20 I'll leave some sandwiches . . . the fridge in case you are hungry when you come in.

21 We'd better start . . . six, because climbing up . . . the gallery takes some time. I hope you don't mind sitting . . . the gallery. ~ No, of course not. When I go . . . the opera I always go . . . the gallery.

22 He is always . . . a hurry. He drives . . . a tremendous speed.

23 When he began speaking . . . English, she looked . . . him . . . amazement.

24 Write . . . ink and put your name . . . the top of the page.

25 We start serving breakfasts . . . 7.30. Shall I send yours up . . . your room, or will you have it . . . the restaurant?

26 He's always . . . a bad temper . . . breakfast time.

27 According . . . the guidebook there are three hotels . . . the town.

28 The pilot climbed . . . 5,000 metres and flew . . . that height till he got . . . the coast. Then he came down . . . 1,000 metres and began to take photographs.

29 I'm interested . . . chess but I'm not very good . . . it.

30 Who is the girl . . . the blue dress, sitting . . . the head of the table?

31 I couldn't offer him a room . . . my flat because . . . that time my mother-in-law was staying with us.

32 The train stopped . . . all the stations, and long before we got . . . London every seat was taken and people were standing . . . the corridors.

33 Shall we discuss it . . . my room, or shall I come . . . your office?

34 . . . my astonishment I was the only person . . . the bar. Everyone else had gone . . . the Casino.

35 The Loch Ness Monster is supposed to live . . . the bottom of the Loch and come . . . the surface from time . . . time.

36 You can't say that he lives . . . luxury. There's hardly any furniture . . . his room. He hasn't even got a desk to write . . . .

109 Prepositions and prepositions/adverbs: at, by, in, into, of, off, on, out (of), to, under, with

☑ PEG 90, 92–4, 95 G

Fill the gaps in the following sentences from the above list.

1 I'm going to Bath . . . Monday . . . Tom. Would you like to come . . . us? ~
Are you going . . . bus? ~
No, we're going . . . Tom's car.

2 I saw him standing . . . the queue but I don't know whether he got
. . . the bus or not.
3 How do you go . . . school? ~
It depends . . . the weather. . . . wet days I go . . . tube; . . . fine
weather I go . . . foot.
4 The car stopped . . . the traffic lights and wouldn't start again, so
the driver got . . . and pushed it . . . the side . . . the road.
5 Someone threw a stone . . . the speaker. It hit him . . . the head and
knocked his glasses . . . .
6 I want to post this . . . a friend . . . Italy. Will he have to pay duty
. . . it?
7 According . . . Tom, it is impossible to live . . . Paris . . . less than
£10,000 a year.
8 Are you . . . your own (alone)? ~
No, I'm . . . a friend . . . mine.
9 You ought to be ashamed . . . yourself for coming . . . my nice clean
kitchen . . . muddy boots.
10 Children get presents . . . Christmas and . . . their birthdays.
11 How would we get . . . . . . (escape from) this room if the hotel were
. . . fire?
12 He arrived . . . London . . . 6 p.m. . . . a foggy November day. We
often have fogs . . . November.
13 The man . . . his back . . . the camera is the Minister . . .
Agriculture.
14 How do I get . . . the Public Library? ~
Go . . . the end . . . this street and turn right; turn left . . . the next
traffic lights and then take the second turning . . . your right. This
will bring you . . . Brook Street, and you'll find the library . . . your
left.
15 Alternatively you could get a 14 bus . . . this stop and ask the
conductor to tell you where to get . . . (alight).
16 The boy was leaning against the wall . . . his hands . . . his pockets.
'Take your hands . . . . . . your pockets,' said his father sharply.
17 As she was getting . . . . . . the car one . . . her buttons fell . . . .
Although we were . . . a hurry she insisted . . . stopping to look for
it.
18 Mr Jones is very keen . . . punctuality. His lessons start dead . . .
time and you get . . . terrible trouble if you're late.
19 The man . . . the pipe and red hair is the brother . . . the girl . . .
blue.
20 Don't leave your luggage . . . the corridor. It'll be . . . everyone's
way. Bring it . . . the compartment and put it . . . the rack.
21 He sits . . . his desk all day . . . his head . . . his hands. It gets . . .
my nerves.
22 . . . mistake I opened Mary's letter instead . . . my own. She was
very angry . . . me and said that I'd done it . . . purpose.
23 I buy a newspaper . . . my way . . . the station and read it . . . the
train. By the time I get . . . London I've read most . . . it.

24 He was charged . . . driving while . . . the influence . . . alcohol.
25 People who drop litter . . . the pavements are liable . . . a fine . . . £50.
26 He accused me . . . selling secret information . . . the enemy.
27 You look worried. Are you . . . some sort . . . trouble? ~
   Yes, . . . a way. I'm . . . debt and my creditors want to be paid . . . the end . . . the month, and . . . the moment I haven't any money . . . the bank.
28 The car skidded . . . the tree, the windscreen was smashed and the driver was cut . . . the face . . . splinters . . . glass.
29 Four people were injured . . . the demonstration. Three . . . them are students . . . the university, the fourth is here . . . holiday. That's him over there . . . his arm . . . plaster.
30 This picture was painted . . . Picasso; and there's another Picasso . . . the opposite wall.
31 The horse stopped suddenly and the rider fell . . . . He couldn't get . . . again without help and there was no one . . . sight.
32 The children hastily changed . . . bathing things and jumped . . . the river . . . shouts of delight.
33 We'll have to go . . . car; we can't go . . . bus . . . account . . . the bus strike.
34 Divers breathing a mixture . . . helium and oxygen can work . . . a depth . . . 100 metres.
35 I'm tired . . . working . . . the suburbs and I've asked to be transferred . . . our central branch.
36 Can I have Monday . . . ? *or* Can I have a holiday . . . Monday?
   I want to go . . . my grandson's wedding.

110 Prepositions and prepositions/adverbs: at, by, during, for, from, in, of, on, over, since, till, under, with

◪ PEG 87, 90–1

Insert suitable words, choosing them from the above list.

1 I've lived . . . this street . . . ten years.
2 He has lived . . . 101 Cornwall Gardens . . . 1966.
3 . . . the age . . . 18 he was sent to prison . . . theft.
4 He was . . . prison . . . two years. . . . that time he became interested . . . pigeons.
5 There is a parcel of books . . . you . . . the table . . . the hall. ~
   Oh, they must be . . . my brother. He always sends me books . . . my birthday.
6 We heard that Bill wasn't . . . arrest but was helping the police . . . their enquiries. The police are interested . . . a bank robbery which took place . . . Bill's last holidays.

7 *Much Ado About Nothing* is . . . Shakespeare, and you'll find more
. . . his plays . . . the bookcase . . . the corner.

8 As the child was too young to travel . . . herself, they arranged . . .
her to travel . . . the care . . . a friend of the family.

9 Have you heard . . . John . . . his return? ~
Yes, I had a letter . . . Monday. He's thinking . . . going back . . .
America.

10 He was ill . . . a week and . . . that week his wife never left his side.

11 Aren't you coming . . . us? ~
No, I'm waiting . . . Tom. ~
But he won't be ready . . . some time. ~
I'm not . . . a hurry. I'll wait till he's ready.

12 I'm very sorry . . . being late. It was good . . . you to wait . . . me.

13 Passengers may leave bulky articles . . . the stairs . . . the
conductor's permission, but the bus company will not be responsible
. . . such articles.

14 Remember to be . . . good time . . . the opera because if you're late
they won't let you . . . . . . the end . . . the act.

15 I want two seats . . . *Romeo and Juliet* . . . Friday night.

16 . . . spite . . . the heat he refused to take . . . his coat.

17 He was wounded . . . the shoulder . . . a bullet fired . . . an upstairs
window.

18 While . . . their way from the coast . . . the mountains they were
attacked . . . a jaguar.

19 What platform does the train . . . York leave . . . ? ~
Platform 8, and you'd better hurry. It'll be leaving . . . a minute.

20 He invited me to dinner . . . his club and . . . the meal he asked me
. . . advice about his investments.

21 He's not independent . . . any means. He depends . . . his father . . .
everything.

22 He has a picture . . . Picasso (*Picasso painted the picture*) and he can't
decide whether to hang it . . . the hall . . . the right as you come . . . ,
or . . . the sitting room . . . the fireplace.

23 I'm tired . . . hearing about Tom and his Picasso. He can hang it . . .
his garage . . . all I care!

24 He said he was . . . debt and asked me . . . a loan . . . £50.

25 What's the cheapest way . . . getting . . . London . . . Edinburgh? ~
Well, you could hitch hike there . . . next . . . nothing, or you could
go . . . coach . . . about £20.

26 I was horrified . . . his appearance. He looked as if he hadn't slept
. . . weeks.

27 When he gets back . . . the office he expects his wife to meet him
. . . the door . . . his slippers, and have a hot meal waiting . . . him.

28 Yesterday the children went . . . a walk and didn't get back . . .
10 p.m. Their mother was furious . . . them . . . coming in so late.

29 Passengers who get . . . or . . . a bus (*i.e. who board or leave it*) except
. . . the official stops do so . . . their own risk.

30 The rows are lettered . . . A to T, beginning . . . the row nearest the stage. So if Tom is sitting . . . B26, and Jack is sitting . . . C26, Tom will be directly . . . front . . . Jack.

31 What's the best way . . . cooking a lobster? ~
Cook it . . . boiling salted water, and serve it cold . . . mayonnaise.

32 He was fined . . . parking his car . . . a no-parking area.

33 He opened the door . . . a rusty key and went down the steps . . . the cellar, followed by Bill . . . a torch.

34 The adults worked . . . 6 a.m. to 6 p.m., . . . an hour . . . lunch. Boys . . . 18 were not supposed to start . . . 8 a.m. (*earlier than 8 a.m.*)

35 He died . . . heart failure . . . Tuesday night. His wife is still suffering . . . shock.

36 The house is . . . fire! Send . . . the Fire Brigade!

111 Prepositions and prepositions/adverbs:
about, at, away (adverb only), **by, for, from, in, into, on, out, to, under, up, with, over**

☑ PEG 96–7

Insert a suitable word in the following sentences.

1 He insisted . . . seeing the documents.

2 They succeeded . . . escaping . . . the burning house.

3 I am not interested . . . anything that happened . . . the very remote past.

4 The children are very fond . . . swimming. . . . summer they spend most . . . their time . . . the water.

5 How are you getting . . . at school? ~
I'm getting . . . all right except . . . English. I'm very bad . . . English; I'll have to work harder . . . it, and spend more time . . . it.

6 Paul goes . . . school . . . you, doesn't he? How's he getting . . . . his English? *or* How's his English getting . . . ? ~

7 I don't know. We're not . . . the same class. But he gets . . . . the other students all right. He has heaps . . . friends.

8 There is no point . . . going . . . car if we can't park near the theatre.

9 She made a point . . . coming late so that everyone would look . . . her.

10 It never occurred . . . me to ask him . . . proof . . . his identity.

11 . . . first, driving on the left is confusing, but you'll soon get used . . . it.

12 I've heard such a lot . . . him that I'm looking forward . . . seeing him very much.

13 He was so absorbed . . . his work that when I came . . . , he didn't even look . . . (*raise his head*)

14 I'm sorry . . . Tom. (*I pity him.*) He has worked . . . Brown and Company . . . ten years and now the firm has been taken . . . by Jones Ltd, and they're going to dismiss him.

15 I'm sorry . . . being late . . . Monday. *Or* I'm sorry . . . Monday.

16 The complete set . . . books can be ordered . . . £10 . . . Jones and Company. (*Jones and Company will send them to you if you write enclosing £10.*)

17 I'm waiting . . . my friend. He'll be here . . . a moment.

18 I see . . . today's paper that you need a secretary . . . a knowledge of French. I should like to apply . . . the post.

19 You can't rely . . . him. He's almost always late . . . appointments.

20 If you do not comply . . . the traffic regulations you will get . . . trouble . . . the police.

21 Wine is good . . . you, but it is expensive . . . England because there is a fairly high tax . . . it.

22 . . . fairy stories, stepmothers are always unkind . . . their stepchildren; but my stepmother has always been very good . . . me.

23 He was so infuriated . . . the play that he walked . . . (*left the theatre*) . . . the middle . . . the first act.

24 My au pair girl takes care . . . my little boys (looks . . . them) . . . the afternoons. She's very good . . . children. (*She can manage them well.*)

25 He threw stones . . . his attackers, trying to drive them . . . .

26 I threw the ball . . . Peter, but instead . . . throwing it back . . . me, he ran . . . and hid it.

27 I object . . . being kept waiting. Why can't you be . . . time?

28 '. . . accordance . . . the wishes . . . my people,' the president said, 'I am retiring . . . public life.'

29 This regulation doesn't apply . . . you. You are . . . (*less than*) 18.

30 I'm not exactly keen . . . cooking; but I prefer it . . . washing up. (*Washing up is worse than cooking.*)

31 I was so afraid . . . missing the train that I took a taxi . . . the station.

32 What . . . taking the day . . . and spending it . . . the seaside?

33 I don't object . . . lending you my pen, but wouldn't it be better if you had a pen . . . your own?

34 Don't ask the office . . . information. I will provide you . . . all the information you need.

35 I disapprove . . . people who make all sorts . . . promises which they have no intention . . . keeping.

36 I was . . . the impression that I had paid you . . . the work you did . . . me.

112 Use and omission of prepositions

■ PEG 88-9

Insert a preposition if necessary. Choose from **at, by, for, in, of, on, past, till/until, to, with.**

1 He asked . . . his father . . . money.
2 They paid . . . me . . . the books.
3 I thought he would offer . . . Ann the job, but he offered it . . . me.
4 Keep . . . me a place, and keep a place . . . Ann too.
5 They showed . . . us photographs . . . their baby.
6 Buying presents . . . children is sometimes very difficult. . . . the end I bought a kite . . . Tom and a torch . . . Ann.
7 Pass the salt . . . your father, Peter, and pass . . . me the pepper, please.
8 When you have lunch . . . a restaurant, who pays . . . the bill? ~ Oh, each . . . us pays . . . what he has had.
9 Paul's a pianist. He sometimes plays . . . us . . . the evening. Last night he played some Chopin.
10 I think I'll be able to find . . . Ann a job. ~ Could you find a job . . . me, too?
11 He sold the picture . . . an American dealer . . . £5,000.
12 He promised . . . us a share . . . the profits.
13 He built a very nice house . . . Jack . . . only £50,000. I wonder what sort . . . house he would build . . . me . . . £30,000.
14 She is knitting socks . . . refugees. I wish she'd knit . . . me some socks.
15 Sitting . . . the floor isn't exactly comfortable. Throw . . . me a cushion, please, Ann.
16 If you are going . . . the Post Office, could you buy . . . me a book . . . stamps?
17 If you write . . . me a song I'll sing it . . . the school concert. I'll get Paul to accompany . . . me . . . the guitar.
18 Could you lend . . . us your lawnmower, please? ~ I'm afraid you'll have to ask . . . someone else to lend . . . you one. We've lent ours . . . Mr Jones and he always keeps it . . . ages.
19 I thought you'd be late . . . dinner, so I ordered some sandwiches . . . you; they're . . . the bar. I haven't paid . . . them: you can pay . . . the barman.
20 I explained . . . him that it was the custom . . . England to wash one's car at the weekend.
21 I described the machine . . . him and asked . . . him if he could make . . . me one like it.
22 She told . . . us that she'd been attacked . . . the street. We asked . . . her to describe her attacker and she said he was a tall man . . . a limp.
23 He told . . . them to wait . . . him . . . the bridge.
24 I cannot repeat . . . you what she said . . . me . . . confidence.

25 The headmaster warned . . . me to work harder. What did he say . . . you, Jack?
26 He advised . . . the strikers to go back . . . work. They received his advice . . . shouts . . . contempt.
27 They don't allow . . . you to smoke . . . cinemas . . . France.
28 He told lies . . . the police. ~
   I'm not surprised. He told . . . me a pack . . . lies yesterday.
29 This film reminds . . . me . . . my childhood.
30 I rely . . . you to remind . . . me to pay Jack . . . the books he bought . . . me.
31 We must try to get . . . home . . . time . . . tea.
32 We didn't reach Berlin . . . after dark, and had some difficulty . . . finding our hotel.
33 If we say 'The manager showed . . . us to our room,' we mean that he led . . . us . . . the door. If we say, 'He showed . . . us the room,' we mean that he entered . . . the room . . . us.
34 I read . . . him the report. He listened . . . me . . . amazement.
35 He ordered . . . us to give . . . him all the maps . . . our possession.
36 He suggested . . . me that we should offer to pay . . . her . . . dollars.

---

113 till/until, to, for, since, then, after, afterwards

Part 1   till, until, to

☑ PEG 92 A, 93

Insert **till**, **until**, **to** where appropriate.

1 Go on . . . the crossroads.
2 Go on . . . you see a church on your right.
3 We work from 9 a.m. . . . 6 p.m.
4 Start now and go on . . . I tell you to stop.
5 I'm going to wait . . . it stops raining.
6 You'll have to stay in bed . . . your temperature goes down.
7 The library is open from 10 . . . 4 o'clock.
8 This train goes . . . York.
9 We have lunch from 12.00 . . . 1.00. Then we start again and go on . . . 5.30.
10 Go back . . . the hotel and wait there . . . I call for you.
11 I'm not going for a walk, I'm only going . . . the bank. ~
   Then you'd better wait . . . the bank opens.
12 If you're going . . . the Post Office would you post a letter for me? ~
   Yes, of course; but it won't go . . . tomorrow.

Part 2 **for, since** (see also Exercise 122)

◪ PEG 91, 187

Insert **for** or **since**.

1 It's a long time . . . I had a good meal. *Or* I haven't had a good meal
. . . ages.
2 I've been waiting for Tom . . . 6.00; I wonder if he's lost his way.
3 Ever . . . his accident he's been afraid of flying.
4 I haven't seen Tom . . . we left school.
5 The astronauts have already been in orbit . . . two days.
6 . . . last year the noise has become very much worse.
7 I've had this toothache . . . the last week.
8 Her husband died last year, and . . . then she has been supporting
the family. *Or* She's been supporting the family . . . the last year.
9 It's three years . . . I did any skiing. *Or* I haven't done any skiing
. . . three years.
10 The windows haven't been cleaned . . . weeks.
11 He has been missing . . . 48 hours.
12 . . . last year we haven't been allowed to park here.

Part 3 **then, after, afterwards**

◪ PEG 92 B

Insert **then, after,** or **afterwards**.

1 We had tea and . . . went for a walk. *Or* . . . tea we went for a walk.
2 We'll have watercress soup to start with. What would you like . . .
that?
3 . . . waiting for half an hour he went home in disgust. . . . (*later on*)
he was sorry he hadn't waited longer.
4 I give all the guests breakfast; . . . I have my own.
5 First you loosen the nuts, . . . you jack up the car, . . . you take the
wheel off.
6 He listened at the keyhole for a minute; . . . he opened the door
cautiously.
7 University administrators sometimes appear more important than
scholars; but the administrators will not be remembered . . . their
death.
8 'Put your toys away,' said his mother, 'and . . . we'll have tea.'
9 In the story, the Princess married the Prince and they lived happily
ever . . . .
10 He wound up the clock, set the alarm for 5.00, . . . got into bed and
fell asleep.
11 He poured the brandy into a glass, warmed it in his hands a little,
. . . drank it slowly.

Prepositions

12 I covered the pudding with cream and decorated it with cherries. ~
    And . . . ? ~
    . . . we ate it, of course.
13 For years . . . people remembered that terrible night.
14 I spoke angrily; . . . (*some time later*) I regretted my words.
15 He looked round to see that nobody was watching; . . . he took a
    piece of bent wire and began trying to open the door.
16 First you say 'Yes', and . . . you say 'No'. You're an impossible
    person to make plans with.

13 Auxiliaries + perfect infinitives

114 Auxiliaries + perfect infinitives

■ PEG 255

Use the perfect infinitive of the verbs in brackets with a suitable auxiliary verb:

I've never seen a London policeman. ~
You (see) one! You've been in London a week already!
You must have seen one.

Note that **not** placed before the verb in brackets refers to the auxiliary verb:

I heard their phone ringing. ~
You (not hear) their phone ringing. They haven't got a phone.
You couldn't have heard their phone ringing.

1 Jack: I've finished.
Ann: But you were only half way through when I went to bed. You (work) all night!

2 The instructions were in French. I translated them into English for him. ~
You (not translate) them. He knows French.

3 Tom: What's happened to Jack? We said 7.30 and now it's 8.00 and there's no sign of him.
Ann: He (forget) that we invited him. He is rather forgetful. I (telephone) him yesterday to remind him. (*It was foolish of me not to telephone.*)

4 Tom: Or he (get) lost. He hasn't been to this house before. I (give) him directions. (*I didn't give him directions, which was stupid of me.*)
Ann: Or he (have) a breakdown or a puncture.
Tom: A puncture (not delay) him so long.

5 Ann: Or he (stop) for a drink and (get) involved in an argument. Jack's arguments go on for hours!
Tom: Or he (run) out of petrol. Perhaps we'd better go and look for him.

6 You (not feed) the bears! (*It was foolish of you to feed them.*) Now they'll be angry if the next campers don't feed them too.

7 Nobody has been in this house for a month. ~
Nonsense! Here's last Monday's paper in the wastepaper basket; somebody (be) here quite recently.

8 Two of the players spent the night before the big match at a party. ~
   That was very foolish of them. They (go) to bed early.

9 He says that when walking across Kensington Gardens he was attacked by wolves. ~
   He (not be attacked) by wolves. There aren't any wolves in Kensington. He (see) some Alsatian dogs and (think) they were wolves.

10 I waited from 8.00 to 8.30 under the clock and he says he waited from 8.00 to 8.30 under the clock, and we didn't see each other! ~
   You (wait) under different clocks! There are two in the station, you know.

11 He set off alone a month ago and hasn't been heard of since. ~
   He (fall) into a river and (be eaten) by crocodiles. ~
   Or (be kidnapped) by tribesmen. ~
   Or (catch) fever and (die) of it.

12 We (start) yesterday (*this was the plan*); but the flight was cancelled because of the fog, so we're still here, as you see.

13 Mary to Ann, who has just toiled up six flights of stairs: You (not walk) up! You (come) up in the lift. It's working now.

14 I left my car here under the No Parking sign; and now it's gone. It (be) stolen! ~
   Not necessarily. The police (drive) it away.

15 He had two bottles of Coke and got frightfully drunk. ~
   He (not get) drunk on Coke. He (drink) gin with it.

16 He was riding a bicycle along the motorway when he was hit by the trailer of a lorry. These big lorries are very dangerous. ~
   Perhaps, but Paul (not ride) a bicycle along the motorway; bicycles are not allowed.

17 I've lost one of my gloves! ~
   The puppy (take) it. I saw him running by just now with something in his mouth. It (be) your glove.

18 We've run out of petrol! ~
   I'm not surprised. I noticed that the tank was nearly empty when we left home. ~
   You (tell) me! We (get) petrol at the last village. Now we've got a 10-mile walk!

19 If the ground hadn't been so soft the horse I backed (win) instead of coming in second. He never does very well on soft ground.

20 I've written to Paul. ~
   You (not write). He's coming here tomorrow. You'll see him before he gets your letter.

21 They (build) a two-storey house (*this was the original plan*), but money ran out so they built a bungalow instead.

22 If the dog hadn't woken us we (not notice) the fire for several hours, and by that time it (spread) the house next door.

23 Why didn't you wait for me yesterday? ~
  I waited five minutes. ~
  You (wait) a little longer!
24 How did Peter get here? ~
  He (come) on a motorcycle. (*This is a possibility.*) ~
  He (not come) on a motorcycle. He doesn't ride one. ~
  He (come) as a pillion passenger.
25 (Alice, staying at a hotel for the first time, carefully washes up the
  early morning tea things.)
  Mother: You (not do) that. The hotel staff do the washing up.
26 Why are you so late? You (be) here two hours ago!
27 Mrs Smith: I've cooked scrambled eggs for Mr Jones, because of his
  diet, and steak and onions for everyone else.
  Mr Jones: You (not cook) anything special for me, Mrs Smith; I'm
  not on a diet any longer.
28 If I'd known we'd have to wait so long I (bring) a book. ~
  If I'd known it was going to be so cold I (not come) at all!
29 Tom (looking out of the window): Fortunately that teapot didn't hit
  anyone, but you (not throw) it out of the window, Ann! You (kill)
  someone.
30 Look at this beautiful painting! Only a very great artist (paint) such a
  picture! ~
  Nonsense! A child of five (paint) it with his eyes shut.
31 I wonder how the fire started. ~
  Oh, someone (drop) a lighted cigarette. Or it (be) an electrical
  fault. ~
32 You don't think it (be started) deliberately? ~
  Well, I suppose it (be). (*It is possible.*) But who would do a thing like
  that?
33 There is only one set of footprints, so the kidnapper (carry) his
  prisoner out. He not (do) it in daylight or he (be) seen. He (wait) till
  dark.
34 I went with him to show him the way. ~
  You (not do) that. (*That wasn't necessary.*) He knows the way.
35 Then an enormous man, ten feet tall, came into the ring. ~
  He (not be) ten feet tall really. He (walk) on stilts.
36 He jumped out of a sixth-floor window and broke his neck. ~
  You say 'jumped'. It (not be) an accident? ~
  No. The window was too small. It (be) deliberate.

115 Auxiliaries + perfect infinitives

■ PEG 255

Use the perfect infinitive of the verbs in brackets with a suitable auxiliary verb.

1 Tom: I had my house painted recently, but when they sent in the bill I was appalled. If I'd known it was going to cost so much I (not have) it done.

2 Peter: But it's your own fault, Tom. You (ask) for an estimate before letting them start.

3 Mother (very anxious about her son, aged ten): Where is he? He (be) here an hour ago? (*It's now 5.00 and he is usually home by 4.00.*)

4 Friend: He (go) to the playground to watch a football match.
Mother: No, if there'd been a match today he (tell) me. He always tells me all the football news.

5 Friend: His teacher (keep) him in as a punishment.
Mother: She (not keep) him in for a whole hour.

6 Friend: Then he (go) to a friend's house.
Mother: Yes, or he (be) knocked down crossing the street. He may be lying unconscious in hospital!
Friend: If that had happened the hospital (ring) you.
Mother: They (not ring) me. My phone isn't working!

7 He jumped out of the aeroplane and landed unhurt! ~
You mean he parachuted down? ~
He didn't say anything about a parachute. ~
He (have) a parachute. Otherwise he (be) killed.

8 I bought a sweater at Marks and Spencer's last Sunday. ~
You (not buy) it on Sunday. Marks and Spencer's is shut on Sundays.

9 Tom's had another accident. He came out of a side road rather fast and a lorry crashed into him. ~
It sounds like Tom's fault. He (wait) till the main road was clear.

10 I wonder who carried the piano upstairs. I suppose it was Paul. ~
Paul (not carry) it by himself. Someone (help) him.

11 I was on the Circle Line and we were just leaving Piccadilly— ~
Then you (not be) on the Circle Line. It doesn't go through Piccadilly. You (be) on the Bakerloo Line or the Piccadilly Line.

12 The plane disappeared two weeks ago and no one knows what happened to it. ~
It (crash) into the sea. If it had crashed on land someone (report) it by now. ~

13 But what do you think caused the plane to crash? ~
Who knows? It (blow) up. Someone (plant) a bomb on board before take-off, or one of the passengers (have) explosives with him.

14 Or someone (try) to hijack the plane. And there (be) a fight during which the plane crashed.

15 Or something (go) wrong with the engines, or it (be) a case of metal fatigue. ~
It (not be) metal fatigue because it was a brand new plane.

16 The pilot (collapse) at the controls. ~
But if that had happened the second pilot (take over).

17 Maria (new to English customs): He said, 'How do you do?' so I told him about my migraine.
Ann: You (not do) that. (*That wasn't the right thing to do.*) You (say), 'How do you do?' too.

18 It was the depths of winter and we had to wait eighteen hours in an unheated station. ~
You (be) frozen by the time the train arrived.

19 I've done all the calculations. Here you are—six pages. ~
But you (not do) all that work! We have a computer to do that sort of thing. ~
You (tell) me! Then I (not waste) all my time!

20 He failed the exam but he (pass) it. (*He had the ability to pass it.*) It's all his own fault; he (work) much harder during the term.

21 He's not here! Yet I locked him in and bolted the door too, so he (not possibly open) the door from inside. And he (not get) out of the window; it's too small. ~

22 Somebody (let) him out. One of his friends (follow) you here and (slip) in when your back was turned.

23 Passenger: Fares are awful! I had to pay £2 for my ticket and £1 for the baby.
Another passenger: But you (not buy) a ticket for the baby. Babies travel free.

24 Immediately after drinking the coffee I felt very sleepy and the next thing I remember is finding myself lying in the middle of the road. ~
They (drug) your coffee and (dump) you there. ~
If I hadn't woken up when I did I (be run) over. ~
That (be) part of their plan. (*It is possible that it was part of their plan.*)

25 I found he knew all my movements for the past week. He (bribe) one of the other students to give him the information. ~
Or he (follow) you himself. ~
No, he (not do) that. (*That is not possible.*) I (see) him.

26 I stamped it and posted it. ~
You (not stamp) it. It was a reply-paid envelope.

27 He walked from London to Cambridge in three hours. ~
He (not do) it in that time! Someone (give) him a lift.

28 I found that everything I said on the phone had been reported to the police. ~
Your phone (be) tapped.

29 My ring's gone! It was on the table by the window only a minute ago! Who (take) it? ~
It (be) a magpie. There are some round here and they like shining

things. A magpie (hop) in through the window and (snatch) it when you were out of the room. (*This is possible.*)

30 I had to walk home yesterday: I had no money for my fare. ~ You (tell) me! I (lend) you the money!

31 I (not take) a taxi. I (walk); it was only a hundred metres. (*I took a taxi but it wasn't necessary.*)

32 The shoplifter thought she was unobserved but when she got to the door a store detective stopped her. They (watch) her on closed-circuit television.

33 When I rang the exchange and asked for the number the operator said, 'You (not ring) the exchange! You (dial) the number direct!' However, he put me through.

34 One moment the conjurer's handkerchief was empty and the next moment it was full of eggs! ~
He (have) the eggs up his sleeve! ~

35 Well, I suppose he (have) eggs up his sleeve: but for his next trick he produced a bowl of goldfish out of the air. He (not have) a bowl of goldfish up his sleeve, now, could he?

36 Mary: My grandmother knew a girl whose fiancé was sent to prison for twenty years. This girl (marry) any one of a dozen men because she was a real beauty, but she waited till her fiancé came out of jail!
Jack: She (love) him very much.
Ann: She (be) an idiot!

116 Auxiliaries + perfect infinitives

■ PEG 114 B, 255

Use the perfect infinitive of the verbs in brackets with the appropriate auxiliary. Phrases in bold type should not be repeated but their meaning should be expressed by auxiliary + perfect infinitive.

You (bought) bread, **which was not necessary**.
You needn't have bought bread.

1 To someone who was not at the party: 'We had a wonderful time; you (be) there.'

2 **It is possible that** Shakespeare (write) it. ~
Shakespeare (not write) it because events are mentioned that didn't occur till after Shakespeare's time.

3 I found this baby bird at the foot of a tree. It (fall) from a nest.

4 I used to visit her and I always wondered why she had those dreadful pictures on the walls. ~
It is possible that she (like) them.

5 During the gale, the captain was on the bridge the whole time. He (be) exhausted afterwards.

6 You (send) a telegram, **which was quite unnecessary**; a letter would have done.

7 You (leave) a note. (**It was very inconsiderate of you not to do so.**)

8 Somebody phoned at lunchtime but I couldn't catch the name. ~
It (be) my brother. He sometimes rings me up then.

9 The lecturer was a tall thin man with white hair. ~
Then it (not be) Dr Fell because he is short and fat. It (be) Dr Jones; I think he is thin.

10 You (not go) out yesterday without a coat. No wonder you caught cold.

11 I saw them in the street but they didn't stop to speak to me. ~
It is possible that they (be) in a hurry.

12 They (be) married next week but now they have quarrelled and the wedding has been cancelled.

13 If we hadn't had this puncture we certainly (be) home by now.

14 You (carry) the dog, **which was unnecessary**. He can walk very well.

15 People were waiting but the bus didn't stop. ~
It is possible that it (be) full.

16 We went sailing on a lake in a London park. I think it was the Round Pond. ~
It (not be) the Round Pond. There are only toy boats there. It (be) the Serpentine.

17 Look, there's a tree right across the road! ~
So there is. It (be) blown down by the gale last night.

18 This building (be) finished by the end of last year (**this was the plan**), but there have been so many strikes that it isn't finished yet.

19 But for the fog they (reach) the top next day.

20 You (cross) the road by the subway. (**but you didn't**)

21 **It is a pity** you (not bring) your kite. It is just the day for kites.

22 **It is possible that** I (be) mistaken.

23 I sat on a seat in the park and now my coat is covered in green stripes. ~
The paint (be) wet.

24 I suppose it was Charles who left the kitchen in such a mess. ~
No, it (not be) Charles. He never has a meal in. It (be) Bill.

25 I know she was in because I heard her radio, but she didn't open the door. ~
Possibly she (not hear) the bell.

26 If you had told me that you were in London I (put) you up. (**This would have been possible.**)

27 If they had gone any further they (fall) over a precipice.

28 He (check) that his brakes were working properly. (**but he didn't**)

29 You (apologize), **which was not necessary**.

30 I can't think why they didn't try to help him. ~
It is possible that they (not realize) that he was drowning.

31 He (thank) us. (**We are offended that he didn't.**)

32 I (go) on Tuesday (**this was the plan**). But on Tuesday I had a terrible cold so I decided to wait till Wednesday.

33 You (warn) him that the ice was dangerous. (but you didn't)
34 If you had kept quiet nobody (know) anything about it.
35 You (bought) a new one, which wasn't necessary. I could have lent
   you mine.
36 As soon as I switched on my new electric cooker there was an
   explosion. ~
   There (be) something wrong with it.

14 Present, past and perfect tenses

117 The simple present and the present continuous

◪ PEG 164–74

Put the verbs in brackets into the correct present tense.

1 Ann sees Paul putting on his coat and says: Where you (go), Paul?
Paul: I (go) to buy some cigarettes. You (want) an evening paper?

2 Ann: No, thanks. You are always buying cigarettes, Paul. How many you (smoke) a day?
Paul: I (not smoke) very many—perhaps 20. Jack (smoke) far more than I (do). He (spend) £10 a week on cigarettes.

3 Mary (see) Peter standing at the bus stop.
Mary: Hello, Peter. What bus you (wait) for?
Peter: Hello, Mary. I (wait) for a 9 or a 14.

4 Mary: You usually (go) to work by car, don't you?
Peter: Yes, but the car (belong) to my mother and she sometimes (want) it. She (use) it today to take Tom to the dentist.

5 Mary: I usually (go) by car too. Jack (take) me because he (pass) my office on his way to the factory. But this week he (work) in a factory in the opposite direction: so I (queue) like you.

6 Peter: Here's a 9 now. You (come) on it or you (wait) for a 14?
Mary: I (think) I'll take the 9. If I (wait) for a 14 I may be late, and if you (be) late at my office everyone (look) at you.

7 Mary and Ann (wait) outside a telephone box. Inside the box a boy (dial) a number.
Mary: You (know) that boy?
Ann: Yes, he's a friend of my brother's. He (phone) his girl friend every day from this box.

8 Mary: Where he (come) from?
Ann: He (come) from Japan. He's a very clever boy; he (speak) four languages.

9 Mary: I (wonder) what he (speak) now.
Ann: Well, his girl friend (come) from Japan too; so I (suppose) he (speak) Japanese.

10 It is 8.30. Tom and Ann (have) breakfast. They both (open) their letters.
Tom: No one ever (write) to me. All I (get) is bills! You (have) anything interesting?

11 Ann: I've got a letter from Hugh. He (say) he (come) to London next week and (want) us to meet him for lunch.

12 Peter: You (have) traffic wardens in your country?
Pedro: No, I (not think) so. You (not see) them in my town anyway.
What exactly a traffic warden (do)?

13 Peter: He (walk) up and down the street and if a car (stay) too long
at a parking place or (park) in a no-parking area he (stick) a parking
ticket to the windscreen.

14 Look! He (put) a ticket on Tom's car. Tom will be furious when he
(see) it. He (hate) getting parking tickets.

15 Customer: I (want) to buy a fur coat. Have you any nice coats for
about £500?
Assistant: I'm afraid we just (close), madam. It's 4.55, and we
always (close) at 5.00 sharp on Fridays as Mr Jones the manager
(not want) to miss his favourite television programme.

16 It is Friday evening and the Brown family are at home. Mrs Brown
(listen) to a concert on the radio; Mr Brown (read) a paper, George
Brown (do) his homework and Ann Brown (write) a letter.

17 Mr Brown always (read) his newspapers in the evenings. Mrs Brown
sometimes (knit) but she (not knit) tonight.

18 Mr Black often (go) to the theatre but his wife (not go) very often.
He (like) all sorts of plays. She (prefer) comedies.

19 Tonight they (watch) a very modern comedy. They (enjoy) it, but
they (not understand) some of the jokes.

20 What (happen) in your class? The teacher (give) lectures every
day? ~
No. He (give) one lecture a week, and on the other days he (show)
films or (discuss) books with us.

21 A bus conductor (get) more exercise than a bus driver. The driver
just (sit) in his cab but the conductor (stand) and (walk) about and
(run) up and down the stairs.

22 Why that man (stand) in the middle of the road? ~
He (try) to get across. He (wait) for a gap in the traffic. ~
Why he (not use) the subway? ~
Lots of people (not bother) to use the subway. They (prefer) to risk
their lives crossing here.

23 You (wear) a new coat, aren't you? ~
Yes. You (like) it? ~
The colour (suit) you but it (not fit) you very well. It's much too big.

24 All the guides here (speak) at least three foreign languages, because
a lot of foreign visitors (come) every summer.

25 Paul (take) a party of French tourists round now and tomorrow an
American party (come).

26 Englishmen very seldom (talk) on the Underground. They (prefer) to
read their newspapers. ~
Those two men in the corner (talk). ~
But they (not talk) English.

27 Jones and Co. (have) a sale at the moment. Shall we look in on our
way home? ~

I'd love to but I'm afraid I won't have time. I (meet) Tom at 5.30. ~
You (go) out with Tom often?

28 I usually (go) by train, but this weekend I (go) by bus. It (take)
longer but it (cost) less.

29 Ann (on telephone): You (do) anything at the moment, Sally?
Sally: Yes. I (pack); I (catch) a plane to New York in three hours'
time.
Ann: Lucky girl! How long you (stay) in New York?

30 Peter: You (go) out tonight, Paul?
Paul: No, I (stay) at home. The neighbours (come) in to watch TV.
Peter: You (invite) the neighbours often?
Paul: No, but they (invite) themselves whenever there is a good
programme.

31 Jack: I just (go) out to get an evening paper.
Ann: But it (pour)! Why you (not wait) till the rain (stop)? (*I advise
you to wait.*)

32 Lucy: Tom (get) up very early but he (wash) and (shave) and (get) his
breakfast so quietly that I (not hear) a thing. But I (hear) him driving
away from the house because his car (make) a lot of noise.

33 Alice: My brother (get) up very early too. But he (make) such a lot of
noise that he (wake) everybody up. He (sing) in his bath and (bang)
doors and (drop) things in the kitchen and (play) the radio very
loudly.

34 Lucy: Why you (not ask) him to be a bit quieter?
Alice: I (mention) it every night but it (not do) any good. He (say)
that he (not make) a sound, and I (think) he really (believe) it.

35 Tom: You (see) that man at the corner? He (keep) stopping people
and asking them questions. You (think) he (ask) for directions?
Jack: No, I (expect) he (make) a survey.
Tom: How you (make) a survey?
Jack: You (stop) people and (ask) them questions and (write) the
answers on a report sheet.

36 In most countries a child (start) school at six and (stay) for about five
years in a primary school. Then he (move) to a secondary school. At
17 or 18 he (take) an exam; if he (do) well in this exam he can go on
to a university if he (wish).

118 The simple present and the present continuous

☑ PEG 164–74

Put the verbs in brackets into the correct present tense.

1 Mrs Jones: My daughter never (write) to me so I never (know) what
she (do). Your son (write) to you, Mrs Smith?
Mrs Smith: Yes, I (hear) from him every week. He (seem) to like
writing letters.

2 These apples (cost) 40p a bag. You (think) that is expensive? ~
It (depend) on the size of the bag.

3 I (see) my solicitor tomorrow (*I have arranged this*); I (change) my
will. ~
You always (change) your will. Why you (not leave) it alone?

4 You (look) very thoughtful. What you (think) about? ~
I (think) about my retirement. ~
But you're only 25. You only just (start) your career. ~
I (know); but I (read) an article which (say) that a sensible man
(start) thinking about retirement at 25.

5 My next door neighbour always (knock) on my door and (ask) me to
lend her 10p pieces. ~
What she (do) with them? ~
She (put) them in her gas meter. I really (not mind) lending her a
few 10p pieces but what (annoy) me is that she (know) how many
she (need) each week but never (take) the trouble to bring the right
number home. ~

6 What she (do) if she (run out) of them when you are away? ~
Oh, she (borrow) from her other neighbour, Mr White; but this (take)
longer because he always (want) her to stay and chat and she (find) it
quite hard to get away from him. ~

7 How much she (owe) you now? ~
I (not know); I (not keep) an account. Anyway she (leave) next week;
she (get) married. I (try) to think of a suitable wedding present. ~

8 Why you (not offer) to cancel her debt? ~
That (sound) rather a mean sort of present. Anyway she probably
(not realize) that she (owe) me money. ~

9 My brother (say) that people who (owe) him money always (seem) to
forget about it, but people he (owe) money to always (remember)
exactly.

10 I (not think) your brother (enjoy) the party. He (keep) looking at his
watch. ~
Oh, I'm sure he (enjoy) it. He always (enjoy) your parties. But I
(know) he (want) to be home early tonight because he (expect) an
important telephone call.

11 Jack: How much longer you (stay) in England?
Paul: Only one more day. I (leave) tomorrow night. I (go) to Holland
for two weeks.

12 Jack: And you (come) back to England after that or you (go) home?
Paul: It (depend) on my father. But if he (agree) to let me go on
studying here I'll certainly come back. And I (expect) he will agree.

13 Paul: By the way, Jack, Ann (see) me off at Victoria tomorrow. Why
you (not come) too? You could have coffee with her afterwards. (*Paul
is advising/inviting Jack to come and see him off.*)

14 You (see) that man at the corner of the street? He is a private
   detective. He (watch) No. 24. ~
   How you (know) he (watch) No. 24? ~
   Because whenever anyone (come) out of, or (go) into, the house he
   (make) a note in his little book.

15 What all those people (do) in the middle of the street? And why they
   (wear) such extraordinary clothes? ~
   They (make) a film. Most of the crowd are local people who (work)
   as extras. ~

16 It (sound) great fun. You (think) I could get a job as a film extra? ~
   I (not know) but I (see) Ann over there; when they (finish) this scene
   I'll ask her if they still (take) on extras. ~

17 Ann (act) in the film? ~
   She has a small part. She (not act) very well. I (imagine) she got the
   part because she (know) the director.

18 My brother (live) next door and his two children (come) and (see) me
   every day. The boy (not bother) to knock at the door; he just (climb)
   in through the window; but the girl always (knock).

19 Tom: We (move) into our new house tomorrow.
   Bill: But why you (leave) your present house? It (suit) you all.
   Tom: Yes, I (know) it (do); but the Council (pull down) all the houses
   on this side. They (widen) the road. They (say) it's a bottleneck.

20 If you (ask) a friend if she (like) your new dress she usually (say)
   'Yes'; so you (not know) whether she really (think) it (suit) you or
   whether she merely (be) polite.

21 If you (want) a candid opinion you'd better ask my sister. She never
   (tell) white lies; she always (say) exactly what she (think).

22 Your sister's frankness (annoy) people? ~
   Yes, it (do). The average person (not want) a truthful answer; he
   (want) you to say something agreeable.

23 I (hear) that you have bought a new house. ~
   Yes, but I (not live) in it yet. They still (work) on it, and the work
   (take) longer than I expected. ~

24 I (think) repair jobs always (take) longer than one (expect). What
   they (do) now? ~
   They (put) in new electric points. They (seem) competent
   electricians but they (smoke) at their work and this (slow) them
   down.

25 They always (hammer) next door. ~
   Yes, that house (keep) changing hands and the new owner always
   (begin) by putting in a new fireplace, and their fireplace is just on
   the other side of this wall so we (hear) everything. The wall (shake),
   too.

26 Ann (stir) something in a saucepan and Mary (stand) beside her
   holding a cookery book.
   Mary: It (say) 'simmer', and you (boil) it, Ann.
   Ann: I (not think) it (matter) if you (cook) it quickly; but I (not know)
   why it (not get) thick. It usually (thicken) at once.

27 The hall (be) painted at the moment, so it (not look) its best. ~
But where are the painters? They (stop) work at 3.00? ~
No, they are in the kitchen. They (have) a tea break.

28 What the word 'Establishment' (mean)? My dictionary (not give) an
explanation. ~
It roughly (mean) the government and people who (have) power and
authority.

29 If we (say) that Mr Brown (belong) to the Establishment we also
(imply) that he (accept) the existing system. He (not try) to
overthrow it. ~

30 All rich men (belong) to the Establishment? ~
Middle-aged rich men probably (do) but rich young men like pop
singers always (jeer) at the Establishment. The word (be used)
chiefly in a pejorative sense.

31 The house opposite the college (be pulled) down. That's why we
(use) the back entrance at present. If you (go) out by the front door
you (get) covered with dust.

32 Tom: I (smell) something burning!
Jack: So (do) I. I (think) it (come) from the kitchen. Ann probably
(iron). She usually (iron) and (watch) TV at the same time and if she
(get) very interested in a programme she (forget) that she (press) a
hot iron on to somebody's shirt. Mother (think) of selling the TV set.

33 Mrs Jones: What you (look) for, Tom?
Mr Jones: I (look) for the garage key. I always (look) for the garage
key, because nobody ever (put) it back on its hook.
Mrs Jones: I always (put) it back on its hook. Why you (not try) your
pockets? (*I advise you to try your pockets*).

34 Imagine that you (travel) by train, in a crowded compartment. One
of the passengers (read) a newspaper; another (do) a crossword
puzzle; another (look out) of the window. Suddenly the train (stop)
with a jerk and your suitcase (fall) off the rack on to somebody's
toes.

35 This is a story about an invalid who (spend) most of the day in bed.
He has a powerful telescope and he (amuse) himself by watching the
activities of the people in the opposite houses. One day when he
(watch) No. 24 he (see) a murder being committed.

36 The cashier used to do the accounts and I used to check his figures;
now the computer (do) it all. ~
And who (check) the computer? ~
No one. The computer (not need) a second opinion. ~
And what (happen) if the computer (make) a mistake?
The computer never (make) a mistake.

119 The simple past and the past continuous

☑ PEG 175–81

Put the verbs in brackets into the correct tense: simple past or past continuous.

1 Peter and Ann (decide) to redecorate their sitting-room themselves.
2 They (choose) cream paint for the woodwork and apricot for the walls. 3 When John (look) in to see how they (get) on, Ann (mix) the paint, and Peter (wash) down the walls. 4 They (be) glad to see John and (ask) if he (do) anything special that day. 5 He hastily (reply) he (go) to the theatre and (go) away at once, because he (know) they (look) for someone to help them.

6 They (begin) painting, but (find) the walls (be) too wet. 7 While they (wait) for the walls to dry, Ann (remember) she (have) a phone call to make. 8 Peter (start) painting while she (telephone), and (do) a whole wall before Ann (come) back. 9 He (grumble) that she always (telephone). 10 Ann (retort) that Peter always (complain).

11 They (work) in silence for some time. 12 Just as they (start) the third wall, the doorbell (ring). 13 It (be) a friend of Peter's who (want) to know if Peter (play) golf the following weekend. 14 He (stay) talking to Peter in the hall while Ann (go) on painting. 15 At last he (leave). 16 Peter (return), expecting Ann to say something about friends who (come) and (waste) valuable time talking about golf. 17 But Ann nobly (say) nothing.

18 Then Peter (think) he would do the ceiling. 19 He just (climb) the step ladder when the doorbell (ring) again. 20 Ann (say) she (get) tired of interruptions but (go) and (open) the door. 21 It (be) the postman with a letter from her aunt Mary, saying she (come) to spend the weekend with them and (arrive) that evening at 6.30.

120 The simple past and the past continuous

☑ PEG 175–81

Put the verbs in brackets into the simple past or past continous.

1 I (walk) along Piccadilly when I (realize) that a man with a ginger beard, whom I had seen three times already that afternoon, (follow) me. 2 To make quite sure, I (walk) on quickly, (turn) right, then left and (stop) suddenly at a shop window. 3 In a few minutes the man with the beard (appear) and (stop) at another shop window. 4 I (go) on. 5 Whenever I (stop) he (stop), and whenever I (look) round he (be) still there. 6 He (look) a very respectable type and (wear) very conventional clothes and I (wonder) if he was a policeman or a private detective. 7 I (decide) to try and shake him off. 8 A 74 bus

(stand) at the bus stop just beside me. 9 Then the conductor (come) downstairs and (ring) the bell; just as the bus (move) off, I (jump) on it. 10 The man with the beard (miss) the bus but (get) into another 74, which (follow) the first. 11 Both buses (crawl) very slowly along Knightsbridge. 12 Every time the buses (pull) up at a stop, the man (look) out anxiously to see if I (get) off. 13 Finally, at some traffic lights, he (change) buses and (get) into mine. 14 At Gloucester Road Underground, I (leave) the bus and (buy) a ticket at a ticket machine. 15 As I (stand) on the platform waiting for a Circle Line train, my pursuer (come) down the stairs. 16 He (carry) a newspaper and when we (get) into the same compartment, he (sit) in one corner reading it, and I (read) the advertisements. 17 He (look) over the top of the newspaper at every station to see if I (get) out. 18 I (become) rather tired of being shadowed like this, so finally I (go) and (sit) beside the man and (ask) him why he (follow) me. 19 At first he (say) he (not follow) me at all but when I (threaten) to knock him down, he (admit) that he was. 20 Then he (tell) me he (be) a writer of detective stories and (try) to see if it was difficult to follow someone unseen. 21 I (tell) him he hadn't been unseen because I had noticed him in Piccadilly and I (advise) him to shave off his ginger beard if he (not want) his victim to know he (be) followed.

121 The simple past and the past continuous

PEG 175-81

Put the verbs in brackets into the correct tense: simple past or past continuous.

1 He (sit) on the bank fishing when he (see) a man's hat floating down the river. It (seem) strangely familiar.
2 It (snow) heavily when he (wake) up. He (remember) that Jack (come) for lunch and (decide) to go down to the station to meet him in case he (lose) his way in the snowy lanes.
3 When I (reach) the street I (realize) that I (not know) the number of Tom's house. I (wonder) what to do about it when Tom himself (tap) me on the shoulder.
4 As the goalkeeper (run) forward to seize the ball a bottle (strike) him on the shoulder.
5 I (look) through the classroom window. A geometry lesson (go) on. The teacher (draw) diagrams on the blackboard.
6 Most of the boys (listen) to the teacher but a few (whisper) to each other, and Tom (read) a history book. Tom (hate) mathematics; he always (read) history during his mathematics lesson.
7 Everyone (read) quietly when suddenly the door (burst) open and a complete stranger (rush) in.

8 I (go) to Jack's house but (not find) him in. His mother (say) that she
   (not know) what he (do) but (think) he probably (play) football.
9 This used to be a station and all the London trains (stop) here. But
   two years ago they (close) the station and (give) us a bus service
   instead.
10 She (promise) not to report me to the police but ten minutes later I
   (see) her talking with a policeman and from the expression on his
   face I am sure she (tell) him all about it.
11 I (pick) up the receiver and (dial) a number. To my surprise I (find)
   myself listening to an extraordinary conversation. Two men (plan) to
   kidnap the Prime Minister.
12 I (meet) Paul at the university. We (be) both in the same year. He
   (study) law, but he (not be) very interested in it and (spend) most of
   his time practising the flute.
13 The train just (start) when the door (open) and two panting
   passengers (leap) in.
14 'What you (do) between 9.00 and 10.00 yesterday?' (say) the
   detective.
   'I (clean) my house,' said Mrs Jones. 'I always clean my house on
   Saturday mornings.'
15 My neighbour (look) in last night and (say) that he (leave) the district
   and (go) to Yorkshire, to a new job. I (say) that I (be) very sorry that
   he (go), and (tell) him to write to me from Yorkshire and tell me how
   he (get) on.
16 They (build) that bridge when I (be) here last year. They haven't
   finished it yet.
17 The dentist's waiting room was full of people. Some (read)
   magazines, others just (turn) over the pages. A woman (knit); a child
   (play) with a toy car. Suddenly the door (open) and the nurse (say),
   'Next, please.'
18 The house next to yours (be) full of policemen and police dogs
   yesterday. ~
   What they (do)? ~
   I (hear) that they (look) for drugs. ~
   They (find) any? ~
   Yes, I believe one of the dogs (discover) some cannabis.
19 Peter (tell) me yesterday that he (make) his own £5 notes. ~
   Don't believe him. He just (pull) your leg.
20 A traffic warden just (stick) a parking ticket to my windscreen when
   I (come) back to the car. I (try) to persuade him to tear it up but he
   (refuse).
21 Ann works in the branch where the big robbery (take) place. ~
   She actually (work) there at the time of the raid?
22 When Ann (say) that she (come) to see me the next day, I (wonder)
   what flowers she would bring. She always brings flowers.
23 While I (wonder) whether to buy the dress or not, someone else
   (come) and (buy) it.

24 He always (borrow) from me (*he borrowed more often than was reasonable*) but when I once (ask) him to lend me something, he (say) he (not have) got it before he even (know) what I (want) to borrow.

25 I (go) home on foot and all the time I (have) the impression that I (be) followed (*passive*). But though I (turn) round several times, I never (see) anybody.

26 I (bump) into Tom yesterday. I (ask) him to join us for lunch tomorrow but he (say) he (have) (*had arranged to have*) lunch with Ann.

27 My dog (attack) the postman as he (put) the letters into the letter box. The man (thrust) a large envelope into the dog's mouth and of course he (tear) it. Unfortunately the letter (contain) my diploma. I (patch) the diploma up with Sellotape but it still looks a bit odd.

28 How you (break) your leg? ~
I (fall) off a ladder when I (put) up curtains. The worst of it (be) that it (be) just before the holidays and I (go) away. (*had planned to go away*) ~

29 So you (not go) away? ~
No, of course not. I (cancel) my bookings and (spend) the holiday hobbling about at home.

30 The curtain just (rise) when somebody at the back of the theatre (shout) 'Fire!' The audience (look) round nervously.

31 As it (rain) the children (play) in the sitting room. Tom was there too. He (try) to write a letter but he (not get on) very well because the children (keep) asking him questions.

32 What you (do) when the doorbell (ring)? ~
I (make) a cake. ~
And what you (do) when you (hear) the bell? ~
I (go) to answer it of course. But when I (open) the door there (be) nobody there.

33 A few minutes later the bell (ring) again and this time I (find) a man in a peaked cap who (say) he (make) a survey.

34 I (say), '(Be) it you who (ring) this bell a minute ago?'
'No,' he (answer), 'but when I (talk) to your neighbour I (see) a man standing at your door. I think he (go) round to the back of your house.'

35 We (not get) much sleep last night because the people next door (have) a noisy party. I (ring) up the landlord and (say) that his tenants (make) too much noise. He (point out) that it (be) Saturday and that people often (have) parties on Saturday nights. I (say) that the people in his house always (have) parties. (*had too many parties*)

36 What you (do) before you (get) this job? ~
I (work) for Brown and Company. ~
And how long you (stay) with them? ~
I (stay) for about six months. I (leave) because they always (go) on strike. It (become) quite monotonous.

122 The present perfect with **for** and **since**

☐ PEG 187

Part 1 Answer the following questions as shown in the examples:

Can you skate? (three years)
Yes, but I haven't skated for three years.
Could you climb a rope? (I left school)
Yes, I suppose I could, but I haven't climbed one since I left school.

1 Can you play chess? (ten years)
2 Can you sing? (I came to England)
3 Could you milk a cow? (I left my father's farm)
4 Can you put up a tent? (I went camping two years ago)
5 Can you make Yorkshire pudding? (over a year)
6 Can you read Latin? (I left school)
7 Could you bath a baby? (fifteen years)
8 Could you repair a radio? (I left the army)
9 Can you ski? (my last holiday)
10 Can you read a map? (quite a long time)
11 Could you make a basket? (I was in hospital)
12 Can you sew on buttons? (I got married)
13 Can you drive a car? (over six months)
14 Could you take someone's temperature? (years)
15 Can you ride a motor cycle? (I was at the university)
16 Can you row a boat? (1977)
17 Can you paint in oils? (some time)
18 Can you type? (years and years)

Part 2 Rephrase the following sentences, using the present perfect tense with **for** or **since**:

I last read a newspaper on June 2.
I haven't read a newspaper since June 2.
It is two years since I saw Tom.
I haven't seen Tom for two years.

19 It's two years since I had a puncture.
20 It's two months since he earned any money.
21 He last shaved the day before yesterday.
22 I last drank champagne at my brother's wedding.
23 It's two years since I was last in Rome.
24 I saw Tom last on his wedding day.
25 I last ate raw fish when I was in Japan.
26 It's years since Mary last spoke French.
27 It's ten weeks since I last had a good night's sleep.
28 He last paid taxes in 1970.
29 I last ate meat five years ago. (*Omit* ago.)
30 It's three months since the windows were cleaned.
31 It's years since I took any photographs.

32 I last watched TV on New Year's Day.
33 It's three months since he wrote to me.
34 I was last paid six months ago. (*My pay is six months in arrears.*)
35 The last time I was abroad was in the summer of 1978.
36 It's ten years since that house was lived in.

123 The present perfect and the simple past

■ PEG 175-7, 182-9

Put the verbs in brackets into the correct tense: present perfect or simple past. (In some cases the present perfect continuous is also possible. This is noted in the Key.)

1 Paul: I (play) football since I was five years old.
Tom: You (play) since you (come) to England?
Paul: Oh yes. I (play) quite a lot. I (join) a club the day after I (arrive).

2 Tom: You (play) any matches?
Paul: We (play) about ten. We have two more to play. We (have) a very good season, we (win) all our matches so far, though we (not really deserve) to win the last one.

3 Tom: I (play) football when I (be) at school but when I (leave) school I (drop) it and (take) up golf.

4 Ann: Hello, Jack! I (not see) you for ages! Where you (be)?
Jack: I (be) in Switzerland. I (mean) to send you a postcard but I (not have) your address with me.
Ann: Never mind. You (have) a good time in Switzerland? How long you (be) there?
Jack: I (be) there for a month. I only just (get) back. Yes, I (enjoy) it thoroughly. I (ski) all day and (dance) all night.

5 Ann: I (ski) when I (be) at the university, but I (break) a leg five years ago and since then I (not do) any.

6 When I first (come) to this house, it (be) a very quiet area. But since then a new housing estate (be) built and it (become) very noisy.

7 My son (not start) work yet. He's still at the High School. ~
How long he (be) at school? ~
He (be) at the High School for six years; before that he (spend) five years at the Primary School in Windmill Street.

8 I just (hear) that Peter is in Australia. ~
Oh, you (not know)? He (fly) out at the beginning of the month. ~
You (hear) from him? Does he like the life? ~
Yes, I (get) a letter last week. He (tell) me about his job. But he (not say) whether he (like) the life or not. Perhaps it's too soon to say. He only (be) there three weeks.

9 I (not know) you (be) left-handed. ~
I'm not left-handed; but my oil-heater (explode) yesterday and I

(burn) my right hand, so I have to use my left.

10 This bicycle (be) in our family for fourteen years. My father (use) it for the first five years, my brother (ride) it for the next five, and I (have) it for the last four.

11 I hear that your MP, Mr Simpson, (make) a very clever speech last night. How long he (be) your MP? ~
Oh, we only (have) him since January. His predecessor Mr Allen (resign) suddenly because of ill-health and there (be) a by-election.

12 I hear that Mr Jones (leave). ~
Yes, he (leave) last week. ~
Anybody (be) appointed to take his place? ~
I believe several men (apply) for the job but so far nothing (be) decided.

13 Peter (meeting Ann at the airport): Hello, Ann. You (have) a good trip?
Ann: The actual flight (be) lovely, one of the best I (have) ever, but it (take) ages to get into the plane. First they (think) that one of us (be) a hijacker and they (search) us all for firearms; then they (announce) that one of the engines (be) faulty. We finally (take off) an hour later.

14 Peter: How you (spend) this extra hour before take-off?
Ann: Oh, they (take) us to the restaurant and (feed) us and we (walk) about and (buy) things we (not need). The time (pass) all right.

15 You (book) your hotel room yet? ~
Well, I (write) to the hotel last week but they (not answer) yet.

16 Peter (meeting Paul unexpectedly in London): Hello, Paul! I (not know) you (be) here.
Paul: Oh, I (be) here nearly two months. I (arrive) on the 6th of January.

17 Peter: When we last (meet) you (say) that nothing would induce you to come to England. What (make) you change your mind?
Paul: I (find) that I (need) English for my work and this (seem) the quickest way of learning it.

18 Peter: You (know) any English when you first (arrive) here?
Paul: No, I (not know) a word.

19 Ann (to Yvonne, who is going to English classes): How long you (learn) English?
Yvonne: I (learn) off and on for about five and a half years. (*Use the continuous form.*)

20 I (begin) English at secondary school and (do) it for three years. Then I (drop) it for a year and (forget) most of it. Then I (spend) two years at a secretarial college, where I (study) commercial English, and for the last six months I (study) in London.

21 At 4 p.m. my neighbour (ring) up and (say), 'Is Tom with you?' Tom, her son, (spend) most of his time in my garden playing with my children, so whenever she (not be able) to find him she (ring) me. 'I'm afraid I (not see) him today,' I (say). 'But my children (go) to the beach this morning and (not come) back yet. Perhaps he (go) with them.'

22 I just (have) my first driving lesson. ~
How it (go)? You (enjoy) it? ~
Well, I not actually (hit) anything but I (make) every other possible mistake.

23 Old Ben (sell) newspapers just inside the station entrance, and my father always (buy) his evening paper from him as he (leave) the station on his way home. But one day my father (arrive) home without his paper. 'Ben (not be) there this evening,' he (say). 'I hope he (not be taken) ill.'

24 On Saturday afternoon I (see) Frederick sitting in his garden.
'I (think) you (work) on Saturdays,' I (say).
'I (work) this morning,' (explain) Frederick, 'but at lunch time the boss (go) off to play golf and (tell) us all to go home. It's about time he (give) us a whole Saturday off actually. I (work) practically every Saturday since the beginning of the year.'

25 Ann: You (be) to Hampton Court?
Jane: Yes, I (go) there last week. The tulips (be) wonderful.
Ann: You (go) by car?
Jane: No, I (go) with my English class. We (hire) a coach.

26 Ann: Where else you (be) to since you (come) to England?
Jane: Oh, I (be) to Stratford and Coventry and Oxford and Canterbury.

27 Ann: You (see) a lot. When you (go) to Stratford?
Jane: I (go) last week. The people I work for (take) me.

28 Ann: You (see) a play at the Royal Shakespeare Theatre when you (be) at Stratford?
Jane: Yes, we (see) *Macbeth*. We were very lucky. We just (walk) in and (ask) if they (have) any returned tickets, and the girl at the box office (say), 'Yes, a man just (return) three stalls.'

29 Ann: You (be) to Wales?
Jane: No, I (be) to Scotland but I (not be) to Wales. I'd like to go.

30 Peter: You (see) any good films lately?
Ann: Yes, I (go) to the National Film Theatre last week and (see) a Japanese film.
Peter: You (like) it?
Ann: Yes, I (love) it, but of course I (not understand) a word.

31 Tom: I hear that Mr Benson just (die). You (know) him quite well, didn't you?
Jack: Yes. We (work) for the same company for ten years. I (not see) so much of him after he (leave) the company but we (keep) in touch.

32 Ann (think) the garage (be) empty, and (turn) off the lights. 'Hey!' (shout) Paul from under the car. 'I'm sorry, Paul,' (say) Ann, 'I (not know) you (be) there.'

33 Father: Tom (not come) back yet?
Mother: Yes, he (come) in an hour ago. He (go) straight to bed.
Father: Funny. I (not hear) him.

34 Paul: That's a live wire. It just (give) me a shock!
Ann: Nonsense! I just (touch) it and I (not feel) anything!

35 When Paul (come) into the room, Ann was sitting in an armchair just
behind the door. Paul, not noticing Ann, (go) to the window and
(look) out. Ann (cough) and Paul (spin) round. 'Hello, Ann!' he
(exclaim), 'I (not see) you!'

36 Jack: You just (agree) to go, so why aren't you getting ready?
Peter: But I (not realize) that you (want) me to start at once!

124 The present perfect and the simple past

◪ PEG 175-7, 182-9

Put the verbs in brackets into the correct tense: present perfect or
simple past.

1 I (buy) a new house last year, but I (not sell) my old house yet, so at
the moment I have two houses.

2 When Ann (be) on her way to the station it (begin) to rain. Ann (run)
back to her flat for her umbrella, but this (make) her late for her
train.

3 She (catch) the next train but it (not get) in till 9.00, so she (arrive) at
her office ten minutes late.

4 Her boss (look) up as she (come) in. 'You (be) late every morning
this week,' he (growl).

5 At 7 a.m. Charles (ring) Peter and (say), 'I'm going fishing, Peter.
Would you like to come?'
'But it's so early,' (say) Peter. 'I (not have) breakfast yet. Why you
(not tell) me last night?'

6 Tom (meet) Paul at lunch time and (say), 'I (not see) you at the bus
stop this morning. You (miss) the bus?'
'I (not miss) it,' (reply) Paul. 'I (not miss) a bus for years. But this
morning George (give) me a lift.'

7 Ann (go) to Canada six months ago. She (work) in Canada for a while
and then (go) to the United States.

8 Mary (be) in Japan for two years. She is working there and likes it
very much. ~
How she (go)? ~
She (go) by air.

9 When I (buy) my new house I (ask) for a telephone. The Post Office
(tell) me to wait, but I (wait) a year now and my phone still (not
come).

10 Bill usually has breakfast at 8.00. Yesterday at 8.30 Peter (meet) Bill
and (offer) him an apple. 'No, thanks,' (say) Bill. 'I just (have)
breakfast.'

11 Just as Ann (arrive) at the airfield a plane (land) and a girl (climb)
out. To her surprise Ann (recognize) her cousin, Lucy. 'Hello, Lucy,'
she (exclaim). 'I (not know) that you (know) how to fly a plane.'
'I only just (learn),' (say) Lucy. 'I (go) solo for the first time last week.'

12 Peter (try) to come in quietly but his mother (hear) him and (call) out, 'Where you (be)? Your supper (be) in the oven for an hour.'

13 You (be) to the theatre lately? ~
Yes, I (go) to *Othello* last week. ~
You (like) it? ~
Yes, but I (not see) very well. I (be) right at the back.

14 Ann (coming out of a bookshop): I just (buy) a copy of *David Copperfield*. You (read) it?
Mary: As it happens it is the only one of Dickens's books that I (not read). I (not even see) the film.

15 You (be) to Cambridge? ~
Yes, I (be) there last month. ~
How you (get) there? ~
My brother (take) me in his car.

16 You (see) Philip lately? I (ring) his flat several times last week but (get) no answer. ~
Oh, he (be) in America for the last month. He (fly) out on the first for a conference and then (decide) to stay for six weeks. ~
You (hear) from him? ~
Yes, I (get) a letter shortly after he (arrive).

17 How long you (be) in your present job? ~
I (be) there for six months. ~
And what you (do) before that? ~
Before that I (work) for Jones and Company.

18 How long you (work) for Jones and Company? ~
I (work) for them for two years. ~
You (like) working for them? ~
No, I (not like) it at all. ~
Then why you (stay) so long?

19 We usually go out on Saturday evenings, but last Saturday (be) so wet that we (stay) in and (play) cards. ~
What you (play)? ~
We (play) poker. I (lose) fifty pence.

20 When you (begin) school? ~
I (begin) school when I (be) five. I (go) to a primary school first. I (stay) there for six years and then I (go) to a comprehensive school.

21 When I (be) seventeen I (start) my university course. ~
When you (get) your degree? ~
Oh, I (not get) my degree yet; I'm still at the university. I only (be) there for two years.

22 Tom (leave) the house at 8.20. At 8.25 the phone in Tom's house (ring), Tom's wife, Mary, (answer) it. 'Could I speak to Tom, please?' (say) the caller.
'I'm afraid he just (go) out', (say) Mary.

23 You (be) to Cornwall? ~
Yes, I (be) there last Easter. ~
You (go) by train? ~
No, I (hitch-hike).

24 I (not see) Charles for some time. ~
He (be) ill, poor chap. He (collapse) at work a fortnight ago and (be
taken) to hospital. They (send) him home after two days but he (not
come) back to work yet.

25 There (be) a very good programme on TV last night. You (see) it? ~
No, I (take) my set back to the shop last week because there (be) so
much distortion; and they (say) it (need) a new part. They (not be
able) to get the new part so far, so I (not watch) television for about
ten days.

26 You (ever) be to France? ~
Yes, I (spend) last July and August in Grenoble. I (go) to improve my
French but everyone I (meet) (want) to improve his English so I (not
get) much practice.

27 The postman usually comes between 8.00 and 9.00 in the morning.
At 8.45 a.m. yesterday Ann (say), 'Are there any letters for me?'
'I don't know,' (say) Mary. 'The postman (not come) yet.'
At 11 a.m. Jack, Mary's husband, (ring) from his office to ask if
there (be) any letters for him. 'No,' (say) Mary. 'Nobody (get) letters
today. The postman (not come).'

28 Mr Speed, Ann's employer, (dictate) three letters and (tell) Ann to
type them as soon as possible. Half an hour later he (ring) Ann's
office. 'You (finish) those letters yet?' he (ask).
'Well,' (say) Ann, 'I (do) the letter to Mr Jones, and I'm now typing
the one to Mr Robinson, but I (not start) the one to Mr Smith yet.'

29 You (find) out yet about the trains to Liverpool? ~
No. I (ring) the station last night but the man who (answer) the
phone (not seem) to be sure of the times. He (say) something about a
new timetable. ~
But the new timetable (be) in operation for three weeks!

30 Tom and Jack work in different offices but go to work in the same
train. One evening Tom's wife (say), 'Jack (move) into his new house
yet?' 'I don't know,' (say) Tom, 'I (not see) Jack today. He (not be)
on the train.'

31 Where you (be)? ~
I (be) shopping in Oxford Street. ~
So I suppose you (buy) shoes? ~
Yes. I (find) a shop where they were having a sale and I (get) three
pairs.

32 In the evenings I often play chess with my next door neighbour. I
(play) chess with him ever since I (come) to live here ten years ago.
He (be) here all his life; he (inherit) the house from his father,
another great chess player. ~
You ever (play) chess with the father? ~
We (play) once or twice but he (die) a year after I (arrive).

33 I can't find my gloves. You (see) them? ~
Yes, you (leave) them in the car yesterday. I (put) them back in your
drawer.

34 I hope you're enjoying your visit to England. You (meet) any Englishmen yet? ~
Yes, I (meet) a man called Smith at a party last night. ~
What you (talk) about? ~
We (talk) about the weather.

35 Mrs Jones: For years I (do) all my washing by hand; then last year I (buy) a washing machine and I must say it (make) washing day much less exhausting. It only takes me an hour now.
Mrs White: I don't like washing machines. I always (do) my washing by hand and I intend to go on doing it. I always (find) it very satisfying work.

36 Tom: Don't you think it's time we (have) something different for Sunday dinner?
Ann: But we (have) roast beef for Sunday dinner ever since we (get) married. Your mother (tell) me that you (be) particularly fond of roast beef.
Tom: But my mother (be) dead for five years and in those five years my tastes (change).

125 The present perfect simple and continuous

■ PEG 182–93

Put the verbs in brackets into the correct tense: present perfect simple or present perfect continuous.

1 Peter: You (telephone) for ages. You not nearly (finish)?
Jack: I (not get) through yet. I (try) to get our Paris office but the line (be) engaged all morning.

2 Ann (fail) her driving test three times because she's so bad at reversing. But she (practise) reversing for the last week and I think she (get) a bit better at it.

3 Tom: I often (wonder) why Bill left the country so suddenly.
Peter: Actually, I just (find) out.

4 He (play) the bagpipes since six o'clock this morning. He only just (stop).

5 Why you (not bring) me the letters for signature? You (not type) them yet?

6 Tom (looking up absent-mindedly as Mary comes in): You (sunbathe)?
Mary (crossly): Don't be ridiculous! It (rain) all day!

7 A pair of robins (build) a nest in the porch since last week. I (watch) them from my window since they began.

8 The police (not find) the murderer yet, but the dead man's brother (be) in the station all day. The police say that he (help) them with their enquiries.

9 They (pull) down most of the houses in this street, but they (not touch) the old shop at the corner yet.

10 Tom is convinced that there is gold in these hills but we (search) for six months and (not see) any sign of it.

11 I (wait) for the prices of the houses to come down before buying a house, but I think I (wait) too long and the prices are beginning to go up again.

12 Peter (be) a junior clerk for three years. Lately he (look) for a better post but so far he (not find) anything.

13 I (do) housework all morning and I (not finish) yet. ~
I (do) mine already. I always start at 6 a.m.

14 I just (pick) ten pounds of strawberries! I (grow) strawberries for years but I never (have) such a good crop before.

15 What you (do) with the corkscrew? The point is broken off. ~
I'm afraid I (use) it to make holes in this tin.

16 She just (sell) two of her own paintings. ~
She's lucky. I (paint) for five years and I (not sell) a single picture yet.

17 They are throwing crockery at each other in the next flat. ~
This (happen) before? ~
Well, they (have) a good many rows but this is the first time they (throw) crockery.

18 What you (do) with my typewriter? I can't find it anywhere. ~
Tom just (go) off with it. He says he'll bring it back when he (finish).

19 He (work) for Crow Brothers for forty years and never once (be) late. The firm just (present) him with a gold watch as a sign of their appreciation.

20 We (mend) sheets all morning but we only (do) three, and now the sewing machine (break) down so we'll be even slower with the next one.

21 George (collect) matchboxes ever since he left school. Now he (collect) so many that he doesn't know where to put them.

22 I (look) through my old photograph album. It's full of photographs of people whose names I completely (forget). I wonder what (happen) to them all.

23 It was lovely at eleven o'clock, but since then the sky (get) steadily darker and the wind (rise). I'm afraid the fine spell (come) to an end.

24 Since he became Mayor, my brother reckons that he (eat) 30 official lunches and 22 official dinners, and he (lose) count of the number of receptions and parties that he (attend). ~
He (put) on a lot of weight?

25 Secretary: Customers (ring) up all morning complaining about getting incorrect bills.
Manager: I know; something (go) wrong with our computer. The mechanic (work) on it. I hope he (find) out what's wrong.

26 Someone (use) my umbrella! It's all wet! And it was wet yesterday and the day before! ~
Well, it wasn't me. I (not be) out of the house for a week!

27 I (stand) in this queue for ages. It (not move) at all in the last five minutes. I think the man in the ticket office just (shut) his window and (go) off for lunch.

28 The Town Council (consider) my application for permission to build a garage for three months. They just (give) my neighbour permission to build one, so I hope they (decide) to let me have one too.

29 You look exhausted! ~
    Yes, I (play) tennis and I (not play) for years, so I'm not used to it.

30 They began widening this road three weeks ago; but the workmen (be) on strike for the last fortnight so they (not get) very far with it.

31 That man (stand) at the bus stop for the last half hour. Shall I tell him that the last bus already (go)?

32 I wonder if anything (happen) to Tom. I (wait) an hour now. He often (keep) me waiting but he never (be) quite so late as this.

33 Mrs Brown (live) next door for quite a long time now but she never (say) more than 'Good morning' to me.

34 I just (remember) that I (not pay) the rent yet. I am surprised that the landlord (not ring) me up to remind me. ~
    It is the first time you (be) late with the rent in 25 years. He probably thinks that you (pay) and he (lose) the cheque.

35 Shop assistant: Could you give me some proof of your identity, madam?
    Customer: But I (shop) here for fifteen years!
    Shop assistant: I know, madam, but apparently the company (lose) a lot of money lately through dud cheques and they (make) new regulations which we (be told) to apply to all customers no matter how long we (know) them.

36 What you (do)? I (look) for you for ages. ~
    I (build) a barbecue in the garden.

126 The simple past and the past perfect, simple and continuous

■ PEG 175–7, 194–7

Put the verbs in brackets into the correct tense.

1 He (give) me back the book, (thank) me for lending it to him and (say) that he (enjoy) it very much; but I (know) that he (not read) it because most of the pages (be) still uncut.

2 When he (see) his wife off at the station, he (return) home as he (not have) to be at the airport till 9.30. 3 He (not have) to pack, for his wife already (do) that for him and his case (be) ready in the hall.
   4 He (not have) to check the doors and windows either, for his wife always (do) that before she (leave) the house. 5 All he (have) to do (be) to decide whether or not to take his overcoat with him. In the end he (decide) not to. 6 At 8.30 he (pick) up his case, (go) out of

the house and (slam) the door behind him.   7 Then he (feel) in his pockets for the key, for his wife (remind) him to double-lock the front door.   8 When he (search) all his pockets and (find) no key he (remember) where it (be).   9 He (leave) it in his overcoat pocket. 10 Then he (remember) something else; his passport and tickets (be) in his overcoat pocket as well.

11   I (arrive) in England in the middle of July. I (be told) that England (be) shrouded in fog all year round, so I (be) quite surprised to find that it was merely raining.   12 I (ask) another passenger, an Englishman, about the fog and he (say) that there (not be) any since the previous February.   13 If I (want) fog, he said, I (come) at quite the wrong time.   14 However, he (tell) me that I could buy tinned fog at a shop in Shaftesbury Avenue.   15 He (admit) that he never (buy) fog there himself but (assure) me that they (sell) good quality fog and that it (not be) expensive. I suppose he was joking.

16   When the old lady (return) to her flat she (see) at once that burglars (break) in during her absence, because the front door (be) open and everything in the flat (be) upside down.   17 The burglars themselves (be) no longer there, but they probably only just (leave) because a cigarette was still burning on an ornamental table.   18 Probably they (hear) the lift coming up and (run) down the fire escape. 19 They (help) themselves to her whisky too but there (be) a little left, so she (pour) herself out a drink.   20 She (wonder) if they (find) her jewellery and rather (hope) that they had.   21 The jewellery (be given) her by her husband, who (die) some years before.   22 Since his death she (not have) the heart to wear it, yet she (not like) to sell it.

23   Now it (seem) that fate (take) the matter out of her hands; and certainly the insurance money would come in handy.

24   I (put) the £5 note into one of my books; but next day it (take) me ages to find it because I (forget) which book I (put) it into.

25   A woman (come) in with a baby, who she (say) just (swallow) a safety pin.

26   I (think) my train (leave) at 14.33, and (be) very disappointed when I (arrive) at 14.30 and (learn) that it just (leave).   27 I (find) later that I (use) an out-of-date timetable.

28   He (park) his car under a No Parking sign and (rush) into the shop. When he (come) out of the shop ten minutes later the car (be) no longer there.   29 He (wonder) if someone (steal) it or if the police (drive) it away.

30   It (be) now 6 p.m.; and Jack (be) tired because he (work) hard all day.   31 He (be) also hungry because he (have) nothing to eat since breakfast.   32 His wife usually (bring) him sandwiches at lunch time, but today for some reason she (not come).

33   He (keep) looking at her, wondering where he (see) her before.

34   I (look) out before I (go) to bed and (see) a man standing on the opposite pavement watching the house.   35 When I (get up) the following morning he (be) still there, and I (wonder) whether he (stay) there all night or if he (go) away and (come) back.

Present, past and perfect tenses

36 When I (open) the door I (see) a man on his knees. 37 He clearly
(listen) to our conversation and I (wonder) how much he (hear).
38 When I (ask) him what he (do), he (say) that he (drop) a 50p piece
outside the door and (look) for it. 39 I (not see) any sign of the
money, but I (find) a small notebook and pencil which he probably
(drop) when the door (open) suddenly. 40 So he (take) notes of our
conversation! 41 The notes (be) written in a foreign language, so I
(turn) to the stranger and (ask) him to translate. 42 But he (pull) my
hat over my eyes and (run) off down the corridor. 43 By the time I
(recover) from the shock he (disappear) round the corner.
44 Curiously enough, when I (move) my foot I (find) that I (stand) on
a 50p piece. 45 Perhaps he (tell) the truth after all!

127 Questions

■ PEG 54–60, 104

Make questions for which the following would be reasonable
answers. Ask about the words in bold type.
> I saw **Tom**. Possible question: *Who did you see?*

When a noun in brackets is placed after a pronoun, use this noun in
the question:
> I saw him (Tom) **today**. Question: *When did you see Tom?*

1 They went **to New York**.
2 It takes **four hours** to get there.
3 I didn't think **much** of it.
4 He earns **a hundred pounds** a week.
5 He (Tom) was fined **ten pounds**.
6 It (my room) is **twice as big as yours**.
7 They left the country **ten years ago**.
8 They came **by bus**.
9 I've been here **for two months**.
10 They (the students) went **to the museum** yesterday.
11 It (the car) does **fifty to the gallon**.
12 He met her **in a coffee bar**.
13 They (the neighbours) complained about **the smell**.
14 He (the clerk) made him **fill up a form**.
15 **The pigs** ate them (the apples).
16 He got in **by climbing over the wall**.
17 **John** bought them (the tickets).
18 They (the roads) were **very crowded**.
19 I smoke **forty** (cigarettes) a day.
20 It (the hotel) was **awful**.
21 It (the market) is **a stone's throw** from here.
22 I've had it (this cough) **since the beginning of October**.

62

23 He (Guy Fawkes) tried **to blow up Parliament**.
24 I'd like to speak to **Mr Jones** please.
25 This is **Tom's**.
26 He stopped it (the train) **by pulling the communication cord**.
27 I've been waiting **for half an hour**.
28 She (Mary) put it **in the dustbin**.
29 I threw it away **because I was tired of it**.
30 There are **four** (hotels in the town).
31 They left it (the lawnmower) **outside**.
32 I found her address **by calling at every house in the village**.
33 She (Ann) gave me **duck and green peas** for lunch.
34 It (the lake) is **very deep indeed**.
35 I borrowed **my brother's** car.
36 He **buried it in the garden**.

128 Questions

☑ PEG 54–60, 104

See previous exercise for instructions.

1 He told me **exactly what happened**.
2 It (the bridge) is built of **reinforced concrete**.
3 We're all going **to watch the cricket match**.
4 He broke it (his leg) **in a skiing accident**.
5 He (Tom) lost his job **because he kept coming in late for work**.
6 I bought **the big one**.
7 It (the new theatre) **looks rather like a factory**.
8 I'd like **about a dozen**.
9 It (the concert) began **at eight p.m.**
10 She went (to the dance) with **George**.
11 He bought one (a car) **because the local railway station closed down**.
12 He's coming **at the end of the week**.
13 **That** one is longer.
14 **Jack** taught me (to play poker).
15 She's broken **another of your best plates**.
16 I'm looking for **a telephone box**.
17 He's borrowed **your** typewriter.
18 She was asking him for **a rise**.
19 He's ringing up **the police**.
20 It (the word 'boss') means **employer**.
21 He escaped **by climbing over the prison wall**.
22 We were talking about **Margaret**.
23 They liked **Ann's** idea best.
24 He complained to **the manager**.
25 It was **about the size of an orange**.
26 They (the students) intend **to demonstrate against the new regulations**.

27 I come from **Scotland**.
28 The best kind costs **about twenty pounds**.
29 He gave it away **because he didn't like the colour**.
30 She (his sister) **is very pretty**.
31 It (this knife) is for **opening oysters**.
32 In the mornings I have to **get the breakfast, make the beds and take Mrs White's children to school**.
33 I like **the black one** best.
34 He comes (to London) **about once a month**.
35 **Your father** told me (about it).
36 He's **quick-tempered and impulsive**.

129 Mixed tenses: letters

☑ Put the verbs in brackets into the correct tense. (A variety of tenses will be needed, as well as some conditionals and imperatives; for **be able** use **can/could** where possible.)

Part 1

Dear Hilda

1 I just (hear) that my mother isn't very well, and I (like) to go and see her. The trouble is I can't take my dog Tim with me. 2 You (think) you (be able) possibly look after him for a week? 3 You (have) him for a week last year, you (remember), and you (say) he (be) no trouble, and (get) on well with your dog.

4 If you (be able) have him, I (be able) bring him along any time that (suit) you. 5 He (have) his own bed and bowl, and I (bring) enough tinned dog food to last him a week.

6 But if it (not be) convenient, (not hesitate) to say so. 7 There (be) quite good kennels near here, and they (take) him if I (ask). 8 He (be) there once before and (seem) to get on all right.

Love

Sarah

Part 2

Dear Sarah

9 I (be) very sorry to hear about your mother's illness, and (be) glad that you (go) to Scotland to see how she is. 10 It (be) nice for her to see you.

11 Of course I (look) after Tim. 12 We thoroughly (enjoy) having him last year and my dog (miss) him when he (leave) and (look) for him everywhere. 13 I'm sure he (be) delighted to see him again.

14 You (bring) him on Tuesday afternoon? Or, if that (not suit), any

time on Wednesday.   15 (not bother) to bring dog food; I (have) plenty.   16 I hope you (have) time to have tea with me when you (bring) Tim, and that by then you (have) better news of your mother.

Love

Hilda

Part 3

Dear Peter

17 You by any chance (know) where Bob is?   18 I (like) to find out because I just (hear) of a job that exactly (suit) him, but if he (not apply) fairly soon of course he (not get) it.

19 I last (see) him about a month ago, when he just (leave) his job with the film company.   20 He (say) he (go) to France (*had decided to go to France*) for a holiday and (promise) to send me a postcard with his French address as soon as he (find) a place to stay.   21 But I (hear) nothing since then and (not know) even whether he (go) to France or not.

22 If you (know) his address I (be) very grateful if you (phone) me. 23 I (try) to phone you several times but your phone (not seem) to be working.

Yours

Jack

Part 4

Dear Sir

24 I (be) interested in the furnished cottage near Dedham which you (advertise) in yesterday's *Telegraph*, for my husband and I (come) to England in June and (require) accommodation for three months. 25 You please (tell) me exactly where it (be) and give me details of bus and train services in the area.   26 I also (like) to know about the local shops.   27 I (be able) to shop without a car?   28 My husband (hope) to hire a car, but I (not drive) and he (not be) free very often to take me shopping, so we (need) a cottage on a bus route.   29 The local shops still (deliver)? I (know) they (do) ten years ago.

30 I (be) grateful also if you (tell) me whether you supply sheets etc. and whether a laundry (call) at the house.   31 The rent you (ask) (sound) reasonable for the size of the cottage. How you (like) it paid? Weekly, monthly or in advance?

32 My husband and I (be) abroad for ten years, but before that we (live) near Dedham, which is why we (want) to spend our holidays there.   33 My husband also (write) a book about Constable and (like) to finish it in the area where he, Constable, (paint) most of his pictures.

34 Mr Jones, the bank manager, (know) us since we (live) in the area

65

and I (be) sure he (recommend) us as suitable tenants. 35 I of course (be willing) to send a deposit.

36 I (be) grateful for an early reply and (enclose) a stamped addressed envelope.

Yours faithfully

Pamela Smith

130 Mixed tenses: letters

☑ Put the verbs in brackets into the correct tense (some present participles will be required).

Part 1

Dear Sir

1 I (write) to you three weeks ago, (ask) about conditions of entry into your college. 2 You (reply), (enclose) an enrolment form, which I (fill up) and (return) without delay. 3 Since then, however, I (hear) nothing and I (begin) to wonder if my application (go) astray.

4 You please (check) that you (receive) it and if you haven't, please send me another enrolment form. 5 If, on the other hand, you (receive) my application but (not decide) whether to accept me as a student or not, I (be) very grateful if you (tell) me when I may expect to hear your decision. 6 Finally, if my application already (be) refused, I (like) to be informed as soon as possible because if I do not get into your college I (have) to apply to another and the sooner I (do) this, the better chance I (have) of being accepted.

Yours faithfully

P. Smith

Part 2

Dear Mr Jones

7 My family and I (suffer) a good deal lately from the noise made by your guests when they (leave) your house on Saturday nights.

8 They (stand) in the street, (laugh) loudly and (call) goodbye to you and to each other. 9 Then they (get) into their cars, (bang) the doors loudly, and finally they (reverse) their cars on to the road. 10 This (sound) a fairly simple manoeuvre, but there is always at least one of your guests who (find) it almost beyond him—whether because he (have) too much to drink or still (learn) to drive I (not know)—but I (know) that it (take) him ages to get out, and all the time we hear his engine (roar) and his friends (shout) advice.

11 By the time all your guests (go) and the road is quiet again, my family all (be) wakened up, and the children often (find) it very hard to get to sleep again.

12 I (be) very grateful if you (ask) your guests to leave more quietly, and perhaps you (be able) persuade any learner drivers to come by taxi.

Yours sincerely

Andrew Brown

Part 3

Dear Ann

13 You (be) free to come to dinner here on Saturday next at 8.00?
14 My brother Paul (come) and (bring) a friend of his called Tom Edwards.   15 You (not meet) Tom but I (think) you (like) him.
16 He is an assistant stage manager at the Gate Theatre and (be able) to tell you about the actors.   17 Paul says Tom (receive) hardly any salary and often (not get) enough to eat, so he (ask) me to have roast beef and Yorkshire pudding for dinner, with apple dumpling to follow.   18 He probably (ring) up between now and Saturday, to say that it (be) a good idea to start with a substantial soup, such as ox-tail!   19 I (know) you not usually (eat) heavy three-course meals of this type, but I (hope) the conversaton (not be) so heavy. Anyway, come if you (be able).

Love

Mary

20 PS. The 14 bus (pass) the door as you probably (remember), and Paul (give) you a lift home.

131 Mixed tenses: telephone conversations

☑ Put the verbs in brackets into the correct tense and fill the spaces with suitable forms.

Part 1

1 Caller: this is Mrs Jones at 22 High Street. . . . I have an appointment for a shampoo and set, please?
2 Receptionist: Yes, Mrs Jones. Who usually (do) your hair?
3 Caller: Peter usually (do) it, but the last time I (come) he (be) on holiday and Ann (do) it. So if Peter (be) not available, Ann (do) very well.
4 Receptionist: When you (want) to come, Mrs Jones?
5 Caller: I (like) to come tomorrow afternoon if possible.
6 Receptionist: I'm afraid that that afternoon is full. Thursday afternoon at 4.00 (suit) you?
7 Caller: I'm afraid it . . . . . My mother-in-law (come) to tea.

Present, past and perfect tenses

8 Receptionist: Then what about Friday afternoon? Peter (be able) (do) you at 4.00.
9 Caller: That (be) splendid. Thank you very much.
10 Receptionist: Thank you, Mrs Jones. We (expect) you at 4.00 on Friday then. Goodbye.

Part 2

11 Tom: . . . I speak to Ann, please?
12 Ann: Ann (speak).
13 Tom: Tom here. Where you (be), Ann? I (try) to get on to you for the last half hour. You (not leave) your office at 5.00?
14 Ann: Yes, I . . ., but today I (go) shopping and only just (get) in. It (be) nice to hear your voice, Tom. I (not know) you (be) in London.
15 Tom: I only (arrive) this morning. I (ring) you before but I (be) terribly busy all day covering a conference. It only just (end). You (do) anything tonight, Ann?
16 Ann: Yes, I (go) to the theatre.
17 Tom: But that (be) terrible! I (be) only here for one night!
18 Ann: I (be) sorry, Tom. If you (tell) me you were coming up, I (keep) the evening free. But you didn't tell me.
19 Tom: I (not know) myself till this morning when the boss suddenly (dash) into the office and (tell) me to rush up here to cover the conference.
20 Ann: I thought Peter usually (do) the conferences.
21 Tom: Yes, he (do) but when he (drive) up here last night he (have) an accident and (take) (*passive*) to hospital. So I (do) it instead. Ann, you really (go) out tonight? . . . (*negative interrogative*) you get out of it?
22 Ann: No, I . . . (*negative*). I'm free tomorrow but I (suppose) that (be) too late.
23 Tom (suddenly changing his plans): No, I (stay) another day. I daresay the boss (get) over it. You (like) to meet me for dinner tomorrow?
24 Ann: I (love) to. But Tom, you (be) sure it (be) all right? I (hate) you to lose your job.
25 Tom: It (be) all right. I (ring) the boss and tell him I (stay) another night. I (stay) an extra night in York last month and he (not seem) too put out about it.
26 Ann: Why you (stay) an extra night in York?
Tom: I (tell) you tomorrow. Goodnight, Ann.

15 Future forms

132 The present continuous and the future simple

◪ PEG 202, 207

Put the verbs in brackets into the correct tense.

1 Tom: Where you (go) for your next holiday? (*Where have you arranged to go?*)
Ann: I don't know yet but we probably (go) to Spain.
2 We (have) a drink with Peter tonight. (*He has invited us.*) It's his last night; he (leave) tomorrow.
3 Ann: Do you think we (see) Bill tomorrow?
Mary: I hope so. He probably (look) in on his way to the airport.
4 I (see) my bank manager tomorrow. (*I have arranged this.*) I'm going to ask him for a loan but I expect he (refuse).
5 I (know) the result tomorrow. As soon as I hear, I (tell) you.
6 Jack's mother: Jack (be) ready in a moment. He is just finishing breakfast.
Jack's father: If I wait for him any longer I (miss) my train. I think I (walk) on; he probably (catch) me up.
7 I probably (come) to London some time next month. I (give) you a ring nearer the time and tell you when I (come). (*when I have decided/arranged to come*)
8 Hotel Porter: You (get) a parking ticket if you leave your car there, sir. If you (stay) the night (*have arranged to stay*) you (have to) put it in the hotel garage.
Tourist: All right. I (move) it as soon as I've arranged about a room.
9 Ann: I've scorched Bill's shirt. Whatever he (say)?
Mary: Oh, he (not mind). He just (buy) another shirt. He has plenty of money.
10 Peter: We'd better leave a message for Jack. Otherwise he (not know) where we've gone.
George: All right. I (leave) a note on his table.
11 Jack: I don't want to get married. I never (get) married.
Mother: You think that now. But one day you (meet) a girl and you (fall) in love.
12 Tom: I (go) to York tomorrow. (*I have arranged to go.*)
Ann: You (come) back the same day? (*Have you arranged to come back?*)
Tom: No. I probably (have) to spend the night there.

13 Peter: You (walk) home? (*Have you decided to walk?*)
   Andrew: Yes. It's too late for a bus.
   Peter: But it's pouring. You (get) soaked! Here, take this umbrella.
   Andrew: Thanks very much. I (bring) it back tomorrow.
14 Jack: I (have) another window put in. (*I have arranged this.*) They
   (start) work on it tomorrow.
   Ann: That (make) the room much brighter.
15 You (take) any exams this term? (*Have you decided to take an
   exam?*) ~
   Yes, I (take) an English exam at the end of the month. ~
   Do you think you (pass)? ~
   I don't know. If I don't, I (take) it again at the end of next term.
16 Where you (meet) Tom? (*Where have you arranged to meet him?*) ~
   We (meet) at Covent Garden. He (take) me to see *The Magic Flute.*
17 What you (do) next weekend? (*What plans have you made?*) ~
   It depends on the weather. If it's fine we (go) somewhere in the car;
   if it's wet we probably (stay) at home.
18 When Jack (arrive)? (*When did he say he'd arrive?*) ~
   Some time this evening. ~
   And how he (get) here? (*How has he arranged to travel?*) ~
   I don't know yet. I suppose he (come) by car.
19 What they (do) for their holidays? (*Have they decided to do?*) ~
   They (go) camping. ~
   And what (happen) to their dog? (*What plans have they made for the
   dog?*) ~
   They (take) the dog with them. I think he (enjoy) it more than they
   will.
20 Don't make a sound or you (wake) the baby; and then he (not get) to
   sleep again.
21 Mary: Don't forget that Tom's four boys (spend) the weekend here.
   I don't know how we (manage) with four boys under our feet in this
   small house.
   Jack: I have an idea. We (turn) the attic into a playroom. Then they
   (be able) to play trains without tripping anyone up.
22 Tom: Peter's just phoned to say that he (catch) (*has arranged to
   catch*) the 8.10 train and (be) here by 9.00.
23 When George (come) out of hospital? (*What date has been fixed?*) ~
   I don't know. They (move) him (*have arranged to move*) to the County
   Hospital next week so I (have) to ask them about coming out dates.
24 I (ring) Peter tonight. (*We have arranged this.*) I (ask) him to ring
   you? ~
   No, don't bother. I (be) away most of the week. I (write) to him. (*not
   a previous decision*)
25 Don't worry about meals tomorrow. Everything's been arranged. We
   (have) breakfast on the train, we (lunch) with the manager—he
   (stand) us lunch—and the Smiths (give) us dinner after the show.

26 Tom (who has just dropped his key on the path): Never mind;
   Mary's at home. She (let) us in and we (find) the key tomorrow when
   it's light.

27 George and Lucy (get) married next week. You (go) to the
   wedding? ~
   No, I wasn't invited. They (have) a big wedding?

28 I (wait) for you? ~
   No, don't bother. This (take) a long time, I'm sure, and I don't want
   you to miss your train.

29 Tom, the host: What you (have), Paul?
   Paul: I (have) the grilled steak, please.
   Tom: And I (have) roast duck. (He gives his orders to the waiter and
   then studies the wine list.) Hm. You (have) steak and I (have) duck.
   We (have) some red wine.

30 Jack: I (give) you a lift to work tomorrow if you like.
   Tom: Have you borrowed a car?
   Jack. No, I've just bought one. I (collect) it this afternoon.

31 Ann: Peter has set his alarm clock for 5 a.m. He (get) up very early,
   isn't he?
   Mother: Early! Do you know what (happen)? The alarm bell (ring),
   Peter (sleep) through it and he (come) down to breakfast at the usual
   time or a little later.

32 Peter: I (be) promoted next week. Mr Jones (leave) and I (take) over
   the department. (These arrangements have already been made.)
   Ann: At this rate you soon (be) a director, and then you (spend) two
   hours a day on business lunches and (lose) your figure.

33 Tom: I (fly) to New York next week. (This has been arranged.)
   Jack: You (take) your wife with you?
   Tom: No. I know that if I take her she (spend) all her time and most
   of my money in the New York shops.

34 Mary: Jack and I (go) out tonight. We (have) dinner at the Festival
   Hall and (go) to a concert afterwards.
   Ann: And what about the children? I (come) and babysit if you like.
   Mary: Oh, my neighbour (come) in to sit with them. But thank you
   for offering, Ann. I (ask) you next time.

35 Nadia: I see that Amadeus (come) to our local cinema next week.
   George: Oh, good. We (go) and see it together on Monday night?
   Nadia. Yes, let's. I (get) the book out of the library and then I (be
   able) to compare the book and the film.
   George: If you do that out loud during the film I (not pay) for your
   supper afterwards.

36 Ann (reading newspaper): It says here that Smith's (open) their new
   department next week, and that they (have) a sale to give it a good
   start. I think I (look) in on Monday at lunchtime.
   Mary: Good idea! I (come) too.
   Peter (entering room): Where you girls (have) lunch today?
   Mary: We (miss) lunch. We (go) to a sale instead.

Future forms

133 The present continuous and **be going to**

☑ PEG 202-6

Put the verbs in brackets into one of the above forms, using the
present continuous wherever possible.

1 Where you (go) for your holidays? ~ I (go) to Norway. ~
   What you (do) there? ~ I (fish).
2 Where you (go) this evening? ~
   I (not go) anywhere. I (stay) at home. I (write) some letters.
3 Take an umbrella; it (rain).
4 How long you (stay) in this country? (*Have you decided to stay?*) ~
   Another month. I (go) home at the end of the month. ~
   What you (do) then? ~
   I (try) to get a job.
5 I (dye) these curtains. ~
   You (do) it yourself, or (have) it done? ~
   I (have) it done. Who should I take them to?
6 I've seen the film, now I (read) the book. I've just got a copy from
   the library. (*I haven't started the book yet.*)
7 You (do) anything next weekend? ~
   Yes, my nephews (come) and I (show) them round London. ~
   You (take) them to the theatre? (*Have you booked seats?*) ~
   No, they're too young for that. I (take) them to the zoo.
8 We (start) early tomorrow. We (go) to Ben Nevis. ~
   You (climb) Ben Nevis? ~
   Not me. Tom (climb) it. I (sit) at the bottom and (do) some
   sketching.
9 Uncle: I hear you (go) to the regatta tomorrow. You (sail) in it?
   Niece: No, but we (take) our cameras. We (try) to photograph the
   winning yachts.
10 You (not ask) your boss to give you a fire in your office? ~
   It isn't worth while. I (leave) at the end of the week. ~
   Really? And what you (do) then? You (have) a holiday? ~
   No, I (start) another job the following Monday.
11 I hear you've bought a caravan. You (use) it for your holidays? ~
   No, I (live) in it. I (start) moving my things next week. ~
   What you (do) with your house? ~
   I (sell) it to the man who sold me the caravan. He (get) married next
   month.
12 Mrs Jones (go) to hospital. She (have) her appendix out. ~
   Who (look) after the children? ~
   Her sister (come) down from Scotland.
13 He isn't happy at his boarding school. I (send) him to a day school. ~
   Have you decided on the other school? ~
   No, but I (see) (*have an appointment with*) the headmaster of the Park
   School this afternoon. I'll probably send him there.

14 Tom (arrive) tomorrow. ~
He (spend) the weekend here or (catch) the night train back as usual? ~
He (spend) the weekend. He (give) a lecture on Friday and (attend) a big reception on Saturday.

15 He (bring) his wife with him? (*Has he arranged to bring his wife?*) ~
Yes. She (do) some shopping while he (give) his lecture.

16 I've just arranged to do a part-time job. I (start) on Monday. ~
What you (do) the rest of the time? ~
I (study).

17 You (go) abroad for your holiday? ~
Well, I (get) a holiday job. I (go) to an agent's on Saturday to find out about it. I (ask) for a job abroad; but of course they may all be taken. ~
You might get a job picking grapes. Jack (join) a camp in the South of France—his university arranged it—and they all (pick) grapes.

18 I (buy) a new coat. The weather report says that it (be) very cold.

19 Ann has won a car in a competition but she can't drive.
Tom: What you (do) with the car? You (sell) it?
Ann: No, I (learn) to drive. I (have) my first lesson next Monday.

20 I hear you've bought a new house. ~
Yes. I (move) in next week. ~
You (have) a house warming party? ~
Not just yet. I (paint) the house first. The paintwork's terrible.

21 You (have) it done? (*Have you arranged to have it done?*) ~
No, I (do) it myself. I (use) that non-drip paint so it shouldn't be too difficult. And the family (help), of course. ~
What about ladders? ~
Oh, I've fixed that. I (hire) from the local do-it-yourself shop.

22 I (do) a lot of work in the garden, too. I (plant) 20 apple trees and (make) a lawn in front of the house. ~
All that digging will take years. You (give) up your job?

23 I (get) some help with the garden. (*I have arranged this.*) Two men (start) work on the hedge on Friday and a lawn expert (come) on Monday to advise me about the lawn.

24 The employers (meet) the strikers again tomorrow. (*This has been arranged.*) ~
They just (repeat) what they said today? Or they (climb) down? ~
I believe that they (offer) a 10 per cent rise plus a productivity bonus.

134 be going to and will + infinitive

◪ PEG 205

Put the verbs in brackets into one of the above forms.

1 Where are you off to with that ladder? ~
I (have) a look at the roof; it's leaking and I think a tile has slipped.

2 We bought our new garage in sections and we (assemble) it ourselves. ~
That sounds rather interesting. I (come) and help you if you like.

3 Why do you want all the furniture out of the room? ~
Because I (shampoo) the carpet. It's impossible to do it unless you take everything off it first.

4 Here are the matches: but what do you want them for? ~
I (make) a bonfire at the end of the garden; I want to burn that big heap of rubbish. ~
Well, be careful. If the fire gets too big it (burn) the apple trees.

5 Have you decided on your colour scheme? ~
Oh yes, and I've bought the paint. I (paint) this room blue and the sitting room green.

6 Why are you asking everyone to give you bits of material? ~
Because I (make) a patchwork quilt.

7 I wonder if Ann knows that the time of the meeting has been changed. ~
Probably not. I (look) in on my way home and tell her. I'm glad you thought of it.

8 Leave a note for them on the table and they (see) it when they come in.

9 I'm afraid I'm not quite ready. ~
Never mind. I (wait).

10 Do you have to carry so much stuff on your backs? ~
Yes, we do. We (camp) out and (cook) our own meals, so we have to carry a lot.

11 I've been measuring the windows. I (put) in double glazing.

12 You (wear) that nice dress in a dinghy? ~
Of course not! I (sit) on the pier and (watch) you all sailing. I (not get) all wet and muddy and pretend that I'm enjoying it!

13 If you leave your keys with the hall porter he (take) the car round to the garage.

14 Shop assistant: We have some very nice strawberries.
Customer: All right. I (have) a pound.

15 Husband: This bread is absolutely tasteless! I wish we could have home-made bread.
Wife: All right. I (start) making it. I (get) a book about home baking today, and from now on I (bake) all our bread!

16 Mary: Ann's busy baking. Apparently she (bake) all their bread from now on.
Jean: She soon (get) tired of that.

17 Why have you brought your camera? You (try) to take photographs?
It's not allowed, you know. ~
No, I (try) to sell the camera. ~
That's not allowed either. If a policemen sees you, he (confiscate)
the camera.

18 Tom to Jack, who has just helped him to change a wheel: I (have) to
leave this at the garage; I don't know how to mend a puncture in a
tubeless tyre.
Jack: But it's quite easy. I (come) round this evening and show you if
you like.

19 Later:
Tom to wife: I (not take) the tyre to the garage. I (mend) it myself.
Jack (help) me.

20 Why are you rolling up the carpets? You (paint) the ceiling? ~
No, I (take) the carpet to the cleaner's.

21 Ann: Here's the letter to the landlord. If there's anything I should
add, say so and I (add) it.
Peter: It's fine, but it's illegible. He (not be able) to read it.
Ann: Oh, I (type) it! (*She had always intended to type it.*)
Peter: Good, then we (have) a copy.

22 Employer: But there are a lot of mistakes in this, Miss Jones.
Miss Jones: Yes, I suppose there are. All right, I (type) it again.

23 Mrs Smith: Your cold's worse, Ann. Go back to bed and I (ring) the
school and tell them you can't come.

24 Mrs Smith was just picking up the receiver when her husband came
downstairs. 'Ann's not well,' she said. 'I (ring) the school and say
that she can't come.'

25 Ann: Why are you taking fishing rods? You (not climb) the mountain
after all?
Tom: We (climb) *and* fish. There's a lake on top and we (try) to get
some fish out of it.
Ann: Well, if you catch any I (cook) them; but I think I (buy) some
all the same.

26 Mary, meeting Jack carrying two buckets of water: Hello, Jack!
Where's the fire?
Jack: I (wash) the car, if you want to know. Would you like to help
me?
Mary: I'm not dressed for it but I (come) and watch.

27 Where are all those children off to with baskets? ~
They (pick) blackberries. They probably (come) back at 6.00 with
their baskets crammed and then their mothers (start) making jam.

28 Ann: You (have) to go now, Tom, or you (be) late.
Mary: But it's pouring. He (get) soaked if he goes out in that.
Tom: You're right. You (let) me stay a little longer?

29 George and Paul find an injured man lying by the roadside.
Paul: I (stay) with him, George, if you go back and get help.
George: All right. I (try) to get a lift back.

30 No, I'm not going away for the weekend. I'm staying at home. I
(start) building my garage. The bricks have come at last. ~
You (do) it all by yourself? ~
No, my nephew (help) me. I suggested it to him yesterday and he
was quite enthusiastic.

31 He says he's tired of writing books about horrible people who get
more and more horrible on every page, and now he (write) about
perfectly charming people who are happily married. ~
I wonder if anyone (buy) it. ~
Oh yes, people (buy) it. He's a famous writer.

32 I hear the farmer down the road has hired a bulldozer. ~
Yes, he (dig) up all his hedges and put in fences instead.

33 The new owner (make) any changes? ~
He's made some already. You should see his new menus. He
(concentrate) more on the restaurant than the shop.

34 What do you want all those corks for? ~
I've bought a cask of wine and I (bottle) it myself.

35 There's someone at the door. ~
I (go). But I expect it's someone for you.

36 Where are you all going? ~
There's nothing to eat or drink here except one chop and a bottle of
champagne, so we (buy) some fish and chips and eat them in the car.
Come with us. ~
No, thanks. I think I (stay) and use up the chop and champagne.

135 The future continuous and **will** + infinitive

◢ PEG 214–15

Put the verbs in brackets into one of the above forms.

1 Jack usually gives me a lift home, but we both (come) home by train
tomorrow as his car is being repaired.

2 He says he (meet) us at the bus stop, but I'm sure he (forget) to turn
up.

3 Don't ring now; she (watch) her favourite TV programme. ~
All right. I (ring) at 8.30.

4 I wonder what I (do) this time next year. ~
I expect you still (work) at the same office.

5 I'd like to double-glaze the bedroom windows. ~
All right. I (get) the materials at once and we (do) it this weekend.

6 Wait a bit. Don't drink your tea without milk. The milkman (come)
in a minute.

7 What are you doing next weekend? ~
Oh, I (work) as usual. I'm always on duty at weekends.

8 Air hostess: We (take) off in a few minutes. Please fasten your seat
belts.

 9 He (come) if you ask him.

10 I arranged to play tennis with Tom at nine tonight. ~
But you (play) in semi-darkness. You won't be able to see the ball.

11 I (get) you some aspirins if you like. The chemist's still (be) open. ~
No, don't bother. The office boy (go) out in a minute to post the
letters; I (ask) him to buy me some.

12 It (be) very late when she gets home and her parents (wonder)
what's happened.

13 I never (be) able to manage on my own. ~
But you won't be on your own. Tom (help) you. Look—his name is
bracketed with yours on the list. ~
Oh, that's all right. But Tom (not help) me: I (help) Tom. He always
takes charge when we're on duty together.

14 I (write) postcards every week, I promise, and I (try) to make them
legible. If necessary I (type) them.

15 Typist: Are you in a hurry for this letter, Mr Jones? Because I (type)
Mr White's letters at four o'clock and if yours could wait till—
Mr Jones: I'd like it a little earlier than four if possible.
Typist: All right. I (type) it for you now.

16 What happened at last night's meeting? I hear there was quite a
disturbance. ~
Come and see me and I (tell) you. I don't want to talk about it on the
phone.

17 I'm going to Switzerland next week. ~
You're lucky. The wild flowers just (come) out.

18 This time next month the snow (melt) and skiing will be over.

19 The first day of the term will be horrible, for everybody (talk) about
their holidays and (show) photographs of marvellous foreign
beaches, and as I haven't been anywhere I (feel) terribly out of it.

20 I (tell) her what you say but she (not believe) it.

21 It's 7 a.m. and here we are on top of a mountain. At home people
just (get) up now.

22 But you can't go to a fancy dress party in a dinner jacket! ~
Why not? ~
Because everyone (wear) fancy dress. ~
All right. I (wrap) the hearthrug round me and (go) as a caveman.

23 The coming election (be) the main topic of conversation for the next
fortnight. The party leaders (speak) on TV and the local candidates
(address) meetings in the constituencies.

24 This time tomorrow everyone (read) of your success, and all sorts of
people (ring) up to congratulate you.

25 That oak tree still (stand) there fifty years from now.

26 You please (forward) my mail to the Grand Hotel? I (stay) there as
usual for the first fortnight in August.

27 Heavens! Look at the time. Your father (come) home in a minute and
I haven't even started getting dinner ready!

28 James (leave) for Australia quite soon. He has got a job there.

29 The car (not start). ~
If you get in, Tom and I (give) it a push.

30 It's nearly Christmas already. Carol singers (come) round soon.

31 On the news tonight they mentioned the possibility of a power strike. Everybody (look) for candles tomorrow.

32 Hotel receptionist on phone to client: What time you (arrive), Mr Jones?
Mr Jones: I (travel) on the 4.30 from Victoria. There (be) taxis at the station?
Receptionist: Don't bother about taxis, Mr Jones. We (send) the hotel car down for you.

33 You (use) your dictionary this afternoon? ~
No. You can borrow it if you like. ~
Thanks very much. I (put) it back on your desk this evening.

34 Ann: This time next week I (have) my first skating lesson.
Tom: And this time next month you (hobble) about, covered in bruises!

35 It's a beautiful drive. I'm sure you (enjoy) the scenery. ~
I (not have) a chance to look at it. I (map-read), and Tom gets so furious if I make a mistake that I (be) afraid to take my eyes off the map.

36 I (write) in code if you insist, but I don't think it's at all necessary.

136 The future continuous and **will** (mostly negative)

☑ PEG 214–15

Put the verbs in brackets into one of the above forms.

1 You ask him. It's no good my asking him. He (not do) anything I say.

2 Ann says she (not come) if Tom is driving. She says she doesn't want to die yet. ~
Well, tell her Tom (not drive). He's had his licence suspended.

3 Pupil to teacher: I (not come) back next term. My parents want me to get a job.

4 Headmaster: I (not have) girls here in slacks. If you come here tomorrow in slacks I'll send you home.
Girl: All right, I (not come) tomorrow. I'll get a job.

5 Mother: I'm so grateful for the help you've given Jack; I hope you'll be able to go on helping him.
Teacher: I'm afraid I (not teach) him next term because I only teach the fifth form and he'll be in the sixth.

6 Schoolboy (in school dining hall): The last week of our last term! I wonder what we (do) this time next year.
Friend: Well, we (not eat) school dinners anyway. That's one comfort.

7 They give very good dinners at the school but my daughter (not eat) them. She prefers to go out and buy fish and chips.

8 Yes, you can stroke the dog; he (not bite) you.

9 Shall we meet him at the station? ~
Oh, he (not come) by train. He never comes by train.

10 I've fished that river every year for the last fifteen years. ~
Well, nobody (fish) it next year. The water's been polluted. All the fish are dead.

11 I'll cook any fish you catch, but I (not clean) them. You'll have to do that yourself.

12 I (not show) any films this time. The projector's broken down.

13 Housewife: This time next week I (not wash) up the breakfast things. I (have) breakfast in bed in a luxury hotel.

14 I (not wear) glasses when you see me next. I'll be wearing contact lenses. You probably (not recognize) me.

15 I'll tell him the truth of course. But it (not be) any good. He (not believe) me.

16 Customer: When you deliver my next order—
Shop assistant: We (not deliver) any more orders, I'm afraid. This branch is closing down.

17 It'll be easy to pick her out in that bright red coat of hers. ~
But she (not wear) the red coat! She's given it away.

18 No, I (not tell) you the end! Go on reading and find out for yourself!

19 You (not use) your car when you're on holiday, will you? ~
No, but don't ask me to lend it to you because I (not do) it. Not after what happened last time.

20 I (have) to be a bit careful about money when I retire because I'll only be getting half my present salary. But of course I (not pay) so much tax.

21 You can either pay the fine or go to prison for a month. ~
I (not pay) the fine. ~
Then you (have) to go to prison.

22 He's a clever boy but he's lazy. He (not work).

23 I wonder how Jack (get on) with the new secretary. ~
Oh, Jack (not work) here after this week. He's being transferred.

24 According to the brochures this hotel prides itself on its service, but the staff not even (show) a guest to his room unless he insists. I (not come) here again.

137 The future perfect

☐ PEG 216

Put the verbs in brackets into the future perfect tense.
will is replaceable by **shall** in 3, 6, 7, 11, 13, 14 and 17.

1 I hope they (repair) this road by the time we come back next summer.

2 By the end of next week my wife (do) her spring cleaning and we'll all be able to relax again.

3 Yes, I make jam every week. I (make) about 200 kilos by the end of the summer.

4 In two months' time he (finish) his preliminary training and will be starting work.

5 He spends all his spare time planting trees. He says that by the end of next year he (plant) 2,000.

6 I'll be back again at the end of next month. ~
I hope I (pass) my driving test by then. If I have, I'll meet your train.

7 Come back in an hour. I (do) my packing by then and we'll be able to have a talk.

8 When he reaches Land's End he (walk) 1,500 miles.

9 He's only 35 but he's started losing his hair already. He (lose) it all by the time he's 50.

10 His father left him £400,000, but he lives so extravagantly that he (spend) it all before he's 30.

11 By the end of next year I (work) for him for 45 years.

12 Everywhere you go in central London you see blocks of flats being pulled down and huge hotels being erected. In ten years' time all the private residents (be driven) out and there'll be nothing but one vast hotel after another.

13 Our committee is trying to raise money to buy a new lifeboat. By the end of the year we (send) out 5,000 letters asking for contributions.

14 By the end of my tour I (give) exactly the same lecture 53 times.

15 A hundred people have died of starvation already. By the end of the week two hundred (die). When are you going to send help?

16 Since he began driving, Tom has driven an average of 5,000 miles a year, and had an average of 2½ accidents a year. So by the time he's 60 he (drive) 200,000 miles and had 50 accidents. Let's try to persuade him to go back to cycling.

17 Did you say you wanted help picking apples? I could come on 1 October. ~
We (pick) them all by then. But come all the same.

18 Apparently Venice is slowly sinking into the sea. Scientists are trying to save it but by the time they've found the answer the city probably (sink).

138 The present simple and continuous, the future simple and conditional

■ PEG 164–7, 172–4, 207–9, 219

Put the verbs in brackets into the correct tense. Note that in nos. 1, 13, 17 and 18 the dramatic present tense is used (see PEG 174 C).

Part 1

1 Ann (look) for a bed-sitter. She (see) an advertisement in the local paper and (ring) up Mrs Smith, the owner of the house. Mrs Smith (answer) the phone.

2 Ann: Good afternoon. I (ring) about the room you advertised.
Mrs Smith: Oh yes.

3 Ann: The advertisement (say) 'Share bathroom and kitchen'. How many other people (use) the bathroom and kitchen?

4 Mrs Smith: Only one other—an Italian girl. And she (use) the kitchen very little. She (eat) out most of the time. I (not think) she (like) cooking.

5 Ann: That (suit) me all right. I (like) cooking. But how we (arrange) about paying for the gas we (use) in the kitchen?

6 Mrs Smith: The rent (include) gas for cooking, also hot water and light. But it (not include) heating. Each room has its own fire and meter.

7 Ann: I (see). And the room (face) the front or the back?

8 Mrs Smith: It (face) the front. It (looks) out on the garden square; and it (get) a lot of sun.

9 Ann: That (sound) very nice. Could I come and see it this evening?
Mrs Smith: Yes, the earlier the better.

10 Ann: 7 p.m. (suit) you? I (not be able to) come before that as I usually (not get) away from the office till 6 p.m.

11 Mrs Smith: 7 p.m. (be) all right. I (not think) you (have) any difficulty in finding us. The 14 bus (pass) the house and (stop) a few doors further along, outside the Post Office.

12 Ann: I'm sure I (find) it all right. I (see) you at 7.00 then, Mrs Smith. Goodbye.

13 At 6.30 Mr Smith (come) home from work. He (ask) his wife about the room.

14 Mrs Smith: I haven't let it yet but a girl (come) to see it at 7.00.

15 Mr Smith: She probably (come) at 7.30 just as we (sit) down to supper. People coming here for the first time always (get) lost. I (not think) you (give) proper directions.

16 Mrs Smith: Oh yes, I (do). But nobody (listen) to directions these days. Anyway I'm sure this girl (be) in time.

17 Just then the doorbell (ring). Mrs Smith (look) at her husband and (smile).

18 'You see,' she (say), and (go) to open the door.

Part 2 Weekend plans.

19 Bill (on phone): Hello, Peter. Bill here. I (speak) from Southwold. I (spend) my holidays here this year in a caravan. You (like) to come for the weekend?

20 Peter: I (love) to. But how I (get) to you?

21 Bill: Get the 8 o'clock train to Halesworth and I (meet) you at the station.

22 Peter: OK. I (do) that. Are you near the sea, Bill?

23 Bill: Yes. When the tide (come) in, I'm almost afloat!

24 Peter: It (sound) marvellous!

25 Bill: It is. Wait till you (see) it!

26 (Friday) Peter's mother: What you (do) this weekend, Peter? (*What plans have you made?*)

27 Peter: I (spend) it with Bill in a caravan on the Suffolk coast.

28 Mother: The east coast in this wind! You (freeze) to death—if Bill's cooking (not kill) you first! How you (get) there? (*What travel arrangements have you made?*)

29 Peter: I (catch) the 8 o'clock train and Bill (meet) me at Halesworth.

30 Mother: Then I (lend) you my alarm clock, and we'd better have breakfast at seven. I (tell) Mary.

31 Peter: Poor Mary! She (like) a lie-in on Saturdays!

32 (Friday evening) Mother: I (give) you a call at 6.30, Peter, in case you (fall) asleep again after your alarm (go) off. By the way, Mary, we (have) breakfast at seven tomorrow as Peter (go) away for the weekend and (catch) an early train.

33 Mary (petulantly): Peter always (go) away. I never (go) anywhere!

34 Mother: When he (come) home on Sunday night and you (hear) how awful it was, you (be) very glad you stayed at home!

16 Conditionals

139 Conditional sentences: type 1

☐ PEG 221

Put the verbs in brackets into the correct form.

1 I'll look for your notebook and if I (find) it I (give) you a ring.
2 If you (smoke) in a non-smoking compartment the other passengers (object).
3 I'll wash the glasses in this nice hot water. ~
   No, don't. If you (put) them into very hot water they (crack).
4 If you (see) Tom tell him I have a message for him.
5 If he (win) he (get) £1,000; if he (come) in second he (get) £500.
6 If you (feel) too hot during the night turn down the central heating.
7 Tom: Jack is a translator; he translates 1,000 words a day and gets £100 a week, which he says isn't enough to live on.
   Bill: Well, if he (want) more money he (have) to do more work. Advise him to translate 2,000 words a day.
8 If you (finish) with your dictionary I'd like to borrow it.
9 Jack (in canoe): Watch me! I'm going to stand up!
   Tom (on the bank): He's an idiot! If he (stand) up in the canoe it (capsize).
10 The lift wasn't working when I was here last. If it still (not work) we (have) to use the stairs.
11 I shan't wake if the alarm clock (not go) off.
12 I shan't wake unless I (hear) the alarm.
13 If you'd like some ice I (get) some from the fridge.
14 He's only sixteen but he wants to leave school at the end of the term. ~
   If he (leave) now he (be) sorry afterwards.
15 I expect it will freeze tonight. ~
   If it (freeze) tonight the roads (be) very slippery tomorrow.
16 That book is overdue. If you (not take) it back to the library tomorrow you (have) to pay a fine.
17 Unless Tom (take) his library book back tomorrow he (have) to pay a fine.
18 You'd better take the day off if you (not feel) well tomorrow.
19 If a driver (brake) suddenly on a wet road he (skid).
20 If you (like) I (get) you a job in this company.
21 If you (like) a job in this company, I'll get you one.
22 My dog never starts a fight. He never growls unless the other dog (growl) first.
23 You can use my phone if yours (not work).
24 If you (not know) the meaning of a word you may use a dictionary.

25 If Jack (refuse) to help we'll have to manage without him.
26 If Jack (not help) we'll have to manage without him.
27 (Tom is putting his coat on.) Ann: If you (go) out would you buy me some cigarettes?
28 Henry can't count. ~
   Why you (employ) him as a cashier if he can't count?
29 The police will test the knife for fingerprints. If your fingerprints are on it you (be) charged with murder.
30 Tom: I hate my job
   Peter: If you (hate) it why you (not change) it?
31 You can ask for a continental breakfast if you (not want) a full breakfast.
32 If you (hear) from Tom could you please let me know?
33 Caller: Could I speak to Mr Jones, please?
   Secretary: If you'd wait a moment I (see) if he's in.
34 I'm not expecting any messages, but if someone (ring) while I am out could you say that I'll be back by 6.00?
35 (Notice in a box of chocolates): Every care has been taken with preparation and packing, but if these chocolates (reach) you in a damaged condition please return them to us and we will send you another box.
36 If you (care) to see some of his drawings I (send) them round to your office.

140 Conditional sentences: type 1

☑ PEG 221

Part 1 Drill: reply to the following sentences as shown in the example:
   If Tom meets us at the station we'll be all right.
   But what'll we do if he doesn't meet us?

1 If he pays me tonight I'll have enough money for the tickets.
2 If I get a work permit I'll stay for another six months.
3 If I pass this exam I'll go to the university next October.
4 If he agrees to let me go on working after marriage I'll marry him (*Use* refuse.)
5 I'm going to say to the boss, 'I can't work with Smith. Either I go or he goes. You'll have to choose between us.'
6 If I can find a cheap room I'll stay a fortnight.
7 Your parachute should open after ten seconds.
8 Provided you remember the password you'll be in no danger. (*Use* forget.)
9 Tell the police the truth. I'm sure they'll believe you.
10 If the baby is a girl we're going to call her Ann.

11 If we get a lift we'll be in time.
12 If London airport is clear of fog we'll land there.
13 If Tom helps us the job will only take half an hour.
14 I haven't got a key but Jack will let us in if he is at home.
15 If the ice is thick enough we'll be able to walk across the river.
16 The sands are quite safe as long as you don't walk on them when the tide is coming in.
17 If it's fine tomorrow we'll go for a walk.
18 Driver (having just changed a wheel): We'll be all right provided we don't have another puncture.

Part 2 Rewrite the following sentences replacing **would like** by **like** and making any necessary changes.

If you'd like to wait you can wait here.
If you like you can wait here or
You can wait here if you like.

1 If you'd like a copy of the book I can get you one. (*If you like I . . .*)
2 If you'd like me to ask if there are any vacancies I will. (*If you like I'll . . .*)
3 If you'd like to see the photographs I'll bring them round tonight.
4 If you'd like me to give you a hand I will.
5 If you'd like to watch the procession from my balcony you can.
6 If you'd like to see London from the air I'll arrange a helicopter trip for you.
7 You knitted a very nice sweater for Tom. ~
   Yes, if you'd like me to knit you one I will.
8 If you'd like to borrow my car you can.
9 I'll come back and finish it tomorrow if you'd like me to.
10 If you'd like Ann to type it again I'll ask her to.
11 If you'd like an application form I'll get you one.
12 If you'd like me to go with you I will.
13 I'll paint the front door blue if you'd like that.
14 If you'd like to leave the washing-up till tomorrow you can.
15 If you'd like to postpone the trip till next week we'll do that.
16 If you'd like me to ask him to our next party I will.
17 If you'd like to meet the President I will arrange it.
18 If you'd like to go sailing tomorrow we will.

141 Conditional sentences: type 2

☑ PEG 222

Put the verbs in brackets into the correct form.

1 Of course I'm not going to give her a diamond ring. If I (give) her a diamond ring she (sell) it.

Conditionals

2 Tom: I woke up to find the room full of smoke; but I knew exactly what to do.
   Ann: If I (wake) up to find the room full of smoke I (have) no idea what to do.
3 Ann: I couldn't live without Tom. If he (go) off with another girl I (pine) away and die. But I have complete confidence in Tom.
4 Husband: But I'm not going on a diet. Why should I go on a diet?
   Wife: If you (go) on a diet you (lose) weight.
5 If someone (say), 'I'll give you £500 to go into court and swear that this statement is true,' what you (do)?
6 If we (work) all night we (finish) in time; but we have no intention of working all night.
7 You must never blow out a gas light. Do you know what (happen) if you (blow) out a gas light?
8 If I (see) a tiger walking across Hyde Park I (climb) a tree. ~
   That (not be) any use. The tiger (climb) after you.
9 If I (come) across two men fighting with knives I (call) the police. ~
   But this is a very peaceful area.
10 Ann: All your clothes are years out of date. Why don't you throw them away?
   Mary: Don't be ridiculous! If I (throw) my clothes away I (have) to ask my husband for £1,000 to buy new ones.
11 Ann: If you (ask) him for £1,000 what he (say)?
12 Mary: He (be) too horrified to speak at first. But when he'd recovered from the shock, he probably (start) talking about a divorce.
13 If someone (ring) my doorbell at 3 a.m. I (be) very unwilling to open the door.
14 If I (see) a python in Piccadilly I (assume) it had escaped from a circus.
15 Tom: The plane was on fire so we baled out.
   Ann: I don't think I (have) the nerve to do that even if the plane (be) on fire.
16 We train the children to file out of the classroom quietly, because if a whole class (rush) at the door someone (get) hurt.
17 Why don't you buy a season ticket? ~
   Because I lose everything. If I (buy) a season ticket I (lose) it.
18 Why don't you bring your car to work? If I (have) a car I (bring) it to work.
19 Jack: They get £150 a week.
   Tom: They can't get £150 a week. If they (do) they (not be) striking for £120.
20 Ann: George is fourteen.
   Tom: He must be older than that. He's in a full-time job. If he (be) only fourteen he still (be) at school.
21 He is staying at the Savoy in London. ~
   Is he very rich? ~
   I suppose he is. If he (be) a poor man he (not stay) at the Savoy.

22 If I (have) heaps of money I (drink) champagne with every meal.

23 If you (drink) champagne with every meal you soon (get) tired of it.

24 Prime Minister on golf course: I'm not at all worried about the situation. If I (be) worried I not (play) golf at this moment.

25 But I don't want to buy an elephant! ~
I know that. But where you (go) if you (do) want to buy one?

26 Why don't you get a cat? If you (keep) a cat the mice (not run) about everywhere.

27 What time of year do you think it is in this picture? Summer? ~
No, it must be winter. If it (be) summer the people (not sit) round that big fire.

28 Tom: Oh yes, I heard the phone ringing.
Peter: Well, if you (hear) the phone ringing why you (not answer) it?
(*Be careful; this is not a true conditional sentence.*)

29 Your notes are almost illegible. Why don't you type them? If you (type) them they (be) a lot easier to read.

30 If only we (have) a light! It's depressing waiting in darkness!

31 A university degree is a useful thing. If I (have) a university degree I now (sit) in a comfortable office instead of standing at a street corner selling newspapers.

32 I (be) very grateful if you kindly (sign) this document and let me have it back as soon as possible.

33 If the earth suddenly (stop) spinning we all (fly) off it.

34 Why are you so late? ~
We got stuck in a snowdrift! Luckily a lorry-driver saw us and towed us out. But for him we still (be) there!

35 We didn't exactly break down. We had a puncture. ~
But if it (be) only a puncture why you (not change) the wheel and come on? (*See 28 above.*)

36 I have no particular desire to win the Football Pools. If I (win) an enormous sum everybody (write) to me asking for money.

142 Conditional sentences: type 2

■ PEG 222

Rewrite these sentences, using an **if** construction.
> He smokes too much; perhaps that's why he can't get rid of his cough.
> *If he didn't smoke so much he might get rid of his cough* or
> *If he smoked less he might (be able to) get rid of his cough.*

1 She is very shy; that's why she doesn't enjoy parties.

2 He doesn't take any exercise; that's why he is so unhealthy.

3 I haven't the right change so we can't get tickets from the machine.

4 They speak French to her, not English, so her English doesn't improve.

5 He doesn't work overtime, so he doesn't earn as much as I do.
6 My number isn't in the directory so people don't ring me up.
7 The police are not armed so we don't have gun battles in the streets.
8 The shops don't deliver now, which makes life difficult.
9 He's very thin; perhaps that's why he feels the cold so much.
10 We haven't any matches so we can't light a fire.
11 It's a pity we haven't a steak to cook over our camp fire.
12 I'm fat; that's why I can't get through the bathroom window.
13 He doesn't help me, possibly because I never ask him for help.
14 I can't drive so we can't take the car.
15 We have no ladder so we can't get over the wall.
16 My friend advised me to sell it. (*My friend said, 'If I . . . you I . . .'*)
17 I haven't much time so I read very little.
18 They don't clean the windows so the rooms look rather dark.
19 He never polishes his shoes, so he never looks smart.
20 He doesn't pay his staff properly; perhaps that's why they don't work well.
21 We haven't got central heating, so the house is rather cold.
22 I have no dog, so I don't like being alone in the house at night.
23 He spends hours watching television; that's why he never has time to do odd jobs in the house.
24 I haven't got a vacuum cleaner; that's why I'm so slow.
25 I don't know his address, so I can't write to him.
26 He never shaves; that's the only reason he looks unattractive.
27 You work too fast; that's why you make so many mistakes.
28 I can't park near my office; that's why I don't come by car.
29 I live a long way from the centre; that's why I am always late for work.
30 I haven't a map so I can't direct you.
31 People drive very fast. That's why there are so many accidents.
32 English people speak very quickly. Perhaps that's why I can't understand them.
33 My house is guarded by two Alsatian dogs. That's the only reason it isn't broken into every night.
34 The flats are not clearly numbered, so it is very difficult to find anyone.
35 You don't wipe your feet, so you make muddy marks all over the floor.
36 I live near my office, so I don't spend much time travelling to work.

143 Conditional sentences: type 3

■ PEG 223

Put the verbs in brackets into the correct tenses.

1 If he (not take) his gloves off he (not get) frost bitten.

2 She was sent to prison only because she refused to pay the fine; if she (pay) the fine she (not be) sent to prison.

3 He didn't tell me that he was a vegetarian till halfway through the meal. If he (tell) me earlier I (cook) him something more suitable.

4 I had no map; that's why I got lost. If I (had) a map I (be) all right.

5 Why didn't you say that you were short of money? If I (know) I (lend) you some.

6 It's lucky he had his torch with him. If he (not have) it he (fall) down the cellar steps.

7 The job is much worse than I expected. If I (realise) how awful it was going to be I (not accept) it.

8 It was the drug, not the disease, that killed him. He would still be alive today if he (not take) that drug.

9 This room's freezing because the fire has only just been lit. ~
If it (be lit) this morning, as I suggested, the room would be warm enough to sit in now.

10 I overslept; that's why I'm half an hour late; and if my phone (not ring) at nine o'clock I might still be in bed.

11 It was rather a dull game so I left before the end; if I (wait) another five minutes I (see) Chelsea scoring a really exciting goal.

12 The paraffin heater was perfectly safe. There (not be) a fire if the children (not knock) it over.

13 It's a pity he never patented his invention. If he (patent) it he (make) a lot of money.

14 The fog came down suddenly and I suppose they didn't know which way to turn; if only they (have) a map and compass with them they (not be) drowned.

15 He asked his parents for a loan but he didn't say what he wanted the money for, so they refused. I think if he (tell) them that he wanted to open a restaurant they (agree).

16 The accident was mainly Tom's fault. He was driving much too close to the car in front. If he (be) further away he (be able) to stop in time.

17 The launching of the rocket was delayed half an hour by bad weather. If the weather (be) good they (launch) it at 8.30 instead of at 9.00.

18 Why did you throw away those newspapers? I hadn't finished with them. ~
I'm sorry. If I (know) you were still reading them I (not throw) them away.

19 I'm sorry you didn't tell me that dogs were allowed in the hotel; if I (know) I (bring) my dog. He (enjoy) the walk.

20 Most people (attend) the union meeting if they had had longer notice of it.

21 He says he refused the job, but that this was nothing to do with the salary. He (refuse) even if they (offer) him twice as much.

22 The club secretary is useless. He never tells anybody anything. We (not know) about this meeting if the chairman (not tell) us.

23 When the director asked her to play the lead she agreed though she didn't know anything about the play. I think that if she (read) the play first she (refuse) the part.

24 The burglar made quite a lot of noise getting into the house; but fortunately for him the family were watching a noisy TV play. If they (play) cards they certainly (hear) him.

25 If you had been there what you (do)?

26 It rained, which spoiled our picnic; but if it (not rain) it (be) a great success.

27 Why are you in such a bad temper? ~
Because I've been waiting for 40 minutes in an icy wind. If you (wait) 40 minutes in an icy wind you'd be bad-tempered, too.

28 You used wet sticks; that's why the fire took so long to light. If you (use) dry sticks it (light) long ago.

29 I didn't recognize him at first because he was wearing dark glasses; if he (not wear) them I (recognize) him immediately.

30 You knew that horse was going to win! ~
Don't be ridiculous! If I (knew) I (back) him myself.

31 Why didn't you phone from the village? ~
Because there was no phone in the village. If there (be) of course we (phone) from there.

32 When the weather got bad the climbing party turned back, all except Tom and his brothers, who decided to go on. If only they (turn) back with the others they would be alive today.

33 He was not very happy at school because he was a bookish boy, not at all interested in games. If he (play) games like the other boys he (have) a much better time.

34 We had to stand almost all the way. It was all Tom's fault. If he (book) seats, as I told him to, we (have) quite a comfortable journey.

35 We were travelling with false passports. That was the trouble. If our passports (be) all right we (not be) arrested.

36 They voted by a show of hands and decided in favour of a strike. But it was by a narrow margin and I think that if they (hold) a secret ballot there (not be) a strike.

144 Conditional sentences: type 3

■ PEG 223

Rewrite these sentences using an **if** construction.
> You didn't tell me we had run out of bread, so I didn't buy any.
> *If you had told me we had run out of bread I'd have bought some.*

1 I didn't see the signal, so I didn't stop.
2 I didn't know your number, so I didn't ring.
3 She didn't know you were in hospital, so she didn't visit you.
4 We only came by bus because there were no taxis.

5 She didn't speak to him, possibly because she was so shy.
6 Landlord: She threatened to set fire to her flat; that's the only reason I asked her to leave.
7 We didn't visit the museum because we hadn't time.
8 I only came up the stairs because the lift wasn't working.
9 We didn't listen carefully; perhaps that's why we made this mistake.
10 We got a lift, so we reached the station in time.
11 You washed it in boiling water; that's why it shrank.
12 We missed the train because we were using an out-of-date timetable.
13 His own men deserted him; that's the only reason why he failed.
14 They were driving very quickly. That's why the accident was so terrible.
15 It was raining. That's the only reason I didn't take the children to the beach.
16 When I bought this house I didn't realize that in summer planes skimmed the roof every five minutes. (*If I* (*knew*) . . . *I* (*not buy*) etc.)
17 Tom's father was on the Board. That's the only reason he got the job.
18 He wasn't looking where he was going. That's why he was run over.
19 I don't like country life, perhaps because I wasn't brought up in the country.
20 I didn't know he was so quarrelsome. I'm sorry now that I invited him.
21 It rained all the time. Perhaps that's why he didn't enjoy his visit.
22 I didn't work hard at school so I didn't get a good job when I left.
23 They used closed-circuit television. That's how they spotted the shop-lifter.
24 They asked him to leave the dining-room because he wasn't wearing a shirt.
25 It took us a long time to find his house because the streets were not clearly marked.
26 We didn't go by air only because we hadn't enough money.
27 The bus didn't stop because you didn't put your hand up.
28 He turned up at the interview looking so disreputable and unshaven that they didn't give him the job.
29 I didn't know how thin the ice was, so I was walking on it quite confidently.
30 The champion didn't take the fight seriously at first; perhaps that's why he didn't win it.
31 They got the children back alive only because they paid the ransom at once.
32 The examiner read the passage very quickly, so the candidates didn't understand it.
33 They weren't wearing life-jackets; perhaps that's why they were drowned.
34 He didn't get to the top of his profession, perhaps because his wife didn't encourage him.

35 The exit doors were blocked so people couldn't escape from the burning hall.
36 The astronauts didn't walk very far on the moon because they were hampered by the thick dust.

145 Conditional sentences: mixed types

■ PEG 221–8

Put the verbs in brackets into the correct forms.

1 I've hung out the clothes. It's lovely and sunny; if it (stay) like this they (be) dry in two hours.
2 French is essential in this job. All the telephonists speak it. If they (not know) French they (not understand) half the callers.
3 How did you do in the car rally? ~
We came in last actually; but only because we got lost. If we (not got) lost we (come) in somewhere in the middle. We certainly (not be) last.
4 I wasn't really surprised that we got lost because I knew that the navigator couldn't map-read. ~
But if you (know) that why you (take) him as navigator?
5 This flat would be all right if the people above us (not be) so noisy.
6 A group of spectators, including myself, left the stand just before the end of the game. When we were half way down the stairs a goal was scored and there was a great cheer from the spectators. If there (not be) a goal the crowd (not cheer).
7 If the crowd (not cheer) we (not run) back up the stairs to see what had happened.
8 If we (not run) back we (not crash) into the rest of the spectators on their way down, and there (not be) this frightful accident.
9 If the pain (return) you'd better take another pill.
10 If you aren't going to live in the house why you (not sell) it? If I (have) a house I couldn't use I (sell) it at once.
11 No, I didn't know any Russian at that time. ~
But if you (not know) Russian why you (offer) to give him Russian lessons? ~
Because I knew that he (refuse). He always rejected my offers.
12 Tell him to bring his bicycle inside. If he (leave) it outside someone (steal) it.
13 Why do people always wear dark clothes at night? If pedestrians (wear) light coloured clothes drivers (see) them much more easily.
14 She must have loved him very much because she waited for him for fifteen years. If she (not love) him she (not wait) so long.
15 He looked so small and weak that nobody asked him to do anything. If he (look) strong he (be) expected to dig all day like everyone else.

16 The government are talking of pulling the village down to make
room for an airport. ~
If they (start) doing it the village people (resist)?

17 If you are catching an early train tomorrow you (like) to have
breakfast at 7.00?

18 We'll have to break the ice on the pond; otherwise the ducks (not be
able) to swim. And if they (not be able) to swim they (not be able) to
get food. (*Use* can/could *forms where possible.*)

19 When he left school he became a fisherman. His family didn't like it
at all. They (be) much happier if he (become) a greengrocer like his
father.

20 They still say that if he (go) into the greengrocery business when he
left school he (be) comfortably off now instead of being poor.

21 But he says that if he (have) his life again he (make) the same choice.

22 So many parcels and no baskets! If I (know) that we were going to
buy so much I (bring) a basket.

23 No one bathes here. The water is heavily polluted. If you (bathe) in
it you (be) ill for a fortnight.

24 I can hear the speaker all right but I wish I could see him too. ~
If he (stand) on a barrel we all (see) him and that (be) much better.

25 Look at poor Tom trying to start his car by hand again! If I (be) Tom
I (get) a new battery.

26 I expect you'll see Jack at the lecture tonight. If you (do) you please
(remind) him about tomorrow's meeting?

27 The headmaster decided that Peter was the culprit and expelled
him from the school. A more intelligent man (realize) that Peter
couldn't have been guilty. (*If the headmaster had been more intelligent
he . . . .*)

28 But I blame the real culprit even more. If he (admit) his guilt Peter
(not be) expelled.

29 The only thing I haven't got is a balcony. If I (have) a balcony I
(grow) plants in pots. Then my flat (be) perfect!

30 Jack rang while you were out. ~
Oh dear! If I (know) he was going to ring I (stay) at home.

31 My unmarried friends are always telling me how to bring up my
children. I sometimes think that if they (have) children they (make)
just as many mistakes as I do.

32 (At a cinema) Ann: Don't worry. They get married in the end.
Mary: Then you've seen it before! If you (tell) me that we (go) to
something else!

33 Be careful about the time. If you (spend) too long on the first
question you (not have) enough time to do the others properly.

34 We had a lot of trouble putting the tent up. If it (not be) so windy
perhaps it (not be) quite so difficult.

35 Ann (sitting beside her open fire): I love open fires; if I (have)
nothing but a radiator to sit beside I (get) quite depressed.

36 Lucy, a student at a residential college: Couldn't I leave the hostel
and get a flat, mother?

Mother: No, you couldn't. I know very well what (happen) if you (have) a flat. You (play) the guitar all night and (miss) your classes in the morning; then you (fail) your exams and (have) to repeat the year. And you (not feed) yourself properly and (get) run down. And then you (catch) some infection and (die) of it, and we (have) to leave this district as the neighbours (keep) saying that we had caused your death by letting you have your own way!

146 Conditional sentences: mixed types

■ PEG 221–8

Finish the following sentences.

1 If you had a carpet on the stairs . . . .
2 If you should see a snake . . . .
3 If I lived in the country . . . .
4 If you want to get to the station in time to catch the 8.10 train . . . .
5 He was sleepwalking. When I saw him going towards the window I stopped him. If I hadn't stopped him . . . .
6 She is simply terrified of rats. If she hears the rats running round your attics she . . . .
7 The milk wouldn't have turned sour if . . . .
8 They were completely lost and didn't know which way to turn; but for the dog . . . .
9 If you took a course in computer programming . . . .
10 Jack (trying to phone Peter): I can hear the phone ringing. Peter must be out. If he were in he . . . .
11 If we have another puncture . . . .
12 I could have walked more quickly if my suitcase . . . .
13 My room would be all right if it . . . .
14 If you aren't going to use the car tomorrow, . . . ?
15 If you don't like films why . . . ?
16 There were plenty of fish in the bay; if we'd had fishing lines . . . .
17 The hijackers threatened to kill the pilot unless he . . . .
18 We'll test your voice and if it is good enough . . . .
19 If buses and trains were free . . . .
20 If children were allowed to do exactly as they liked in school . . . .
21 I'd have taken a photograph if . . . .
22 Your job sounds awful. If I were you . . . .
23 If you thought he was unreliable why . . . ?
24 If I'd known that there was going to be an electricity strike I . . . .
25 If the price of petrol goes up . . . .
26 You can camp in this field provided . . . .
27 Unless you isolate people with infectious diseases . . . .
28 Everyone was going much too fast. The pile-up wouldn't have been nearly so terrible if the drivers . . . .

29 They would have paid you more if . . . .
30 If you don't boil the water before you drink it . . . .
31 He expected absolute punctuality. He was furious if . . . .
32 If you lived on the 40th floor and there was a power strike . . . .
33 We could have got seats . . . .
34 Mother to little boy: If you don't eat up your nice rice pudding . . . .
35 Tom (looking at his watch): We'll have to go without Peter if . . . .
36 If you breathe a word of this to anybody . . . .

147 will and shall

■ PEG 201, 207–8, 223, 282

Insert either **will** or **shall** in the spaces; in some examples, **shall**
would be correct in formal English but **will** is used in conversation.
In these cases, the answer **shall/will** will be given in the key.

1 I . . . know tomorrow. It . . . be in the papers.
2 These pigeons are quite tame; they . . . take crumbs from your
fingers.
3 . . . I call for you? ~
No, I . . . get a taxi and meet you at the station.
4 Hold the door open for me, . . . you?
5 Loudspeaker announcement at an air terminal: '. . . Mr Jones,
passenger to New York, please come to Gate 3.'
6 The Head of the Department has just told me that I . . . (not) have
any nine o'clock classes next term. So I . . . (not) have to get up
early, which . . . be a comfort. And I . . . have time to read the paper
at breakfast.
7 Zoo keeper: In spite of all the notices, people . . . feed these animals.
8 Committee regulations: Ten persons . . . constitute a quorum.
9 You can trust me; nobody . . . know that you are here. (*I promise to
keep it secret.*) I . . . (not) even tell my wife.
10 Shop assistant: The small ones are £1 each and the large ones are £2.
Customer: I . . . have six small ones, please.
11 . . . we stop here for a drink? ~
If we do we . . . miss the overture, and they probably . . . (not) let us
in till the end of the act.
12 . . . you have another piece of pie? ~
Yes, please.
13 Jones: Stand away from that door! You can't keep me here against
my will!
Smith: You . . . (not) go till you have given me an explanation! (*I
won't let you go.*)
14 Police Officer (in a loud-speaker van beside a motorway in thick
fog): They are going much too fast. I keep warning them to reduce
speed but they . . . (not) do it.

15 Extract from a club's regulations: Club officers . . . be elected yearly and . . . (not) be eligible for re-election at the end of that year.

16 The train . . . be very crowded, I'm afraid. I expect we . . . have to stand most of the way.

17 Ann (on phone): You left your gloves here last night. . . . I post them to you?
Mary: No, don't bother. I . . . pick them up some time this evening. You . . . be in, . . . (not) you?

18 Tom (at the races): Who won?
Jack: I don't know; it was a photo-finish. But we . . . see in a moment. They . . . put the winner's number up.

19 Ann: She says she'd rather go to prison than pay the fine.
Tom: She . . . (not) go to prison. (*I won't let this happen.*) I . . . pay her fine for her!

20 Where . . . we go to get shoes? ~
What about Oxford Street? ~
Oxford Street? Are you mad? It's Saturday morning! The shops . . . be packed.

21 I . . . (not) see her, I'm sorry to say. She . . . have left by the time I arrive.

22 Secretary: There's a Mr Peterson in the outer office, sir. He says he has an appointment. . . . you see him now?
Mr Smith: I . . . (not) see him now or at any other time. I told him so when we last met. And he hasn't an appointment!

23 Angry villagers, who have just heard that the government intends to pull down their houses and build an airport: They . . . (not) build an airport here! We . . . fight for our village!

24 I am determined that my son . . . have the best possible education.

148 would and should

■ PEG 160, 222–4, 232, 235–7

Insert **would** or **should** in the spaces in the following sentences.

1 Let's go shopping. The shops . . . not be crowded. Monday morning's usually quiet.

2 Why . . . everyone be promoted except me? It's not fair.

3 He used to have a day off once a week, and on that day he . . . get up early, have a hasty breakfast and set out for the river.

4 . . . n't it be better to roll up the carpet before painting the ceiling?

5 I know that it will be difficult to pick him out in such a crowd, but if you . . . happen to see him give him this packet.

6 The car . . . n't start so we had to ring for a taxi.

7 If you . . . wait a moment, I'll ring our stockroom and see if we have another bale of this material.

8 I . . . tell him the truth if I were you.

9 I wish he . . . get up earlier. He's late for work every day.

10 It is astonishing that a person of your intelligence . . . be taken in so easily.

11 The people in the flat above us were members of a band. We liked them very much but they . . . practise the drums at night. Nothing we said made any difference.

12 . . . you like to come with us? There is plenty of room in the car.

13 Do you know where Tom is? ~
He . . . be in the canteen. He's usually there between twelve and one.

14 She asked what she . . . do if any letters came for me while I was away. I told her that my brother . . . come every day to pick up my mail.

15 . . . you like some cake? ~
Yes, please, though I . . . n't eat it really as I'm on a diet.

16 He always carried food for himself and his horse in case they . . . have to spend a night away from camp.

17 Have I spelt it right? Or . . . there be another 's'?

18 If Tom were here he . . . know what to do.

19 Bill proposed that women . . . be allowed to join the club.

20 It . . . take too long to handsew it; we'll have to hire a machine.

21 It is only fair that you . . . know what people are saying about you behind your back.

22 It is essential that everyone . . . be able to see the stage.

23 They . . . n't allow parking in this street at all. It's much too narrow.

24 I hoped they . . . be pleased when they saw the photographs.

25 . . . you mind opening the windows? It's very stuffy in here.

26 Have you a screwdriver? ~
Yes, there . . . be one in that drawer.

27 I suggested that they . . . have a hot breakfast and a cold supper.

28 You . . . love your father. (*It is natural and right.*) ~
Why . . . I love him? I've never seen him.

29 The headmaster suggested that the school . . . buy its own minibus.

30 I wish you . . . tell me what he said in his letter.

31 He . . . n't use the electric blanket. He said it was faulty.

32 They used to work in pairs. One . . . pretend that he wanted to buy something while the other helped himself from the shelves.

33 Small children . . . n't be left alone in a house. They might set themselves on fire.

34 'You . . . n't leave a small child alone. (*You are far too conscientious.*)

35 Father to child: You . . . be in bed. What are you doing running about at this hour?

36 There . . . be a switch somewhere. Ah yes, here it is.

17 Gerund, infinitive and present participle

149 Gerund, infinitive and present participle

■ PEG 266–71

Put the verbs in brackets into the correct forms. Note that sometimes a bare infinitive will be required.

1 'I was lonely at first,' the old man admitted, 'but after a time I got used to (live) alone and even got (like) it.'
2 Before trains were invented people used (travel) on horseback or in stage coaches. It used (take) a stage coach three days (go) from London to Bath.
3 I meant (buy) an evening paper but I didn't see anyone (sell) them.
4 Tom: I want (catch) the 7 a.m. train tomorrow.
  Ann: But that means (get) up at 6.00; and you're not very good at (get) up early, are you?
5 He accepted the cut in salary without complaint because he was afraid (complain). He was afraid of (lose) his job.
6 She remembers part of her childhood quite clearly. She remembers (go) to school for the first time and (be) frightened and (put) her finger in her mouth. And she remembers her teacher (tell) her (take) it out.
7 Did you remember (lock) the car? ~
  No, I didn't. I'd better (go) back and (do) it now.
8 No, I didn't move the bomb. I was afraid (touch) it; I was afraid of (be) blown to pieces!
9 Next time we go (house-hunt), remember (ask) the agent for clear directions. I wasted hours (look) for the last house.
10 Tom: Let's (go) for a swim.
  Ann: I'm not particularly keen on (swim). What about (go) for a drive instead?
11 The hunters expected (be paid) by the foot for the snakes they caught. This meant (take) the snakes out of the sack and (measure) them. They seemed (expect) me (do) it; but I wasn't particularly anxious (be) the first (die) of snakebite.
12 After (spend) two days (argue) about where to go for their holidays, they decided (not go) anywhere.
13 He is talking about (give) up his job and (go) (live) in the country.
14 I was just about (leave) the office when the phone rang. It was my wife; she wanted me (call) at the butcher's on my way home.

15 He said, 'I'm terribly sorry to (keep) you (wait).'
I said, 'It doesn't matter at all,' but he went on (apologize) for nearly
five minutes!

16 The lecturer began by (tell) us where the island was, and went on
(talk) about its history.

17 My father thinks I am not capable of (earn) my own living, but I
mean (show) him that he is wrong.

18 Tom: I can't get my car (start) on cold mornings.
Jack: Have you tried (fill) the radiator with hot water? That
sometimes helps.

19 Did he manage (carry) the trunk upstairs? ~
No, he didn't. He isn't strong enough (move) it, let alone (carry) it
upstairs.

20 Jack: Don't forget (take) a hacksaw with you.
Ann: What's a hacksaw? And why should I (take) one with me?
Jack: It's a tool for (cut) metal. You see, Tom is bound (get) into
trouble for (take) photographs of the wrong things, and you'll be
arrested with him. With a hacksaw you'll be able (saw) through the
bars of your cell and (escape).

21 Peter: Wouldn't it be better (ask) Tom (leave) his camera at home?
Jack: It would be no good (ask) Tom (do) that. It would be like (ask)
a woman (travel) without a handbag.

22 I've got the loaf; now I'm looking for a breadknife (cut) it with. ~
I saw Paul (sharpen) a pencil with the breadknife a minute ago.

23 We stopped once (buy) petrol and then we stopped again (ask)
someone the way.

24 When I caught them (cheat) me, I stopped (buy) petrol there and
started (deal) with your garage instead.

25 Do you feel like (dine) out or would you rather (have) dinner at
home? ~
I'd like (go) out. I always enjoy (have) dinner in a restaurant.

26 Your hair needs (cut). You'd better (have) it done tomorrow—unless
you'd like me (have) a go at it for you.

27 I tried (convince) him that I was perfectly capable of (manage) on my
own, but he insisted on (help) me.

28 Jack: I don't mind (travel) by bus, but I hate (stand) in queues.
Tom: I don't care for (queue) either; and you waste so much time
(wait) for buses. I think it's better (go) by tube, or taxi.

29 He took to (follow) me about and (criticize) my work till I threatened
(hit) him.

30 I have (stay) here; I'm on duty. But you needn't (wait); you're free
(go) whenever you like.

31 In *Animal Farm* the old pig urged the animals (rebel) against man
but he warned them (not adopt) man's habits.

32 There is no point in (arrive) half an hour early. We'd only have
(wait). ~
I don't mind (wait). It's better (be) too early than too late.

33 I always try (come) in quietly but they always hear me (go) upstairs. It's impossible (climb) an old wooden staircase at night without (make) a noise.
34 If you agree (work) for me I'll see about (get) you a work permit.
35 We'd better (start) early. We don't want (risk) (get) caught in a traffic jam.
36 He suggested (call) a meeting and (let) the workers (decide) the matter themselves.

150 Gerund, infinitive and present participle

■ PEG 266–71

Put the verbs in brackets into the correct forms. Remember that sometimes a bare infinitive is required.

1 We suggested (sleep) in hotels but the children were anxious (camp) out.
2 Paul: Would you like (come) to a lecture on Wagner tonight?
Ann: No, thanks. I like (listen) to music but I don't like (listen) to people (talk) about it.
3 If you want the milkman (leave) you milk in the morning, remember (put) a milk bottle outside your door.
4 They let us park motorcycles here but they won't allow us (park) cars.
5 They don't allow (smoke) in the auditorium; they don't want (risk) (set) it on fire, but you can (smoke) in the foyer during the interval.
6 Mr Shaw is very busy (write) his memoirs. He is far too busy (receive) callers (*he is so busy that he can't receive callers*), so you'd better just (go) away.
7 What about (buy) double quantities of everything today? That will save (shop) again later in the week.
8 The inspector asked (see) my ticket and when I wasn't able (find) it he made me (buy) another. ~
He probably suspected you of (try) (travel) without one.
9 Would you like me (turn) down the radio a bit? ~
No, it's all right. I'm used to (work) with the radio on.
10 One of the gang suggested (take) the body out to sea, (drop) it overboard and (pretend) that it had been an accident.
11 I want the boy (grow) up hating violence but his father keeps (buy) him guns and swords. ~
It's almost impossible (prevent) boys (play) soldiers.
12 Would you children mind (keep) quiet for a moment? I'm trying (fill) in a form. ~
It's no use (ask) children (keep) quiet. They can't help (make) a noise.

13 I'm thinking of (go) to Oxford tomorrow on my motorbike. Would
you like (come)? ~
No, thanks. I want (go) Oxford, but I'd rather (go) by train. I loathe
(travel) by road.

14 Let's (go) (fish) today. There's a nice wind. What about (come) with
us, Ann? ~
No, thanks. I'm very willing (cut) sandwiches for you but I've no
intention of (waste) the afternoon (sit) in a boat (watch) you two
(fish).

15 He resented (be) asked (wait). He expected the minister (see) him at
once.

16 The police have put up a railing here (prevent) people (rush) out of
the station and (dash) straight across the road.

17 All day long we saw the trees (toss) in the wind and heard the waves
(crash) against the rocks.

18 I didn't mean (eat) anything but the cakes looked so good that I
couldn't resist (try) one.

19 Do you feel like (walk) there or shall we (take) a bus? ~
I'd rather (go) by bus. Besides, it'll take ages (get) there on foot.

20 All right. When would you like (start)? In a few minutes? ~
Oh, let's wait till it stops (rain); otherwise we'll get soaked (walk) to
the bus station.

21 The old miser spent all his time (count) his money and (think) up
new hiding-places. He kept (move) it about because he was terrified
of (be robbed). He used (get) up at night sometimes (make) sure it
was still there.

22 Jack suggested (let) one flat and (keep) the other for myself. But
Tom advised me (sell) the whole house.

23 The child used (lean) on the gate (watch) the people (go) to work in
the mornings and (come) home in the evenings. And he used to hear
them (shout) greetings to each other and (talk) loudly.

24 He soon got (know) most of them and even managed (learn) the
greetings. Then they began (greet) him too on their way to work and
sometimes would stop (talk) to him on their way home.

25 He succeeded in (untie) himself, (climb) out of the window and
(crawl) along a narrow ledge to the window of the next room.

26 Did you have any trouble (find) the house? ~
No, but I had a lot of difficulty (get) in. Nobody seemed (know)
where the key was.

27 Bill couldn't bear (see) anyone (sit) round idly. Whenever he found
me (relax) or (read) he would (produce) a job which, he said, had (be)
done at once. I wasted a morning (perform) his ridiculous tasks and
spent the rest of the weekend (keep) out of his way.

28 After (spend) a week in the cottage, he decided that he didn't really
enjoy (live) in the country and began (think) of an excuse for (sell)
the cottage and (return) to London.

29 It's no use (argue) with him. You might as well (argue) with a stone
wall. He is incapable of (see) anyone else's point of view.

30 I'm delighted (hear) that you can come on Saturday. We are all looking forward to (see) you. Remember (bring) your rubber boots.
31 He has been charged with (receive) and (sell) stolen goods. He has admitted (receive) but denies (sell) them. The fact is that he hasn't had time (sell) them yet.
32 He noticed the helicopter (hover) over the field. Then, to his astonishment, he saw a rope ladder (be) thrown out and three men (climb) down it. He watched them (run) across the field and out through a gate. Later he saw a car with four men in it (come) out of the lane (lead) to the field.
33 He admitted that it was possible that the car happened (be passing) and that the three men persuaded the driver (give) them a lift; but he throught it much more likely that they had arranged for the car (pick) them up and that the driver had been waiting in the lane for the helicopter (drop) them.
34 What about (have) a picnic in Piccadilly Circus? ~
What an extraordinary place (have) a picnic! Fancy (sit) there with the traffic (swirl) round you and the pigeons (take) bites out of your sandwiches!
35 Would you mind (write) your address on the back of the cheque and (show) us some proof of your identity?
36 Let's (swim) across. ~
I'm not really dressed for (swim). What's wrong with (go) round by the bridge?

18 Unreal pasts and subjunctives

151 Unreal pasts and subjunctives

■ PEG 228, 292, 297–8, 300

Put the verbs in brackets into the correct forms.

1 It's just struck midnight. It's high time we (leave)!
2 If only we (have) a phone! I'm tired of queuing outside the public phone box.
3 You (have) better take off your wet shoes.
4 He walks as if he (have) a wooden leg.
5 He talks as if he (do) all the work himself, but in fact Tom and I did most of it.
6 Father: I've supported you all through university. Now I think it's time you (begin) to support yourself.
7 I wish I (know) what is wrong with my car.
8 It looks like rain; you (have) better take a coat.
9 I wish I (ask) the fishmonger to clean these fish. (*I'm sorry I didn't ask him.*)
10 It's time we (do) something to stop road accidents.
11 The cheese looks as if rats (nibble) it.
12 It's high time they (mend) this road.
13 He always talks as though he (address) a public meeting.
14 He treats us as if we (be) all idiots.
15 Wife: I'd like to get a job.
   Husband: I'd much rather you (stay) at home and (look) after the house.
16 If you (tie) the boat up it wouldn't have drifted away.
17 I wish you (not give) him my phone number. (*I'm sorry you gave it to him.*)
18 If only he (know) then that the disease was curable!
19 Suppose you (not know) where your next meal was coming from?
20 You talk as though it (be) a small thing to leave your country for ever.
21 I hate driving. I'd much rather you (drive).
22 If only I (be) insured! (*But I wasn't insured.*)
23 If you (not take) those photographs we wouldn't have been arrested.
24 I wish transistor radios never (be) invented.
25 If only I (keep) my mouth shut! (*I said something which made matters much worse.*)
26 I'll pay you by cheque monthly. ~
   I'd rather you (pay) me cash weekly.

27 When someone says something to me, I translate it into French, and
   then I think of a reply in French, and then translate it into English
   and say it. ~
   It's high time you (stop) doing all this translation and (start) thinking
   in English.

28 I said 'Sunday'. ~
   I wish you (not say) Sunday. We'll never be ready by then.

29 But I told you what to do. ~
   I know you did. If only I (take) your advice!

30 A flower pot fell off the balcony on to the head of a man who was
   standing below. It was most unfortunate that he happened to be
   standing just there. If he (stand) a foot to the right or left he'd have
   been unharmed.

31 That man has brought us nothing but trouble. I wish I never (set)
   eyes on him.

32 Can I take your best umbrella? ~
   I'd rather you (take) the other one.

33 If you (have) a peep hole in your door you would have seen who was
   standing outside and kept the door shut.

34 I wish I (not try) to repair it. I only made it worse.

35 If I (not have) rubber gloves on I would have been electrocuted.

36 He looks as though he never (get) a square meal, but in fact his wife
   feeds him very well.

152 would rather + subject + past tense

☑ PEG 297–8

Answer the following questions by expressing a preference for a
different action.
   Question: Can I write my essay on the back of an envelope?
   Possible answer: *I'd rather you wrote it on a sheet of foolscap.*
Similarly:
   Can we bring our pet snake to your party?
   I'd rather you didn't or *I'd rather you left it at home.*

It would also of course be possible to answer with **prefer** + object +
infinitive:
   I'd prefer you to write it on foolscap.
   I'd prefer you to leave it at home.

Use **you** in all answers.

1 Can I go by bus?
2 Can I go alone?
3 Can we start tomorrow?
4 Can I ring New York on your phone?

5 Can we sleep in the garden tonight?
6 Can we cook our steak by holding it in front of your electric fire?
7 Can we use your scissors to cut this wire?
8 Can I leave school at sixteen?
9 Can we come in late tomorrow?
10 Shall I wake you up when I come in and tell you what happened?
11 Can I clean my motorcycle in the kitchen?
12 Can I tell Tom what you've just told me?
13 Can I go barefoot?
14 Can I have a snake tattooed round my ankle?
15 Shall we paint your door pink with yellow stars?
16 Shall I ring you at 3 a.m.?
17 Shall I threaten to burn down his house?
18 Can we bathe after dark?
19 Can I park my helicopter on the roof of your house?
20 Can I put the goldfish in the bath?
21 Can we hitch-hike to Rome?
22 Can I borrow your best umbrella?
23 Will it be all right if I write it in longhand?
24 Can I leave the washing up till the day after tomorrow?

153 wish + subject + past, past perfect or conditional

◰ PEG 300–1

Rewrite the following using a **wish** construction (phrases in brackets should be omitted).

1 I'm sorry I haven't got a washing machine.
2 I'm sorry I don't live near my work.
3 I'm sorry our garden doesn't get any sun.
4 I'm sorry I called him a liar.
5 I'm sorry I don't know Finnish.
6 I'm sorry I didn't book a seat.
7 I'm sorry I haven't got a car.
8 I'm sorry I can't drive.
9 I'd like Tom to drive more slowly (*but I haven't any great hopes of this*).
10 I'd like you to keep quiet. (*You're making so much noise that I can't think.*)
11 I'm sorry we accepted the invitation.
12 I'm sorry that theatre tickets cost so much.
13 It's a pity that shops here shut on Saturday afternoon.
14 It's a pity he didn't work harder during the term.
15 I'm sorry you didn't see it.
16 It's a pity you are going tonight.
17 It's a pity I haven't got a work permit.

18 I would like it to stop raining (*but I'm not very hopeful*).
19 I'd like you to wait for me (*even though you are ready to start now*).
20 I'm sorry I didn't bring a map.
21 I'm sorry I ever came to this country.
22 I'm sorry I left my last job.
23 I'm sorry I didn't stay in my last job.
24 I'd like him to cut his hair (*but I don't suppose he will*).
25 I'd like him to stop smoking in bed (*but I haven't any great hopes*).
26 I'm sorry he goes to bed so late.
27 Motorist in fog: It's a pity we don't know where we are.
28 It's a pity we haven't a torch.
29 I'm sorry I didn't know you were coming.
30 I'm sorry you told Jack.
31 I'm sorry I didn't ask the fishmonger to open these oysters.
32 I'm sorry I can't swim.
33 I'm sorry you aren't coming with us.
34 I'm sorry you aren't going to a job where you could use your English.
35 It's a pity you didn't ask him how to get there.
36 I would like every country to stop killing whales (*but have no real hope of this*).

19 The passive

154 Active to passive

■ PEG 302-6

Put the transitive verbs into the passive voice. Do not mention the agent unless it seems necessary.

1 The milkman brings the milk to my door but the postman leaves the letters in the hall.
2 In future, perhaps, they won't bring letters to the houses, and we shall have to collect them from the Post Office.
3 People steal things from supermarkets every day; someone stole twenty bottles of whisky from this one last week.
4 Normally men sweep this street every day, but nobody swept it last week.
5 The postman clears this box three time a day. He last cleared it at 2.30.
6 Someone turned on a light in the hall and opened the door.
7 Women clean this office in the evening after the staff have left; they clean the upstairs offices between seven and eight in the morning.
8 We never saw him in the dining-room. A maid took all his meals up to him.
9 Someone left this purse in a classroom yesterday; the cleaner found it.
10 We build well over 1,000 new houses a year. Last year we built 1,500.
11 We serve hot meals till 10.30, and guests can order coffee and sandwiches up to 11.30.
12 Passengers leave all sorts of things in buses. The conductors collect them and send them to the Lost Property Office.
13 An ambulance took the sick man to hospital. (*Mention* ambulance.)
14 We kill and injure people on the roads every day. Can't we do something about this?
15 Dogs guard the warehouse. The other day a thief tried to get in and a dog saw him and chased him. (*A thief who . . .*)
16 The watchman called the police. The police arrested the man.
17 Tom had only a slight injury and they helped him off the field; but Jack was seriously injured and they carried him off on a stretcher. (*Tom, who had . . . , but Jack, who was . . .*)
18 You can't wash this dress; you must dry-clean it.
19 They are demolishing the entire block.
20 He recommends fitting new tyres. (*Use* should; *see Exercise 157.*)
21 He suggested allowing council tenants to buy their houses.

22 Men with slide rules used to do these calculations; now a computer does them.
23 The court tried the man, found him guilty and sent him to prison.
24 The hall porter polishes the knockers of all the flats every day. ~ Well, he hasn't polished mine for a week.
25 They are repairing my piano at the moment.
26 Passengers shouldn't throw away their tickets as inspectors may check these during the journey.
27 They invited Jack but they didn't invite Tom.
28 The guests ate all the sandwiches and drank all the beer. They left nothing.
29 Has someone posted my parcel?
30 Why did no one inform me of the change of plan?
31 Tom Smith wrote the book and Brown and Co. published it.
32 We shall have to tow the car to the garage.
33 I'm afraid we have sold all our copies but we have ordered more.
34 We will prosecute trespassers.
35 Someone stole my car and abandoned it fifteen miles away. He had removed the radio but done no other damage.
36 You must keep dogs on leads in the gardens.

155 Active to passive

■ PEG 302–6

Put the transitive verbs into the passive voice. Do not mention the agent unless it seems necessary.

1 They haven't stamped the letter.
2 They didn't pay me for the work; they expected me to do it for nothing.
3 He escaped when they were moving him from one prison to another.
4 She didn't introduce me to her mother.
5 A frightful crash wakened me at 4 a.m.
6 When they have widened this street the roar of the traffic will keep residents awake all night.
7 They threw away the rubbish.
8 A Japanese firm makes these television sets.
9 An earthquake destroyed the town.
10 A machine could do this much more easily.
11 Visitors must leave umbrellas and sticks in the cloakroom.
12 We ask tenants not to play their radios loudly after midnight.
13 We can't repair your clock.
14 We cannot exchange articles which customers have bought during the sale. (*Articles* . . .)
15 We have to pick the fruit very early in the morning; otherwise we can't get it to the market in time.

16 The police shouldn't allow people to park there.
17 They are watching my house.
18 The examiner will read the passage three times.
19 Candidates may not use dictionaries.
20 You need not type this letter
21 This used to be number 13, but now I see that someone has crossed out '13' and written '12A' underneath.
22 You mustn't move this man; he is too ill. You'll have to leave him here.
23 They searched his house and found a number of stolen articles.
24 Nobody has used this room for ages.
25 They took him for a Frenchman, his French was so good.
26 You should have taken those books back to the library.
27 They brought the children up in Italy.
28 They have taken down the For Sale notice, so I suppose they have sold the house.
29 Someone broke into his house and stole a lot of his things.
30 We have warned you.
31 A lorry knocked him down.
32 They returned my keys to me; someone had picked them up in the street.
33 We had to give the books back; they did not allow us to take them home.
34 You shouldn't leave these documents on the desk. You should lock them up.
35 They handed round coffee and biscuits.
36 They have tried other people's schemes. Why have they never tried my scheme?

156 Active to passive with phrasal verbs

■ PEG 302–6

In this exercise most of the sentences contain a verb + preposition/adverb combination. The preposition or adverb must be retained when the combination is put into the passive.
In most of the sentences it is not necessary to mention the agent.

1 The government has called out troops.
2 Fog held up the trains. (*agent required*)
3 You are to leave this here. Someone will call for it later on.
4 We called in the police.
5 They didn't look after the children properly.
6 They are flying in reinforcements.
7 Then they called up men of 28.
8 Everyone looked up to him. (*agent required*)
9 All the ministers will see him off at the airport. (*agent required*)

10 He hasn't slept in his bed.
11 We can build on more rooms.
12 They threw him out.
13 They will have to adopt a different attitude.
14 He's a dangerous maniac. They ought to lock him up.
15 Her story didn't take them in. (*agent required*)
16 Burglars broke into the house.
17 The manufacturers are giving away small plastic toys with each packet of cereal.
18 They took down the notice.
19 They frown on smoking here.
20 After the government had spent a million pounds on the scheme they decided that it was impracticable and gave it up. (*Make only the first and last verbs passive.*)
21 When I returned I found that they had towed my car away. I asked why they had done this and they told me that it was because I had parked it under a No Parking sign. (*four passives*)
22 People must hand in their weapons.
23 The crowd shouted him down.
24 People often take him for his brother.
25 No one has taken out the cork.
26 The film company were to have used the pool for aquatic displays, but now they have changed their minds about it and are filling it in. (*Make the first and last verbs passive.*)
27 This college is already full. We are turning away students the whole time.
28 You will have to pull down this skyscraper as you have not complied with the town planning regulations.

157 Active to passive with changes of construction

■ PEG 119, 235, 302–6

Some of the following sentences when put into the passive require or can have a change of construction.

1 **believe**, **claim**, **consider**, **find**, **know**, **say**, **suppose** and **think** when used in the passive can be followed by an infinitive:
    They say he is a spy = *He is said to be a spy.*
    They say he was a spy = *He is said to have been a spy.*
It is said that he is/was . . . is also possible.

2 Subject + **be supposed** + infinitive often conveys an idea of duty, particularly when the subject is **you**:
    It is your duty to obey him = *You are supposed to obey him.*

3 Infinitives after passive verbs are normally full infinitives.

4 Note the use of **have** + object + past participle:
   Get someone to mend it = *Have it mended.*
(See PEG 119.)

5 Note the use of should in the passive. (See PEG 235.)

Put the following sentences into the passive, using an infinitive construction where possible.

1 We added up the money and found that it was correct.
2 I'm employing a man to tile the bathroom.
3 Someone seems to have made a terrible mistake.
4 It is your duty to make tea at eleven o'clock. (*Use* suppose.)
5 People know that he is armed.
6 Someone saw him pick up the gun.
7 We know that you were in town on the night of the crime.
8 We believe that he has special knowledge which may be useful to the police. (*one passive*)
9 You needn't have done this.
10 It's a little too loose; you had better ask your tailor to take it in. (*one passive*)
11 He likes people to call him 'sir'.
12 Don't touch this switch.
13 You will have to get someone to see to it.
14 It is impossible to do this. (*Use* can't.)
15 Someone is following us.
16 They used to make little boys climb the chimneys to clean them. (*one passive*)
17 You have to see it to believe it. (*two passives*)
18 You order me about and I am tired of it. (*I am tired of . . .*)
19 He doesn't like people laughing at him.
20 You don't need to wind this watch.
21 They shouldn't have told him.
22 They decided to divide the money between the widows of the lifeboatmen. (*They decided that the money . . .*)
23 People believe that he was killed by terrorists.
24 They are to send letters to the leaders of charitable organizations.
25 We consider that she was the best singer that Australia has ever produced. (*one passive*)
26 We don't allow smoking.
27 We know that the expedition reached the South Pole in May.
28 Before they invented printing people had to write everything by hand.
29 They urged the government to create more jobs. (*two ways*)
30 They suggested banning the sale of alcohol at football matches.

20 Indirect speech

158 Indirect speech: statements

☑ PEG 307–8, 313–14

Note applying to all indirect speech exercises

When the speaker says **you**, and the person spoken to is not identified, it is good practice for the student to assume that the remark was made to himself. **you** will then become **I/me** or **we/us**. (Answers in the key will be given in first person forms.)

'You can phone from the office,' he said.
He said I could phone from his office.

This must not, of course, be done when the person spoken to is identified:

'You can phone from my office, Ann,' he said.
He told Ann that she could phone from his office.

Note that when **you** stands for **one**, it is reported unchanged:

'You can't bathe in the rivers,' he said, 'they're full of piranhas.'
He said that you couldn't bathe in the rivers as they were full of piranhas.

Put the following statements into indirect speech.

1 'I'm going out now, but I'll be in by nine,' he said. (*Omit* now.)
2 'I'm working in a restaurant, and don't much care for it,' she said.
3 'I can't live on my basic salary,' said Peter. 'I'll have to offer to do overtime.'
4 'My young brother wants to be a tax inspector,' said Mary. 'I can't think why. None of my family has ever been a tax inspector.'
5 'We're waiting for the school bus,' said the children. 'It's late again.'
6 'I've made a terrible mistake!' said Peter.
'You're always making terrible mistakes,' I said. 'You should be used to it by now.'
7 'We make £450 a week,' said one of the men, 'and send most of it home to our wives.'
8 'It's lonely being away from our families,' said another, 'but we earn three times as much in this factory as we would in our own country.'
9 'We've been here for two and a half years,' said the man who had spoken first, 'and we're going to stay another six months.'
10 'I've got a job on an oil-rig,' said Paul.
'That'll be very hard work,' I said.
'I know it'll be hard,' he replied, 'but I don't mind hard work, and it'll be a good experience.'

11 'The ice will soon be hard enough to skate on,' said Tom.
   'I'll look for my skates when I get home,' Ann said.
12 'I'm living with my parents at present,' she said, 'but I hope to have
   a flat of my own soon.'
13 'I'm leaving tomorrow,' she said, 'by the 4.30 from Victoria.'
   'We'll come and see you off,' we said.
14 'I've just bought a car,' said Peter, 'but it's not insured yet so I can't
   take you for a drive.'
15 'I'd like to speak to Susan,' said Mary, 'but I'm bathing the babies
   and they will drown if I leave them alone in the bath while I go to
   the phone.'
16 Mary has just received a postcard from Ann, beginning, 'I'm coming
   up to London next week. I hope you and Jack will meet me for lunch
   one day.' (*Imagine that Mary is reading this card to Jack. Begin:* Ann
   says . . .)
17 'Nothing ever happens in the village,' she said. 'It's like a dead
   village. All the young people have drifted away to the towns.'
18 'I've missed my train,' said Bill. 'Now I'll be late for work and my
   boss will be furious.'
19 'We'll wait for you if you're late,' they said.
20 'They are supposed to be landing at London airport,' I said. 'But if
   the fog gets any thicker the plane may be diverted.'
21 'If you lend me the chainsaw,' said Mary, 'I'll bring it back the day
   after tomorrow.'
22 'I hate getting up on dark mornings,' grumbled Peter.
   'It is horrible,' agreed his wife, 'but the mornings will be lighter
   soon and then it won't be quite so bad.'
23 'The sales are starting tomorrow,' said the typist. 'As soon as we
   finish work the whole typing pool is going to make a dash for the
   shops.'
   'I hope you'll all get what you want,' I said.
24 'I wish I had something to eat,' said Peter.
   'You've only just had lunch,' said his sister. 'I don't know how you
   can be hungry again so soon.'
25 'If you're short of money I can lend you £50,' said my aunt, 'and you
   can take your time about paying it back.'
26 'I usually take my dog out for a walk when I come home from work,'
   he said.
27 'I have a message for your brother,' I said.
   'He isn't at home,' said Ann. 'He left two days ago.'
28 'I bought this bag in Milan,' I said.
   'You shouldn't have bought that colour,' said Peter. 'It doesn't go
   with your coat.'
29 'I must hurry. My father is always furious if any of us are late for
   meals,' she said.
30 'If you want to smoke you'll have to go upstairs,' said the bus
   conductor.

31 'I'm building myself a house,' said Charles. 'I won't show it to you just yet but when the roof is on you can come and see it.'

32 'The lake will probably freeze tonight,' said Peter. 'It's much colder than last night.'
'I'll go out and look early in the morning,' said Mary, 'and if it's frozen I'll make some holes in the ice so that the ducks can feed.'

33 'Even if the strikers go back to work tomorrow it will be some time before things return to normal,' said the official.

34 'Someone is trying to murder me!' said Mrs Jones. 'I keep getting threatening letters.'

35 'I'm taking my children to the zoo tomorrow,' she said, 'to see the baby polar bear.'

36 'All I can hear,' says Ann, 'is a high-pitched buzz. I wonder if it's some sort of signal.'

159 Indirect speech: statements

■ PEG 120, 287, 307–14

See note to Exercise 158.

had better
'You'd better' can also be reported unchanged (though the pronoun may change) but can also be reported by **advise**:
He said, 'You'd better tell Tom.'
He said I'd better tell Tom or
He advised me to tell Tom.
'**I/we had better**' will normally be reported unchanged (though the pronoun may change):
He said, 'I'd better wait.'
He said he'd better wait.
'**I should . . . (if I were you)**' is best reported by **advise**:
I said, 'Shall I write to Ann?' 'I should phone her (if I were you),' said Peter.
I asked if I should write to Ann and Peter advised me to phone her.

Put the following into indirect speech.

1 'There's been an accident, and the road is blocked,' said the policeman. 'It won't be clear for some time. You'd better go round the other way.'

2 'Let's light a fire and cook our sausages over it,' said the children.

3 'I was thinking of going by bus,' said Paul.
'I shouldn't go by bus (if I were you),' said his aunt. 'It's an awfully bad service.'

4 'You'd better take sleeping bags; you may have to sleep out,' he warned us.

5 'I've left some books on your table,' said Peter. 'I think you'll find

them useful. You can keep them as long as you need them but I'd like them back when you've finished with them.'
'Thank you very much,' I said. 'I'll take great care of them.'

6 'If children can learn a complicated language like Japanese by the time they are five,' said the Japanese professor, 'they should be able to learn the language of music. At the moment I'm teaching a class of forty three-year-olds to play the violin,' he added.

7 'The puppy can sleep on our bed,' said Tom.
'I'd rather he slept in a basket,' said his wife. 'That puppy will soon be a very big dog and then there won't be room for all three of us.'

8 'I'll try by myself first,' said Ann, 'and if I find that I can't manage I'll ask Tom to help me.'

9 'Let's camp by this stream,' said Mary. 'If we go on, it may be dark before we find another good place.'

10 'I wish we'd brought our guitars,' said the students. 'Then we could have offered to play in the restaurant and perhaps they'd have given us a free meal.'

11 'I booked a double room on the first floor,' said Mr Jones.
'I'm afraid we didn't get your letter,' said the receptionist, 'and all the first and second floor rooms have been taken. But we could give you two single rooms on the third floor.'
'That wouldn't do me at all,' said Mr Jones.

12 'I've had gypsies on my land for two years,' said the farmer, 'and they've given nobody any trouble; but now the Council have asked me to tell them to move on. I don't see why they should be asked to move and I'm writing to my MP about it.'

13 'This letter is full of mistakes!' snorted Mr Jones.
'I did it in rather a hurry,' admitted the typist. 'I suppose I'd better type it again.'

14 'If you'd like to go on any of these tours,' said the receptionist, 'the hotel will arrange it.'
'We'd like to go on them all,' said the American couple.

15 'We'll try to find your passport,' said the policeman, 'but it'll be very difficult because a lot of suspicious characters sleep on the beach in summer and any one of them might have robbed you.'

16 'Let's go to the races!' said Ann. 'We might make our fortunes. I've been given a very good tip for the 2.30.'
'I've had "good tips" from you before,' said Paul. 'And they were disastrous.'

17 'I don't know why you waste so much time polishing the car,' said Mr Jones.
'The neighbours all polish their cars,' said Mrs Jones, 'and I don't want our Mini to look like a poor relation. If you were any good you'd help me instead of standing there criticizing,' she added.

18 'I'm sorry for not having a tie on,' said Peter. 'I didn't know it was going to be a formal party.'

19 'I'd have enjoyed the journey more if the man next to me hadn't snored all the time,' said Paul.

20 'I was thinking of going alone,' I said.
'You'd better take someone with you,' said the old man. 'It's safer with two. One can keep watch while the other sleeps.'

21 (Paul is speaking to Mary on the phone, and Mary is repeating his words to Ann, who is standing beside her.)
Paul: The plans have been changed. We're going tomorrow now, not on the next day. I want you to meet me at Victoria tonight.
Mary: Paul says . . .

22 'If I want a hot bath I have to put ten pence in the meter,' said Tom, 'and even then it's not very hot.'
'That's ridiculous,' I said; 'It's high time you left that place.'

23 'I know the umbrella belongs to you, but I thought it would be all right if I borrowed it,' said my nephew, 'because you aren't going out tomorrow and I am.'

24 'Let's put your tape-recorder under the table,' said Tom, 'and make a recording of their conversation. It would be very useful to know what they are planning.'
'But my recorder makes a distinct hum,' I said. 'They'd be sure to hear it and look under the table; and then they'd find the recorder and ask all sorts of embarrassing questions.'

25 'Whenever my father was unhappy,' said the girl, 'he would go out and buy something, usually something large and useless. That's why our rooms are full of things we can't use.'
'I'm sorry for your father,' said Tom, looking round. 'He must have been a very unhappy man.'

26 'You can leave your motorcycle in my garage if you like,' he said. 'I'll keep an eye on it while you're away.'

27 'If you want a job you should read advertisements and write letters and ring people up,' he said to Ann. 'It's no use sitting at home, expecting employers to form a queue outside your door.'

28 'This used to be a lovely quiet street,' he said, 'but now it is impossible. When summer comes you'll have to keep the windows shut all the time because of the noise.'

29 'You must leave a note for your mother,' said Peter, 'otherwise she'll be terribly worried when you're not in at your usual time.'

30 'A letter marked "Urgent" has just arrived for Albert,' said Mary, 'and he's on holiday. I wonder if I should ring him up and tell him about it or wait till he comes back.'

160 Indirect speech: questions

◪ PEG 317

See note to Exercise 158.
Put the following questions into indirect speech.

1 'Who has been using my typewriter?' said my mother.

2 'Do you want to see the cathedral?' said the guide.
3 'Do you mind working on the night shifts?' he asked.
4 'Would you like to come with us?' they said.
5 'Who did you give the money to?' asked Ann.
6 'How long does it take to get to Edinburgh by coach?' asked the tourist.
7 'How much do you think it will cost?' he said.
8 'What did you miss most when you were in prison?' Mary asked the ex-convict.
9 Another passenger came in and said, 'Is this seat taken?'
10 'How do you get on with your mother-in-law?' said Paul.
11 'How did you get into the house?' they asked him.
12 'What were you doing with these skeleton keys?' said Mr Jones. 'Were you trying to get at the secret files?'
13 'Did you sleep well?' asked my hostess.
14 'Have you been here long?' the other students asked him.
15 'Can you tell me why Paul left the university without taking his degree?' Paul's sister asked.
16 'How many people know the combination of the safe?' said the detective.
17 'Are there any letters for me?' said Mary.
18 'How long have you been learning English?' the examiner said.
19 'Why aren't you taking the exams?' said Paul.
20 'Are these free-range eggs?' said the customer.
21 'Where are you going for your summer holidays?' I asked them.
22 'Will it be all right if I come in a little later tonight?' asked the au pair girl.
23 'Have you ever seen a flying saucer?' said the man.
24 'Where can I park my caravan?' she asked the policeman.
25 'Would you like a lift?' said Ann. 'Which way are you going?' I said.
26 'Who do you want to speak to?' said the telephonist.
27 'Does anyone want tickets for the boxing match?' said Charles.
28 'What are you going to do with your old car?' I asked him.
29 'Do you grow your own vegetables?' I asked.
30 'What train are you going to get?' my friend inquired.
31 'Could you change a five-pound note? I'm afraid I haven't got anything smaller,' said the passenger to the conductor.
32 'How many sleeping pills have you taken?' said the night sister. 'I have no idea,' said Mr Jones sleepily.
33 'Could we speak to the manager, please?' said the two men. 'Have you an appointment?' said the secretary.
34 'Do you think you could live entirely on your own for six months,' said Tom, 'or would you get bored?'
35 'Did any of you actually see the accident happen?' said the policeman.
36 'Could I see Commander Smith?' the lady asked. 'I'm afraid he's in orbit,' I said. 'Would you like to leave a message?'

161 Indirect speech: questions, advice, requests, invitations, suggestions

■ PEG 283, 286–7, 289, 317–18, 322

'**What about**' often introduces a suggestion and is then reported by **suggest**:

'What about flying?' he said.

He suggested flying.

'I can't come at 1.00,' said Ann. 'Then what about 2.00?' said Tom.

Ann said she couldn't come at 1.00, so Tom suggested 2.00.

'**Why don't you**' often introduces suggestions or advice and is then reported by **suggest** or **advise**:

'I wonder if Tom is coming,' said Ann.

'Why don't you ask him?' I said.

Ann wondered if Tom was coming. I advised her to ask him or *I suggested (her) asking him.*

'**Could I have**' is normally reported by **ask for**:

'Could I have a cup of coffee?' she said.

She asked (me) for a cup of coffee.

'**Could you**' used for requests is reported by **ask** + object + infinitive:

'Could you sign the book, please?' he said.

He asked me to sign the book.

But when '**Could you**' introduces an ordinary question the verb is reported unchanged:

'Could you live entirely on you own?' he said.

He asked if I could live entirely on my own.

'**Would you mind waiting/signing**' etc. can be reported:

He asked me to wait/sign etc. or

He asked if I would mind waiting/signing etc.

offer can be used in two constructions:

'Would you like a drink?'

He offered me a drink.

'Shall I wait for you? I'll wait for you if you like.'

He offered to wait for me.

When the infinitive is used it must be placed directly after **offer**. The person addressed is not mentioned in this construction.

Put the following into indirect speech.

1 'Shall we have dinner somewhere after the theatre?' said Peter.
'Yes, let's,' said Ann. 'What about going to that place Jack is always talking about?' (*For* Yes, let's *put* Ann agreed.)

2 'Jack's parents have asked me to supper tomorrow night,' said Ann.
'What shall I wear?'
'I should wear something warm, dear,' said her mother. 'It's a terribly cold house.'

3 'I'm broke,' said Jack.
  'Shall I lend you some money?' said Peter.
4 'It will take a little time to look up your file,' said the clerk. 'Is it
  worth waiting,' said Ann, 'or shall I go away and come back later?'
5 'Shall I have to do the whole exam again if I fail in one paper?' said
  the student.
  'Yes,' said the teacher.
6 Where will you be tomorrow,' I said, 'in case I have to ring you?'
  'I shall be in my office till six,' said the old man, 'and after that at
  my flat. I shan't be going to the club.'
7 'What shall I do with this cracked cup?' Mary asked.
  'You'd better throw it away,' said her mother.
8 'Shall I ever see him again?' she wondered.
9 'Would you mind getting out of the car?' said the driver. 'I have to
  change a wheel.'
  'Shall I help you?' I said.
10 'I've run out of petrol,' said the man. 'Could you possibly give me a
   lift to the next village?'
11 'Shall we go for a walk?' said Peter.
   'I like walking,' said Ann, 'but at the moment my only comfortable
   walking shoes are being mended. What about going for a drive
   instead?'
12 You've got a lot of parcels,' he said. 'Shall I carry some of them for
   you?'
13 'Shall we be in time?' muttered Tom, looking at his watch. (*Use*
   wonder.)
14 'What shall I do with all this foreign money?' said Peter.
   'Why don't you take it to the bank and get it changed?' said Mary.
15 'Would you like a cigarette?' said Peter.
   'No, thanks,' said Jack. 'I don't smoke.'
16 'Would you like to come with us?' they said. 'There's plenty of room
   in the car.'
   'I'd love to,' said Ann.
17 Ann (on phone): Could you do without me today, Mr Jones? I've got
   an awful cold and I think it might be better if I stayed at home.
   Mr Jones: I should certainly stay at home, Ann. And you'd better
   take tomorrow off too if you aren't better.
18 Mary (on phone): Paul, I've just come back to my flat to find a
   complete stranger asleep in my chair. He's still here, and still asleep!
   What shall I do?
   Paul: Why don't you wake him up and ask him who he is? There's
   probably some quite simple explanation.
19 'I'm not quite ready,' said Peter. 'Could you wait a few minutes?'
   'I can't wait long,' said Jack. 'The train goes at ten.'
20 'Would you mind taking off your hat?' I said to the woman in front
   of me.
   'But the theatre's almost empty!' she said. 'Why don't you move
   along a bit?'

21 'I often see lights in the empty house across the road,' said Albert.
'Do you think I should report it?'

22 'If this house was yours what changes would you make?' I said.
'I'd pull it down and build a modern one on the same site,' said the
window-cleaner. 'The site's all right.'

23 'Could I have your name and address, please?' said the travel agent.

24 'Shall I send it round to your hotel, sir?' the shop assistant asked the
tourist.
'I'm not staying in the town,' said the tourist. 'I'll take it with me.'

25 'How long will you go on looking for them?' I asked one of the
search party.
'We don't search at night. We'll stop when it gets dark and start
again at first light tomorrow.'

26 'We can't discuss this over the phone. Shall we meet here in my flat
tomorrow?' I said.
'I'd rather you came to my office,' he said. 'Could you get here in
half an hour?'

27 'Could I have 40p, please?' said the boy. 'I want to buy an
ice-cream.'

28 'Would you like to sleep on the floor of my flat?' he asked us.
'Or would you rather go to a hotel?'

29 'Could you help me with my luggage, please?' she said. 'If you take
the two big ones I'll take the small one.'
'It's ridiculous to take three suitcases for a weekend,' I said.
'Couldn't you manage with two?'
'No,' she said.

30 'I couldn't come on Monday,' said Ann.
'Then what about Tuesday?' said Peter.
'All right,' said Ann.

162 Indirect speech: commands, requests, invitations, advice

■ PEG 283–4, 286, 320

Put the following sentences into indirect speech, using
tell/order/urge/ask/beg/invite/advise/warn/remind + object +
infinitive, or **ask** (+ object) + **for**, or, in some cases, **ask** +
infinitive.

1 'Don't put sticky things in your pockets,' said his mother.
2 'Please, please don't do anything dangerous,' said his wife.
3 'Go on—apply for the job,' said my friend. 'It would just suit you.'
4 'I should say nothing about it if I were you,' said my brother.

5 'Would you please wait in the lounge till your flight number is called?' she said.

6 'Don't lend Harry any money,' I said to Ann. 'He never pays his debts.'

7 'Could you please ring back in half an hour?' said the secretary.

8 'Would you mind moving your case?' said the other passenger. 'It's blocking the door.'

9 'Remember to book a table,' said Ann.

10 'Get into the right lane,' said the driving instructor.

11 'Avoid Marble Arch,' said the policeman. 'There's going to be a big demonstration there.'

12 'Hold the ladder,' he said. 'It's rather unsteady.'
'Why don't you tie it at the top?' I said. 'It's much safer than way.'

13 'Read the questions twice,' said the teacher, 'and don't write in the margin.'

14 'You'd better not leave your money lying about,' said one of the students.

15 'Why don't you open a bank account?' said another. (*Use* advise.)

16 'Would you like to have lunch with me today?' said Tom.
'I'm afraid I couldn't; I can't leave the office,' said the girl.

17 'Don't take more than two of these at once,' said the doctor, handing me a bottle of pills.

18 'Could I speak to Albert, please?' I said.
'He's still asleep,' said his mother.
'Then please wake him,' I said. 'I have news for him.'

19 'I'd buy the big tin if I were you,' said the grocer.

20 'You're being exploited,' said the other au pair girls. 'You ought to leave your job.'

21 'Fasten your seat belts; there may be a little turbulence,' said the air hostess.

22 'Don't drive through fog with only a fog light on,' he said, 'or oncoming drivers may take you for a motorcycle.'

23 'Could I see your driving licence?' said the policeman.

24 'You'd better sweep up that broken glass,' I said.

25 'The bathroom's empty now,' she said. 'Will you put the light out when you've finished?'

26 'Remember to insure your luggage,' my father said.

27 'Please don't drink any more,' said his wife. 'Don't forget that we have to drive home.'

28 'Do go to a dentist, Tom, before your toothache gets any worse,' I said.

29 'Why don't you cut your hair?' he said. 'You'd find it much easier to get a job if you looked tidy.'

30 'Could I have some more pudding, please?' said the boy.

163 Indirect speech: commands, requests, advice, suggestions

■ PEG 289, 320-2

Read notes to previous exercises.
Put the following into indirect speech, using either constructions recommended in Exercise 162, or (for commands): **say (that)** + subject + **be/should** + infinitive or (for suggestions): **suggest** + gerund or **that** + subject + **should**.

1 'Would you please fill in this form and then join the queue by the door?' said the clerk.
2 'Could you read the last sentence again, please?' said the examiner.
3 'Could I have a new cheque book, please?' said the girl.
'Could you show me your old cheque book?' said the bank clerk.
4 Postcard: Be ready to move off at very short notice. Tom.
Ann (reading it to Mary): Tom says that we . . .
5 'Please, please don't tell my mother,' begged the boy.
6 'Don't fire except in self-defence,' said the police sergeant.
7 'Why don't you take the rest of the day off?' said my assistant.
8 'Will you help me to move the piano, please?' said my aunt.
9 'Don't drive too close to the car in front,' said the driving instructor.
10 'Don't smoke near the petrol pump,' said the mechanic.
11 'When you've chosen a book, bring it to me and I'll stamp it,' said the librarian.
12 'Show the boarding card to the man at the foot of the gangway,' said the clerk.
13 'Reduce speed now,' said a huge notice. (*Omit* now.)
14 'Could I see your ticket, please?' said the inspector.
15 'Keep an eye on your luggage,' he said. 'This place is full of thieves.'
16 'When you have read this, pass it on to the next person on the list,' he said.
17 'Why not light a fire on the bank and cook the fish at once?' suggested the fisherman.
18 'Whenever you see the number "7" on the screen, press this button,' he said.
19 'Sit down and tell me what is worrying you,' he said to her.
20 'Walk along the line of men,' said the police sergeant 'and if you recognize your attacker, just nod. Don't say anything.'
21 'Even if you feel hungry don't eat anything between meals,' said the dietician.
22 'Could you ring up the taxi rank and order a taxi for me?' said Tom.
'Why don't you go by tube?' said Ann. 'It's much quicker.'
23 'Let's buy some yeast and make our own bread,' said Mary.
'The bread we're getting now is absolutely tasteless.'
24 'If you have to use the river water,' said the guide, 'boil it first. Don't drink it unboiled.'

25 'Let's not tell anyone,' said Tom, 'till we are quite certain that the report is true.'

26 Tom (on phone to Ann): I've got the tickets. Meet me at the air terminal at 6.30.
   (*Imagine that you are Ann. Report this message to Mary, who is standing beside you. Begin:* Tom says . . .)

27 'Let's show that we are united,' urged the shop steward, 'by voting unanimously to continue the strike.'

28 'Will customers please count their change,' said a notice above the cashier's desk, 'as mistakes cannot be rectified afterwards.'

29 'Don't clap yet,' warned my friend. 'She hasn't finished. Singers loathe people who clap too soon,' he added.

30 'Don't forget to put your name at the top of the page,' he said.

164 Indirect speech: mixed types

■ PEG 307–24

Read the notes to previous indirect speech exercises.
Note that **want** or **would like** is often useful when the speaker reports a request made to himself or made through him to someone else:

> Tom (on the phone to Ann): Could you book me a room in a hotel for tonight?
> Ann (telling Mary about this): *Tom wants me to book him a room for tonight.*

(*Tom said that I am to book* would also be possible but more authoritative.)
Similarly:

> Mrs Jones (on the phone to Mary): Could you ask Mrs Smith to ring me back?
> Mary (telling Mrs Smith about it): *Mrs Jones rang. She wants/would like you to ring her back.*

(*She says that you are to ring* would be possible but very authoritative.)

1 Letter (from Paul to Ann): Please get me a small tent and camping equipment for two people.
   Ann (telling Mary about this): Paul wants . . .

2 Mr White (on phone to Mr Black's secretary): Ask Mr Black to meet me at six in the bar on the ground floor.
   Secretary (reporting this to Mr Black): Mr White would like . . .

3 'Shall I go and get a candle?' said Ann when the light went out suddenly.
   'I'd rather you got another bulb,' said Mr Jones.
   'But there aren't any,' said Ann, 'and the shops are shut.'

4 'Don't worry about a few mistakes,' said Peter. 'I make mistakes all the time.'
'Do you learn from your mistakes?' I asked. 'Or do you keep making the same ones?'

5 'I'm looking for a man called Albert, who drinks in this bar,' I said.
'I should keep away from Albert if I were you,' said the barman. 'He doesn't like strangers and might turn nasty.'

6 'Could I have a look at your paper for a moment?' said the man.
'I just want to see the football results.'
'I haven't quite finished with it,' I said. 'Could you wait a moment?'
'I can't wait long,' he said. 'I'm getting off at the next stop.'

7 'You woke everyone up last night,' said my mother. 'You must try to be quieter tonight.'
'We will,' I promised.

8 'The soup's cold again,' complained Mr Jones. 'Why do I never have hot soup?'
'Because the kitchen's so far from the dining room,' explained his wife. 'If you insist on living in a castle you must put up with its disadvantages.'
'What about getting an ex-Olympic runner as an au pair girl?' said Mr Jones.
'She wouldn't stay,' sighed his wife.

9 'Your licence is out of date,' said the policeman.
'It is,' I admitted, 'but I've applied for a new one.'
'Next time,' he said severely, 'apply for a new one before your current one has expired.'

10 'I'll have the money for you next week. Shall I post it to you?' I said.
'Could you keep it in your safe till I can come and collect it?' said Tom. 'A lot of my mail has been going astray lately and I'd hate to lose one of your large cheques.'

11 'Could I borrow your map again?' said Peter.
'You're always borrowing it. Why don't you get one of your own?' I said.

12 'When you hear the fire bell,' he said, 'shut the windows and go downstairs.'
'And what shall we do if the stairs are blazing?' I asked.

13 'Can you hear that noise?' Ann said. 'What do you think it is?'
'I think it's only rats running up and down inside the wall,' I said.
'I think it's someone trying to get in,' she said. 'You'd better go and see.'

14 'It's your turn to baby-sit tonight,' they told Ann.
'It can't be!' said Ann indignantly. 'I baby-sat last night! And the night before! And I'm only supposed to do two nights a week!'
'Could you possibly do it just this once?' they said. 'And we promise not to ask you to do any next week.'

15 'This is the best restaurant in town,' said the taxi driver. 'The only problem is that they expect guests to wear ties.'
'Then why have you brought us here?' said the tourists indignantly.
'Don't get excited,' said the taxi-driver, opening a box. 'I keep ties specially for gentlemen in your predicament. What colour would you like? They're all the same price.'

16 'Shall I start tomorrow?' I said.
'I'd rather you started today,' said Tom.

17 'Why don't you go and see the film? It may help you to understand the book,' I said.
'But the film's quite different from the book,' Ann pointed out.

18 'I saw the two climbers,' said the helicopter pilot. 'And one of them sat up and waved to me.'
'Which one of them waved?' I said.
'I don't know,' he answered. 'I wasn't near enough to see them clearly.'

19 'What caused the ship to sink?' I said.
'She must have struck the submerged wreck,' said the coxswain of the lifeboat. 'But I can't understand it, because the wreck is very clearly marked with buoys.'

20 'My car won't start!' exclaimed Mary. 'The battery's flat again! Could you possibly give me a push just to start me down the hill?'
'Why don't you sell that car?' said Bill.
'Nobody would buy it,' said Peter. 'What about just putting a match to it?'

21 'I've been given so many bottles of wine lately that I'll have to buy another wine rack,' said Mr Jones.
'Why don't you throw a party and save yourself the expense of a wine rack?' I suggested.

22 'Press button A to start the engine,' he said.
'But last time you told me to press button B!' I said.
'That was on a slightly different type of machine,' he explained.

23 'Don't brake if you find yourself skidding,' said Tom. 'That only makes it worse. Try to steer into the skid.'
'I know what I *should* do,' I said. 'But when I start skidding I get so excited that I do the exact opposite.'
'Then stop and let me take over,' said Tom. 'We're just coming to an icy bit and I don't want to die just yet.'

24 'I've run out of stamps,' said my father. 'Have you got any?'
'No, but I'll go out and get you some if you like,' I said.
'Don't bother,' he said. 'I've missed the post anyway.'

25 'Repairs to cars rented from us must be arranged through our office,' he said. 'So if anything goes wrong with the one you've hired, please ring the number printed on your card. The office is open from nine to six, Monday to Friday.'
'But what shall I do if something goes wrong with it outside office hours?' I said.

26 'Why didn't you signal to the tanker that she was coming too close?'
I said.
'We did signal,' said the pilot, 'but she came on in and ran aground.'
'What's going to happen to her?' I said.
'We're going to try to tow her off at the next high tide,' he said.
'But if we don't get her off tonight she'll be here till she breaks up,
and there'll be an oil slick all along the coast.'

27 'Why are you spending so long on those accounts?' I asked.
'Because I can't make them balance,' he said. 'I seem to be £13
short; and that means that I'll have to put in £13 of my own money
to make it up.'
'Would you like me to go through them and see if I can find a
mistake?' I said.
'No,' he said, 'but I'd like you to lend me £13.'

28 'Why are you looking so depressed, Jack?' I said.
'Because I've just asked Ann to marry me and she's refused,' he
said sadly.
'I think she prefers clean-shaven men,' I said. 'Why don't you cut
your hair and shave off your beard and try again?'

29 'How did you get up that tree?' Mary asked.
'I used a ladder, of course,' he snapped. 'But someone went off with
it when I was sawing. Go and get another one and don't just stand
there asking silly questions.'

30 'Are you ill?' he said coldly.
'No.' I said.
'Did you sleep well last night?'
'Yes,' I said.
'Then why are you sitting about when all the others are working? Go
out at once and give them a hand.'

31 'Will passengers with nothing to declare please go through the green
door?' said a customs official.
'You'd better go through the green door, Mary,' said Peter, 'but I'll
have to go through the other one. I'll take a bit longer than you will,
so wait for me at the other end.'

32 (Imagine that you have received the following postcard from your brother
Tom. Report it at once to the other members of the family. Begin: Tom
says . . .)
Don't worry about me. I wasn't badly injured and I'm being very
well looked after. I'm coming back next Wednesday on the nine
o'clock flight from Zurich. Could you please meet the plane?

33 'What shall I do with my wet shoes?' said the boy.
'You'd better stuff them with newspaper and put them near the fire,'
said his mother. 'But don't put them too near or they'll go hard.'

34 'Let's drive on to the next village and try the hotel there,' he said.
'But what'll we do if that's full too?' I asked.
'We'll just have to sleep in the car,' he said. 'It will be too late to try
anywhere else.'

35 'They have a rather fierce dog,' said Ann; 'but he's a heavy sleeper,

and with any luck he won't hear you breaking in.'
'What'll I do if he wakes up?' I said.
'If he starts growling, give him some of these biscuits,' said Ann.
'How do you know that he likes these particular biscuits?'
'All dogs like them,' Ann assured me. 'It says so on the packet.'

36 'If you even touch one of the pictures,' warned the attendant, 'alarm
bells will ring all over the gallery and you will be arrested instantly.'
'Are you serious?' I said.
'Try it and see,' he answered with a glint in his eye.

165 Indirect speech: sentences with let

■ PEG 322

1 **He said, 'Let's go'** usually becomes:
    (a) *He suggested going*
though possible in certain cases are:
    (b) *He suggested that they should go*
    (c) *He urged/advised them to go.*
He said, 'Let's not go' can be expressed by any of these
constructions in the negative; but **suggest** + negative gerund is
slightly less usual than the others and is often replaced by the (b)
type of construction or by:
    He was against going/against the idea/against it.
    He was opposed to the idea/He opposed the idea etc.

2 **He said, 'Let them go,'** can become:
    (a) *He suggested that they should go/suggested their going*
but usually it expresses an obligation and becomes:
    (b) *He said that they should go/ought to go.*
Very occasionally it expresses a command and becomes:
    (c) *He said that they were to go.*
    'Let him/them' can also express the speaker's indifference:
    'Everyone will laugh at you,' I said. 'Let them!' he retorted.
    He expressed indifference/said he didn't mind.

3 **let** is also an ordinary verb meaning **allow**:
    'Let me go!' the boy said to the policeman.
    The boy asked the policeman to let him go.

Put the following into indirect speech.

1 'Let's go to the cinema,' said Ann. 'Yes, let's,' I said.
2 The Prime Minister said, 'Let us show the nation that we are worthy
of their confidence.' (*Use* urged.)
3 'Let me stay up a little longer tonight, mother,' begged the child.
4 'Let's eat out tonight,' said Ann. 'Too expensive,' objected Tom.
'Why don't we go back to your flat and have scrambled eggs?'

5 The police officer said, 'Let's leave the wrecked car here for a bit. It may remind other drivers to be more careful.'
6 'The neighbours will object!' said Ann.
  'Let them,' said Tom.
7 'Let's go on a diet,' said Ann.
  'All right,' said Mary reluctantly.
8 'Tom made this mess. Let him clear it up,' said his father.
9 'It's Mothering Sunday tomorrow,' said the boy. 'Let's buy Mum some flowers.'
10 'Let's take a tent and camp out,' said Bill.
  'Let's go to a nice hotel and be comfortable,' said Mary.
11 'Let's give a party,' said Ann.
  'Let's not,' said her husband.
12 I said, 'Let's not jump to conclusions. Let's wait till we hear confirmation of this rumour.'
13 'The newspapers will say it's your fault,' warned his colleagues.
  'Let them say what they like,' he said.
14 'Let the nations forget their differences and work together for peace,' said the preacher.
15 'Let me explain,' she said. 'Don't be in such a hurry.'
16 'Let the children play in the garden if they want to,' she told the gardener. 'I'm sure they won't do any harm.'
17 'Let's stay here till the storm has passed,' I said.
18 'It's the government's fault. Let them do something about it,' grumbled my father.

166 Indirect speech: sentences with **must**, **needn't** and **have to**

■ PEG 325

must (first person)
'I must' can remain unchanged but usually becomes **had to** though **would have to** is better for an obligation which has only just arisen or is likely to arise in the future.

> Reading the letter he said, 'Good heavens! I must go at once!'
> He said, 'If she gets worse I must stay with her.'

These would become respectively:

> *He said that he'd have to go* and
> *He said that he'd have to stay.*

'must I?' usually becomes **had to**.
'I must not' usually remains unchanged.

must (second and third persons)
'you/he must' usually remains unchanged.
'must you/he?' usually becomes **had to**.

'you/he must not' remains unchanged or becomes **weren't to/wasn't to**.
must used for permanent commands or prohibitions or to express
advice always remains unchanged.
must used to express deduction never changes.

needn't

'I needn't' can change to **didn't have to/wouldn't have to** in the same
way that **'I must'** changes to **'had to/would have to**, but it very often
remains unchanged.
'you/he needn't' usually remains unchanged.
'need I/you/he?' remains unchanged or becomes **had to**.

have to

Forms with **have to** follow the usual rules. Remember that **'had to'**
in direct speech will become **had had to** in indirect:

He said, 'After the lecture I had to rush home.'
He said that after the lecture he had had to rush home.

Put the following into indirect speech.

1 He said, 'If what you say is true I must go to the police.'
2 He said, 'I must be at the docks at six a.m. tomorrow.'
3 'Must you make such a noise?' he asked.
4 'You mustn't come in without knocking,' he told us.
5 'Your ticket will cost £5,' I said.
   'In that case,' said my nephew, 'I must go to the bank tomorrow.'
6 Park notice: Dogs must be kept on a lead.
7 His father said, 'Tom must work harder next term.'
8 'You needn't come in tomorrow,' said my employer. 'Take the day off.'
9 'I must go to the dentist tomorrow,' he said. 'I have an appointment.'
10 Notice: Passengers must not lean out of the window.
11 He said, 'There must be someone in the house; there's smoke
   coming from the chimney.'
12 She said, 'When you are a big boy you'll have to tie your own shoes.'
13 'Port wine must never be shaken,' my wine-merchant said.
14 'He hasn't had anything to eat since breakfast; he must be starving,'
   she said.
15 The official said, 'This passport photo isn't like you at all. You must
   have another one taken.'
16 'You mustn't play with knives, children,' said their mother.
17 'I needn't get up till nine tomorrow,' I said.
18 Railway regulations: Passengers must be in possession of a valid
   ticket before travelling.
19 'How did you get your bulldog up the escalator?' I said.
   'I carried him,' said Tom.
   'You must be very strong,' I said admiringly.
20 'You mustn't tell anyone what I've just told you,' she said to me.
21 'Need I eat it all, mummy?' said the child.
   'Yes, dear, you must,' she said.
22 'I had to drive your pigs out of my garden,' she said.

23 'Sticks and umbrellas must be left at the desk,' said the notice in the museum.
24 'Must you do it all tonight? Couldn't you leave some for tomorrow?' I asked her.
25 'When you go through Bayeux you must see the tapestry,' he told me.
26 He said, 'You must walk faster; you are far too slow.'
27 'You mustn't forget to put the stamp on or your friend will have to pay double postage,' he told me.
28 'I needn't tell you how grateful I am,' he said.

167 Indirect speech to direct speech

■ PEG 307–25

Put the following into direct speech with the appropriate punctuation.

1 She asked if he'd like to go to the concert and I said that I was sure she would.
2 She told me to look where I was going as the road was full of holes and was very badly lit.
3 They said that while they were bathing they saw someone examining their clothes.
4 I asked if she had looked everywhere and she said that she had.
5 He suggested giving her a bottle of wine.
6 He said that the new carpet had arrived and asked where he was to put it.
7 He said that two days previously an enormous load of firewood had been dumped at his front gate and that since then he hadn't been able to get his car out.
8 They offered me some more wine and I accepted.
9 He said that if I found the front door locked I was to go round to the back.
10 She asked the burglars who they were and who had let them in. They told her to sit down and keep quiet unless she wanted to get hurt.
11 He asked what the weather had been like during my holiday and I said that it had been awful.
12 He suggested going down to the harbour and seeing if they could hire a boat.
13 He said that if I didn't like escalators I could go up the emergency staircase. I thanked him and said that I would do that.
14 He suggested that Tom and I should go ahead and get the tickets.
15 He said that he thought my electric iron was unsafe and advised me to have it seen to.

16 He said that if war broke out he would have to leave the country at once.

17 I asked him if he had enjoyed house-hunting and he said that he hadn't.

18 She said that she was surprised to see that the grandfather clock had stopped and asked if anyone had been fiddling with it.

19 She said that she had tried to ring up her mother several times on the previous day but had not succeeded in getting through.

20 I asked her if she'd like to borrow the book but she thanked me and said that she had already read it and hadn't liked it very much.

21 He wanted to know if I was going to the dance and suggested that we should make up a party and go together.

22 I told her to stop making a fuss about nothing and said that she was lucky to have got a seat at all.

23 The clerk in the booking office inquired if I wanted a single or return ticket. I asked if a return was any cheaper. He said it made no difference.

24 My employer hoped I would not be offended if he told me that, in his opinion, I would do better in some other kind of job.

25 The AA man told the woman that if her wheels had gone a couple of inches nearer the edge, the car would have plunged into the ravine.

26 He said I mustn't mind if the first one wasn't any good.

27 He asked the crowd if they thought that he was a liar and the crowd shouted that they did.

28 I stopped a man in the street and asked him to help me with my car. The man asked if it would take long, explaining that he was on his way to catch a train.

21 Time clauses

168 Time clauses

☐ PEG 342

Put the verbs in brackets into the correct tense.

1 Heat the oil till it (begin) to smoke.
2 I'll stay here till Tom (get) back.
3 We'll go out as soon as the shops (open).
4 You drive first, and when you (be) tired, I'll take over.
5 The sooner we (start), the sooner we'll get there.
6 We will send you the goods as soon as we (receive) your cheque.
7 I'll wait as long as you (like).
8 Whip the whites of the eggs till they (be) quite stiff.
9 Shall I jump out when the bus (slow) down at the next corner? ~
10 No, you'd better wait till it (stop) at the traffic lights.
11 You are too young to understand. I (explain) it to you when you (be) older.
12 Tom: Brown is the best poet in the university.
Ann: Now read Smith's poems. When you (read) them you'll say that he is better.
13 Tom: I can't get used to driving on the left.
Jack: When you (be) here for another week you'll find it quite easy.
14 The room doesn't look particularly attractive now but when I (clean) and (paint) it, it will look quite different.
15 Pour boiling water on the coffee grounds, wait till the grounds (settle), then strain the coffee into a jug.
16 As soon as they (see) the river the children will want to bathe.
17 When we (see) the cathedral we'll go to the museum.
18 What will you do when you (finish) painting the bridge? ~
19 Oh, this bridge is so long that by the time we (reach) the other end it will be time to start again at this end.
20 Serve the meal and wash up. When you (do) the washing up you can go home.
21 The plane won't take off till the fog (lift).
22 Tom will start as soon as his visa (arrive).
23 I'm glad you're learning French. When you (know) French I (give) you a job.
24 Shall I boil the baby's milk? ~
Yes, but don't give it to him till it (cool).
25 Don't start smoking till the others (finish) their meal.

26 By the time you (give) the children their meal you won't have any appetite left.

27 I don't want anyone to overhear us, but I (tell) you what happened when we (be) alone.

28 How do you like your new job? ~
I've only just started so I really can't say. When I (be) in it for a fortnight I (let) you know.

29 My instructor says that when I (fly) another ten hours, he'll let me fly solo.

30 They say that when the 100 k.p.h. speed limit (be) in operation for a year, they will be able to judge whether it is effective or not.

31 Sculptor's friend: I suppose that when I (come) back next year you will still be working on this horse.

32 Sculptor: Oh no, I (finish) it long before I (see) you again, but as soon as I (finish) one thing I (start) on another, so there'll be something else for you to look at.

33 All the flats are exactly alike so when you (see) one you've seen them all.

34 Advertisement: When you (drive) a Jaguar once, you won't want to drive another car.

35 He's asleep now but I (give) him the letter as soon as he (wake) up.

36 She bought beer and made sandwiches because she knew that when they (arrive) they would be hungry and thirsty.

169 Time clauses

☐ PEG 342

Put the verbs in brackets into the correct tense.

1 When it (get) dark we'll have to stop. We can't work in the dark.

2 Go on till you (come) to a square with a statue in the middle; then turn left and you'll find the theatre on your right.

3 Immediately the train (stop) we'll jump out.

4 I'll help you with your homework as soon as I (do) my own.

5 He was determined to keep the two dogs apart because he knew that the moment they (see) one another they'd start barking.

6 I know the coat's unfashionable but I'm not going to throw it away. I'll keep it till that style (come) into fashion again.

7 Tourist: Can we get to the top of the tower?
Guide: Yes, but be careful when you (go) up because the steps are very uneven.

8 Tourist (puffing up the steps): I'll be glad when I (get) to the top!
Guide: When you (see) the view you'll be glad you made the effort.

9 Mother (to child setting out for school): When you (come) to the main road remember to stop and look both ways before you (cross).

10 'Give this letter to your teacher as soon as you (arrive) at school,'
   said his mother.
   'All right,' said the boy, running out.
   'I bet it will still be in his pocket when he (get) home tonight,' said
   his father.

11 Tom: I'm going to New York by sea. I'm leaving tomorrow.
   Jack: I'm going by air. When I (sit) in my comfortable plane I'll
   think of you tossing about on a stormy sea.
   Tom: When I (walk) about the deck enjoying the fresh air and blue
   sea I'll think of you shut up in a flying box and seeing nothing.

12 But there's someone in the phone box! You can't rush in and grab
   the receiver. You'll have to wait till he (finish).

13 The ladder looks a bit unsteady. ~
   Yes, but before he (start) working he will tie the top end to the tree.

14 The house won't be entirely mine until I (pay) off the mortgage.

15 You'll find that the staff will clock in very punctually but that they
   won't do any work till the boss (arrive).

16 When I (work) here for fifteen years I'll be entitled to a pension.

17 When you (do) the bedrooms, remember to sweep under the beds.

18 When you (do) all the upstairs rooms, come down and give me a
   hand with the lunch.

19 Mother to child: I won't let you watch TV until you (finish) your
   supper.

20 We'll talk business when we (have) dinner, but not during dinner. I
   never talk business at meals.

21 Young man: Weren't you astonished when she said that?
   Old man: When you (be) married as long as I have, you won't be so
   easily astonished.

22 When you (read) the book, leave it in the hospital for someone else
   to read.

23 He said he would give me a ring as soon as he (reach) Paris.

24 Some people say that a man shouldn't think of marrying till he (save)
   up enough money to buy a house.

25 You're an idiot to go into teaching. I'm going into business. In ten
   years' time when you (queue) at the bus stop I'll be driving by in my
   Bentley.

26 When you are picking fruit in the holidays to eke out your salary I
   (cruise) round the Greek islands in my private yacht.

27 I visit a new country every year. By the time I (be) sixty I shall have
   visited all the most interesting countries in the world.

28 When I (see) all there is to see I'll buy a small island and settle down
   there.

29 He saves £500 a year. By the time he (retire) he'll have saved
   £20,000.

30 By the time he (save) £20,000, the value of the money will have gone
   down so much that he'll have to go on working.

31 Ann hoped that it would go on raining. She knew that the moment it
   (stop) Tom would want to go out.

32 I expected that Jack would be there when the train (arrive), but there was no sign of him.

33 The boys worked slowly for they knew that as soon as they (finish) one exercise the teacher would tell them to do the next.

34 I'll take the paper with me. I'll read it while I (wait) for the bus.

35 The window-cleaner was in fact one of a gang of safe crackers. He hoped that while he (clean), or (pretend) to clean, windows he would be able to have a look at the safe.

36 He said that he would lend me money whenever I (need) it.

170 when, whenever and as (= while, because)

☐ PEG 332–3

Use **when, whenever** or **as** to fill the gaps in the following.

1 . . . (*Because*) there were no buses we had to take a taxi.

2 . . . he grew older his temper improved. (*His temper got better every year.*)

3 . . . he grew older (*he reached the age of, say, 40*) his temper improved.

4 . . . the doors opened the crowd began pouring in. (*They didn't wait for the doors to open fully.*)

5 . . . it became dark (*after dark*), he left his hiding place.

6 . . . the sun went down, great bars of red covered the western sky.

7 . . . he left the house (*while he was still in the doorway*) he suddenly remembered where he'd seen her before.

8 . . . he left the house (*after leaving it*) he turned right.

9 . . .we have a puncture (*every time we have one*) she just sits in the car while I change the wheel.

10 Don't exhaust yourself. Sit down . . . you're tired. (*as soon as you're tired*)

11 . . . (*Because*) we were tired we sat down beside the stream.

12 . . .we approached the town (*came gradually nearer to it*) we wondered whether there'd be room in the hotel.

13 . . . we reached the town (*after arriving*) we sent Tom to find out about hotels.

14 I'll have to buy a map . . . (*because*) I don't know the area.

15 . . . you don't know a district it is always a good thing to have a map.

16 . . . the manager is out (*every time he is out*) his assistant signs the letters.

17 . . . (*Because*) the manager is out today I'll sign the letters.

18 The phone rang just . . . I got into my bath. (*I was in the act of getting in.*)

19 I've given your old jacket away . . . (*because*) it was too tight for you.

20 A revolver appeared round the edge of the door . . . it swung open. (*The revolver appeared before the door was fully open.*)

21 . . . the evening wore on there were fewer and fewer people in the streets.

22 . . . he is determined to get something he usually succeeds. (*Every time he is determined etc.*)

23 He happened to look in at the window . . . he walked past. (*in the act of walking past*)

24 . . . she finished her training she got a job. (*after she had finished*)

25 I'll write in Spanish . . . (*because*) he doesn't understand English.

26 The atmosphere became stuffier . . . more and more people crowded into the carriage. (*The more people came in, the stuffier the atmosphere became.*)

27 He sang . . . he worked. (*while*)

28 . . . the sun rose the fog dispersed. (*the more sun, the less fog*)

29 . . . a kettle boils steam comes out of the spout. (*every time*)

30 . . . you're ready I'll bring in the tea. (*as soon as*)

31 . . . he walked along people began to stare and point. (*while*)

32 . . . I didn't see him I can't very well describe him. (*because*)

33 . . . I've learnt English I'll go to France and learn French. (*as soon as*)

34 . . . the meat was cooked I took it out of the oven. (*as soon as*)

35 . . . the meat was cooked I took it out of the oven. (*because*)

36 . . . I reached the box office all the tickets had been sold.

22 Phrasal verbs

171 Combinations with **get** and **be**

☑ PEG chapter 38

Put in the correct prepositions or adverbs.

1 Is Mary in? ~
   No, she's . . . and won't be . . . till nine o'clock.
2 What shall we do now? ~
   I'm . . . keeping quiet and saying nothing.
3 If you got . . . . . . your work instead of talking you'd be finished in
   half the time.
4 He promised to act as chairman, so I'm afraid he can't get . . . . . . it
   now. There's no one else to do it.
5 She wants to do all the work herself but I don't think she is . . .
   . . . it.
6 He leaves his car at a parking meter for over two hours and always
   gets . . . . . . it. (*is never caught*) When I do that, I am fined.
7 I don't think they'll be . . . yet. It's only five o'clock in the morning.
8 They didn't want the news of their engagement to get . . . till it was
   officially announced.
9 The office closes early on Fridays and we get . . . at five o'clock
   instead of six.
10 If you don't give the children something to do, they'll be . . . . . .
   some mischief.
11 The car stopped in front of the bank messenger and two men with
   guns got . . . .
12 She is a friendly girl who gets . . . . . . everyone she meets.
13 As soon as the examinations are . . . we are going away on holiday.
14 It took her a long time to get . . . the death of her husband.
15 We usually get . . . a play among ourselves at the end of the term.
16 I'm going to Berlin on business and I shall be . . . for a week.
17 Tom hasn't been working; he won't get . . . his examinations.
18 The police knew he had committed the crime but he got . . . as there
   was not enough evidence against him.
19 Shall I marry him? ~
   Well, it is . . . . . . you. I can't very well decide for you.
20 I tried to ring him up but I couldn't get . . . ; I think some of the
   lines are down after last night's storm.
21 She talks so much that it is difficult to get . . . from her.
22 Why not have your operation at once and get it . . .?
23 He got . . . his bicycle to pick up his pump.

24 Mary wants to study medicine but she is not very clever. I don't think she is . . . . . . it.
25 The train was delayed and only got . . . at midnight.
26 When winter is . . . I am going to have the house painted.
27 If you don't get . . . (*leave*) I'll send for the police.
28 I am . . . doing the washing up first and watching TV afterwards.
29 Get . . . the bus at Victoria Station.
30 How are you getting . . . with your work?
31 I don't think she is . . . . . . the level of the rest of the class.
32 I left my umbrella in the bus but I got it . . . from the Lost Property Office.
33 I am not getting . . . very fast because I can only type with two fingers.
34 The dog got . . . . . . a string of sausages from the butcher's.
35 We got . . . late because we missed the last bus.
36 Don't worry about my snake. He can't get . . . . . . his box.

172 Combinations with **look** and **keep**

☑ PEG chapter 38

Put in the correct prepositions or adverbs.

1 He wanted to talk to me but I kept . . . working and refused to listen.
2 She is a good secretary but she is kept . . . by her ignorance of languages.
3 The country was in a state of rebellion and was only kept . . . by repressive measures.
4 Look . . . the baby while I am out.
5 She kept the children . . . all day because it was so wet and cold.
6 You must look . . . and make plans for the future.
7 'Keep . . .!' he said. Don't come any nearer.'
8 If you look . . . it carefully you will see the mark.
9 I told the children to keep . . . . . . the room that was being painted.
10 Looking . . . , I see now all the mistakes I made when I was younger.
11 I have started getting up at five a.m. to study but I don't know if I can keep this . . . .
12 He had an unhappy childhood and he never looks . . . on it with any pleasure.
13 The man walked so fast that the child couldn't keep . . . . . . him.
14 She looked . . . to see who was following her.
15 There were so many panes of glass broken that the windows couldn't keep . . . the rain.
16 I've been looking . . . a cup to match the one I broke.
17 Look . . . . . . me at the station. I'll be at the bookstall.
18 Look . . .! You nearly knocked my cup out of my hand.

19 He was kept . . . in his research by lack of money.
20 Tom is looking . . . . . . his first trip abroad. (*expecting with pleasure*)
21 Look . . . on your way home and tell me what happened.
22 Before putting any money into the business, we must look very carefully . . . the accounts.
23 I look . . . her as one of the family.
24 My windows look . . . . . . the garden.
25 He asked me to look . . . the document and then sign it.
26 He looked . . . the book to see if he had read it before.
27 If you can afford a new car your business must be looking . . . .
28 You can always look . . . her address in the directory if you have forgotten it.
29 He looked me . . . and . . . before he condescended to answer my question.
30 I am looking . . . . . . seeing your new house.
31 Children have a natural inclination to look . . . . . . their parents.
32 You will see I am right if you look . . . the matter from my point of view.
33 He looks . . . . . . me because I spend my holidays in Bournemouth instead of going abroad.
34 If he doesn't know the word he can look it . . . in a dictionary.
35 The crowd looked . . . while the police surrounded the house.
36 Since our quarrel she looks . . . me whenever we meet.

173 Combinations with **go** and **come**

■ PEG chapter 38

Put in the correct prepositions or adverbs.

1 It was some time before he came . . . after being knocked out.
2 I had to wait for permission from the Town Council before I could go . . . with my plans.
3 He came . . . to my way of thinking after a good deal of argument.
4 The guard dog went . . . the intruder and knocked him down.
5 He had a sandwich and a cup of coffee, then went . . . working.
6 It's no use trying to keep it secret; it's sure to come . . . in the end.
7 I went . . . the proposal very carefully with my solicitor and finally decided not to accept their offer.
8 The gun went . . . by accident and wounded him in the leg.
9 The question of salary increases will come . . . at the next general meeting.
10 Wearing black for mourning went . . . many years ago.
11 She went . . . . . . a beauty contest and got a prize.
12 Those rust marks will come . . . if you rub them with lemon.
13 The price of tomatoes usually goes . . . in summer in England.
14 If there isn't enough soup to go . . . just put some hot water in it.

139

15 Seeing me from across the room, she came . . . . . . me, and said that she had a message for me.

16 The early colonists of Canada went . . . many hardships.

17 You can't go . . . . your promise now; we are depending on you.

18 I have changed my mind about marrying him; I simply can't go . . . . . . it.

19 The aeroplane crashed and went . . . in flames.

20 He came . . . a fortune last year. (*He inherited it.*)

21 Wait till prices come . . . again before you buy.

22 I refuse to go . . . now. I'm going on.

23 They have gone . . . all the calculations again but they still can't find the mistake.

24 The party went . . . very well; we all enjoyed ourselves.

25 Come . . . . It's far too cold to wait here any longer.

26 Mary went . . . in such a hurry that she left her passport behind.

27 The handle of the tea-pot came . . . in my hand as I was washing it.

28 Why don't you go . . . . . . stamp collecting if you want a quiet hobby?

29 I came . . . a vase exactly like yours in an antique shop.

30 Her weight went . . . to 70 kilos when she stopped playing tennis.

31 Don't go . . . food if you want to economize. Just drink less.

32 The sea has gone . . . considerably since last night's gale.

33 I'm at home all day. Come . . . whenever you have time.

34 She went . . . . . . her work after the interruptions.

35 She goes . . . a lot. She hardly every spends an evening at home.

36 I suggested that we should all take a cut in salary. Naturally this didn't go . . . very well. (*wasn't well received*)

174 Combinations with **take** and **run**

☑ PEG chapter 38

Put in the correct prepositions or adverbs.

1 I couldn't take . . . the lecture at all. It was too difficult for me.

2 He is inclined to let his enthusiasm run . . . . . . him.

3 When he offered me only £3, I was too taken . . . to say a word.

4 He has already run . . . the money his father left him two years ago.

5 Now he is running . . . bills all over the town.

6 She took . . . riding because she wanted to lose weight.

7 I can't start the car; the battery has run . . . .

8 The policeman ran . . . the thief.

9 He takes . . . his mother; he has blue eyes and fair hair too.

10 I forgot to turn off the tap and the wash-basin ran . . . .

11 That blouse is easy to make. You could run it . . . in hour.

12 I am sorry I called you a liar. I take it . . . .

13 Reformers usually run . . . . . . opposition from all kinds of people.

14 He took . . . going for a walk every night before he went to bed.
15 Don't run . . . . . . the idea that Scotsmen are mean. They just don't like wasting money.
16 I wish we could sell the grand piano; it takes . . . too much space here.
17 She is always running . . . her friends behind their backs. She soon won't have any friends left.
18 You'd better take . . . your coat if you're too hot.
19 Just run . . . the music of this song for me.
20 We took . . . each other the first time we met and have been friends ever since.
21 When his father died, Tom took . . . the business.
22 What I saw in the water was only an old tree. I took it . . . the Lock Ness Monster.
23 I ran . . . an old school friend in the tube today.
24 I can't go more than 50 k.p.h. as this is a new car and I am still running it . . . .
25 People often take me . . . my sister. We are very like each other.
26 My neighbour is always running . . . . . . .bread and borrowing some from me.
27 He always takes . . . his false teeth before he goes to bed.
28 I took . . . Tom at chess and beat him.
29 If a bull chased me I'd run . . . .
30 Even a child wouldn't be taken . . . by such an obvious lie.
31 You're looking rather run . . . ; I think you need a holiday.
32 The policeman took . . . the number of the stolen car.
33 If she takes . . . the job of director she'll have to work harder.
34 My car skidded and ran . . . a wall.
35 She makes a little extra money by taking . . . paying guests in summer.
36 A hen ran in front of my car and I'm afraid I ran . . . it.

175 Combinations with **turn**, **call** and **break**

▨ PEG chapter 38

Put in the correct prepositions or adverbs.

1 He broke . . . completely on hearing of his daughter's death.
2 He wasn't rich by any means, but he never turned . . . anyone who needed help.
3 On his way to work he called . . . the florist's and ordered a dozen red roses.
4 Burglars broke . . . the house and stole some jewellery.
5 I turned . . . (*refused*) the job because it was badly paid.
6 We called . . . a specialist when he grew worse.
7 When the police questioned him he broke . . . and confessed.

8 Turn . . . the radio if you're not listening.
9 War broke . . . in 1939.
10 The secretary was then called . . . to read the minutes.
11 He carried on the business alone for years before his health broke . . . .
12 The lion turned . . . the lion-tamer and knocked him senseless.
13 Can you be ready at six? He is calling . . . us then to take us out.
14 Mary has broken . . . her engagement to Charles.
15 I haven't much time for housework but I try to turn . . . one room in the house every week.
16 She called . . . for a few minutes to return a book.
17 The lift broke . . . and we had to use the stairs.
18 The representative of the computer company called . . . all the factories in the district.
19 The situation is difficult and calls . . . great tact.
20 They broke . . . their conversation when I came in.
21 The school broke . . . for the holidays at the end of July.
22 In this book the mysterious stranger turns . . . to be the long-lost son of the duke.
23 The fireman had to break . . . the door to rescue the children.
24 The garden party was called . . . because of the rain.
25 A good horse can be ruined if it is not carefully broken . . . .
26 He was called . . . at the age of eighteen and spent a year in the army.
27 She was plain as a child but she turned . . . remarkably pretty.
28 Negotiations between the two countries were broken . . . following the murder of the ambassador.
29 Mrs Jones rang. She wants you to call her . . . .
30 The family was broken . . . after the death of the parents.
31 The new factory turns . . . surgical instruments as well as cutlery.
32 He broke . . . the conversation to remind us it was getting late.
33 The boat turned . . . and threw us all into the water.
34 We arranged to meet at the theatre but she didn't turn . . . .
35 The three men who broke . . . . . . prison yesterday were later recaptured.
36 A huge crowd turned . . . to see the international football match.

176 Combinations with **give**, **put** and **make**

☑ PEG chapter 38

Put in the correct prepositions or adverbs.

1 He won £100 and gave it all . . . .
2 Put . . . the clock, it is twenty minutes fast.
3 Riding is getting too expensive; I'll have to give it . . . . .
4 I'll put . . . my visit to the Royal Mint till you can come with me.

5 The roads were crowded with people making . . . the coast.
6 He gave . . . all the books he had borrowed.
7 She had invited me to dinner but had to put me . . . as she was taken ill.
8 I can't make . . . the postmark on the letter; it looks like Basingstoke.
9 Put . . . the light it's getting quite light again.
10 After four days of freedom, the escaped prisoner gave himself . . . to the police.
11 That vase is very valuable. Put it . . . before you drop it.
12 She makes . . . very skilfully. She looks much younger than she is.
13 Your secret is safe with me. I won't give you . . . . (*betray you*)
14 He was very much put . . . when she rang off angrily in the middle of their conversation.
15 It's time they made . . . that silly quarrel.
16 I wish you would put . . . the dishes instead of leaving them on the table.
17 He's not really angry. He's only putting it . . . .
18 He didn't want to go to the cinema but they begged so hard that he gave . . . and went with them.
19 I don't believe that story. I am sure you made it . . . .
20 The house itself is quite attractive but the fact that it's near a busy airport put me . . . .
21 The boy is hyperactive. I put it . . . . . . wrong diet.
22 They put . . . a statue of Florence Nightingale after her death.
23 The diver's supply of oxygen gave . . . and he had to be brought to the surface as quickly as possible.
24 I asked him to put . . . the lights if he was the last to leave.
25 I don't know how you put . . . . . . the noise; it would drive me mad.
26 After his fourth attempt he gave . . . trying to pass the driving test.
27 Here's a crash helmet. Put it . . . .
28 He should try to make . . . . . . his loss of sleep by going to bed early.
29 If you can't find a room in a hotel, I could always put you . . . .
30 The names of the winners were given . . . on the radio.
31 The shortage of eggs has put . . . their price considerably.
32 The government put . . . the rebellion with great severity.
33 If you want to save money, give . . . eating in expensive restaurants.
34 This clock is always slow; I put it . . . ten minutes every morning.
35 There was a man giving . . . leaflets outside the church.
36 He put . . . his name for the excursion.

177 Combinations with clear, cut, fall, hold, let and hand

☑ PEG chapter 38

Put in the correct prepositions or adverbs.

1 Clear . . . your books. I want to set the table for lunch.
2 The army fell . . . when the enemy attacked.
3 You should cut . . . this tree. It is too near the house.
4 The examination was so easy that all the candidates handed . . .
   their answer papers after the first hour.
5 My plans for starting a restaurant fell . . . for lack of capital.
6 Our water supply was cut . . . because the pipe burst.
7 At the end of term attendance at these classes usually falls . . . .
8 The wall was covered with pictures of pop stars which Mary had cut
   . . . . . . magazines.
9 I hope the the rain holds . . . until my washing is dry.
10 They won't let you . . . if you aren't a member of the club.
11 The mounted police cleared . . . the crowds.
12 A heavy snowfall held . . . the trains from the north.
13 If you really want to slim you must cut . . . on sweets.
14 The two brothers fell . . . over their father's will. (*quarrelled*)
15 You would recover your sense of taste if you cut . . . smoking
   altogether.
16 If you will hold . . . I'll put you through to Enquiries.
17 If he refuses to fall . . . . . . my plans I can probably find someone
   more co-operative.
18 These folk songs have been handed . . . from generation to
   generation.
19 She has has grown so much that her mother will have to let . . . all
   her dresses.
20 Children, you must clear . . . this mess before going to bed.
21 I was cut . . . in the middle of my call because I ran out of money.
22 How did you get this expensive tool-kit? ~
   It fell . . . the back of a lorry.
23 The retiring minister handed . . . to his successor.
24 I should feel very cut . . . if I lived more than twenty kilometres
   from the town.
25 The soldiers fell . . . and marched off.
26 In the film the train was held . . . and robbed by four armed men.
27 The mystery of his sudden disappearance was never cleared . . . .
28 He didn't dismiss the man; he let him . . . with a warning.
29 I hope the weather will clear . . . soon. I want to go out.
30 He let the rest of the team . . . by not turning up for the match.
31 Deaf people often feel very cut . . . from others by their disability.
32 When she got fatter her clothes were too tight and she had to let
   them all . . . .
33 If the word-processor breaks down, we'll have to fall . . . . . . our old
   typewriter.

34 The survivors of the plane crash were able to hold . . . till help came.
35 Could you hand . . . the photographs so that everyone can see them?
36 You'll need somewhere to keep your books. I'll clear . . . this cupboard for you.

178 Mixed combinations

◪ PEG chapter 38

Put in the correct prepositions or adverbs.

1 I don't care . . . the expense; I want the party to be a real success.
2 I can't account . . . the disappearance of the pictures; they were all there yesterday.
3 If passports were done . . . . . . (*abolished*), travel would be much simpler.
4 You will have to allow . . . some extra expenses on the train.
5 They set . . . on their camping trip with great enthusiasm.
6 When you have thought . . . what I have said, you will understand.
7 He doesn't care . . . continental cookery. He thinks it's too rich.
8 The car pulled . . . beside me and the driver asked me the way to Piccadilly.
9 You can throw . . . the packet; it's empty.
10 They set . . . at six and reached their destination before dark.
11 The doctor thinks he'll pull . . . now. His temperature has gone down.
12 I don't know how she manages to care . . . ten children without help.
13 My children are picking . . . English very quickly but I find it more difficult.
14 She fainted but they brought her . . . by throwing cold water on her face.
15 The teacher pointed . . . several mistakes that the student had not corrected.
16 You need capital before you can set . . . on your own in any kind of business.
17 He suddenly threw . . . his job and went to Australia.
18 Don't make up your mind at once; talk it . . . with your lawyer first.
19 The room needs doing . . . ; it's very shabby.
20 The factory will have to close down if production is not stepped . . . .
21 His final argument brought me . . . to his point of view.
22 We must get the roof mended before the wet weather sets . . . .
23 I don't like the look of these men hanging . . . outside my gate.
24 He picked . . . all the biggest ones for himself.
25 You must carry . . . the instructions on the packet exactly.
26 After the music had died . . . there was a storm of applause.
27 The mob burnt . . . several important buildings in the riots.

145

28 The wearing of national costume has largely died . . . in Europe.
29 These children are very polite; they have obviously been well brought . . . .
30 She carried . . . with her work in spite of all interruptions.
31 You can stay . . . till your father comes home and then you must go to bed.
32 When the rebellion had died . . . things quickly returned to normal.
33 I'll pick you . . . at your office and take you straight to the station.
34 Several new records were set . . . at the last Olympic Games.
35 He advises me to hang . . . . . . (keep) those pictures as they will be valuable one day.
36 At the committee meeting the question of repairs to the roof was brought . . . .

179 Mixed combinations

■ PEG chapter 38

Put in the correct prepositions or adverbs.

1 Blow . . . the candles on the cake before you cut it.
2 He used to be very shy but he has grown . . . . . . it now.
3 A number of oil tankers have been laid . . . recently. Too many of them had been built.
4 Don't let him order you . . . like that; he's not your employer.
5 I can pay . . . the money you lent me after I've been to the bank.
6 Applications for the job must be sent . . . before next Wednesday.
7 The fireworks factory was practically wiped . . . by the explosion.
8 We must keep on working; it's too soon to sit . . . . (relax)
9 The terrorists blew . . . the railway line.
10 He wanted to ask her to marry him but he was too shy to do it at once. He led . . . . . . it by saying he often felt lonely.
11 I had to send . . . an electrician to mend the switch.
12 After nursing the whole family when they had 'flu she was completely worn . . . .
13 My nephew wants to be an explorer when he grows . . . .
14 The house stood . . . in the dull street because of its red door.
15 After the owner's death the business was wound . . . and the shop sold.
16 The little girl couldn't blow . . . the balloon.
17 Children's clothes have to be strong to stand . . . . . . hard wear.
18 As soon as the decorators have finished work in my new house, I'll move . . . .
19 He was laid . . . for six weeks with two broken legs.
20 The idea has gradually grown . . . that the State should look after every citizen from the cradle to the grave.

21 They always lay . . . a large supply of tinned food in winter in case they are snowed up.
22 You can't move into this flat till I move . . . .
23 He thinks I broke his window and threatens to pay me . . . for it.
24 I asked the hotel to send . . . any letters which came after I had gone.
25 BBC stands . . . British Broadcasting Corporation.
26 The inscription on the tombstone had been worn . . . by the weather and could scarcely be read.
27 He's going to turn this old building . . . a block of flats.
28 My shoes wear . . . very quickly since I started walking to the office.
29 I'll start laying . . . my new garden next spring.
30 On a touring holiday you can move . . . to a new place every day if you want to.
31 The lifeboat is standing . . . in case it is necessary to take off the crew of the damaged ship.
32 Don't sit . . . for me. I shall probably be back very late.
33 Contact lenses may feel uncomfortable at first but this feeling soon wears . . . .
34 She was the only one to stand . . . . me. No one else said anything in my defence.
35 He was sent . . . from the university for drug-pushing.
36 The strike was called . . . when the management agreed to the strikers' demands.

180 Mixed combinations

■ PEG chapter 38

Put in the correct prepositions or adverbs.

1 I left the milk heating for too long and it all boiled . . . .
2 When we had worked . . . the cost of a holiday abroad, we decided to stay at home.
3 Ring this number and ask . . . (*to speak to*) Bill.
4 The shop is closing down and selling . . . all the stock at reduced prices.
5 I always mix . . . the painters Monet and Manet. (*confuse*)
6 His description of the accident was borne . . . by other witnesses.
7 I'll do the shopping if you see . . . the lunch.
8 He read the novel, missing . . . the dull descriptive passages.
9 I have fixed . . . my holiday and I can't change the date now.
10 I asked him . . . for a cup of coffee.
11 She left the potatoes cooking for so long that the water boiled . . . and the potatoes were burnt.

12 I can see . . . her sudden friendliness; she wants me to look after her parrot while she is away.

13 You mustn't answer . . . like that when your mother scolds you.

14 Workmen don't always clean . . . very thoroughly after they have made a mess.

15 The news of his marriage to another girl was a shock to her but she bore . . . bravely and went on as if nothing had happened.

16 Ring up the station and find . . . what time the train goes.

17 He stopped to pick . . . a hitch-hiker.

18 He would like to ask her . . . but he is too poor to pay for meals in restaurants.

19 The committee left him . . . . . . the team as he had refused to practise.

20 I couldn't get any bread. All the bakers' shops were sold . . . .

21 I thought he was mad and backed . . . nervously.

22 James was asking . . . you today. He says he hasn't seen you for weeks.

23 He wasn't walking very fast. You'll catch . . . . . . him if you start at once.

24 It would be safer to get your solicitor to draw . . . the contract.

25 She'll be busy seeing . . . the children's clothes before they go back to school.

26 He has got mixed . . . . . . a very odd set of people. I hope they won't have a bad influence on him.

27 All passengers must fill . . . this disembarkation form before they leave the ship.

28 He supported the idea at first but backed . . . when he found he'd have to contribute towards the cost.

29 I've been invited . . . to Brighton this week-end.

30 This stove must be cleaned . . . once a week or it gets choked with ashes.

31 He got out as soon as the train drew . . . .

32 Everyone drew . . . in alarm when smoke began to pour out of the parcel.

33 He doesn't like being seen . . . . He prefers to go to the station alone.

34 The music faded . . . in the distance as the street players moved on.

35 Nobody backed me . . . when I complained about the food in the canteen, so nothing was done about it.

36 I'll see you . . . when you leave. It's easy to get lost in this enormous building.

181 Mixed combinations

■ PEG chapter 38

Put in the correct prepositions or adverbs.

1 If the business continues to lose money, I'm afraid we'll have to close . . . .
2 He joined . . . only because several of his friends had joined the army, too.
3 If the weather doesn't clear up we'll have to knock . . . early; we can't work in the rain.
4 I think Tom is living in York now. I must look him . . . next time I'm there.
5 You'd better ring her . . . and tell her you'll be late.
6 It isn't fair to shout the speaker . . . without giving him a chance to explain.
7 Most au pair girls have to live . . . .
8 The guide rounded . . . the party of tourists and led them to the cathedral.
9 'I've made a mistake; I must rub it . . .' said the child.
10 The car-park attendant said, 'You are too far from the next car; could you close . . . a little?'
11 Drop . . . any time you're passing, and have a cup of tea.
12 She was offered a flat in a modern block and jumped . . . the chance.
13 The last person to go to bed usually locks . . . at night.
14 I'll pay for both of us and you can settle . . . afterwards.
15 The hero in the book was tied . . . by his enemies and left in a gas-filled room, but he managed to escape.
16 They offered to pay half the expenses and he closed . . . the offer at once.
17 He won't buy the car without trying it . . . on the road first.
18 Mother's having a day's holiday; we are waiting . . . her for a change.
19 She rang . . . angrily before I could explain why I hadn't turned up.
20 That's poison; you should lock it . . . where the children can't touch it.
21 Since she got married she seems to have dropped . . . of all social activities.
22 The boxer was knocked . . . in the second round and lost his title.
23 Whales live mainly . . . plankton.
24 An English husband usually helps his wife to wash . . . after a meal.
25 It takes some time to settle . . . to work again after a holiday.
26 My horse was entered . . . the Derby, but he came in last.
27 The porter was told to watch . . . . the people who tried to gate-crash.
28 He had to rub . . . his French to help his son when he started to learn it at school.
29 She took . . . her glove so that she could show . . . her diamond ring.

Phrasal verbs.

30 I tried . . . several coats but none of them suited me.
31 If you can't afford it, you'll have to do . . . it.
32 Watch . . .! That man tried to take your purse out of your shopping-bag.
33 Several gambling clubs have been shut . . . recently for breaking the regulations.
34 This is a clockwork toy. You have to wind it . . . .
35 I pointed . . . all her mistakes but she didn't seem very grateful.
36 I don't think I'd like to share a flat with her. I'd find it difficult to live . . . . . . her standards of tidiness.

182 Mixed combinations with compound prepositions/ adverbs

■ PEG chapter 38

Put in the correct prepositions or adverbs. Note that two words are required.

1 Once he has signed the agreement, he won't be able to back . . . . . . the scheme.
2 Watch . . . . . . the signpost. I don't want to miss the turning.
3 That chair is not very strong. Do you think it is . . . . . . your weight?
4 After drinking half a bottle of whisky he felt able to stand . . . . . . his employer.
5 The Italian course started in September and it's now March. I'm afraid you won't be able to catch . . . . . . the class now.
6 Whenever he runs . . . . . . a difficulty he always comes to me for help.
7 A mother will usually stand . . . . . . her children, no matter what they have done.
8 There's no point in doing . . . . . . the old regulations if you are going to introduce equally stupid new ones.
9 I'm afraid there's no milk left; we'll have to fall . . . . . . dried milk for our tea.
10 It's your turn to make some suggestions; I've run . . . . . . ideas.
11 He may be sorry but that won't make . . . . . . the damage he has done.
12 Some people can break the law and get . . . . . . it. Others get punished.
13 He pretended to fall . . . . . . my plan but secretly he was working against it.
14 Don't tell me any of your secrets. I don't want to be mixed . . . . . . your affairs.
15 He would get . . . . . . his work better if you left him alone.

150

16 Why do you hang ... ... those old magazines? Give them away if you don't need them.

17 Don't run ... ... the idea that I disapprove completely. I'm only trying to point out the disadvantages.

18 He wanted to borrow money and led ... ... it by saying that times were very hard.

19 He has gone ... ... his promises so often that no one trusts him now.

20 Look ... ... me at the station; I'll be carrying the *Financial Times*.

21 He will come ... ... your way of thinking in time.

22 The Minister was very glad to hand ... ... his successor before the crisis got any worse.

23 Children used to look ... ... their parents; now they are inclined to regard them as equals.

24 The astronaut got ... ... his rocket and found himself in the middle of a vast plain.

25 He only puts ... ... his secretary's bad spelling because he can't find a better one.

26 My legs are too short; I can't keep ... ... you if you walk so fast.

27 Once a man gets a reputation for being amusing he has to try and live ... ... it.

28 I suppose you'll look ... ... me when I tell you I prefer kippers to caviare.

29 I've had a busy day and I'm looking ... ... going to bed early.

30 Shall I make the cheque ... ... you or to your firm?

31 The government won't go ... ... this new legislation if public feeling is against it.

32 It took him a long time to grow ... ... the habit of biting his nails.

33 My room is rather dark because it looks ... ... a blank wall.

34 We'll settle ... ... you when you produce all the bills.

35 He looked his son ... and ... and said, 'Aren't you a bit too old now to wear those odd clothes?'

36 She goes ... ... yoga and spends ten minutes every day standing on her head.

183 Substituting phrasal verbs for other expressions

■ PEG chapter 38

Replace the words or phrases in bold type by phrasal verbs. Some of the sentences may sound awkward as they stand.

1 Can he **give a good explanation for** his extraordinary behaviour?

2 He mended the tyre of his bicycle and then **filled** it **with air**.

3 They were having a violent quarrel but **stopped suddenly** when I came in.

4 The meeting was **cancelled** because of the 'flu epidemic.

5 If you refuse to **perform** my orders you'll be dismissed.

6 I don't think you can **overtake** them; they left two hours ago.

7 Sherlock Holmes was often able to **solve** a mystery without leaving his rooms in Baker Street.

8 I **found** a twenty-pound note **by chance** in the street. What should I do with it?

9 If my scheme had **succeeded**, I should have made a profit of a thousand pounds.

10 He **recovered consciousness** when the doctor had applied artificial respiration.

11 The road safety campaign had succeeded in **reducing** road deaths by 10 per cent.

12 Three thousand students **are candidates for** the examination every year but very few pass.

13 He tried to **alight from** the bus while it was still moving and was badly hurt.

14 My sister promised to sing at the concert and though she doesn't want to now, she can't **free herself from the obligation**.

15 They **announced** the names of the winning horses on the radio.

16 If cigarettes get any dearer, I shall have to **abandon the habit of** smoking.

17 Prices always **increase**; they never **become less**.

18 The police **investigated** the case very thoroughly but finally said there was no suspicion of foul play.

19 He **started his journey** in a great hurry.

20 He needs more exercise; he should **start playing** tennis.

21 It is difficult to **train** children well.

22 The train was **delayed** by fog and arrived late.

23 I waited for her for ages but she didn't **come**.

24 She is good at languages. She **learnt** Spanish **without effort**, in a few months.

25 It is **your responsibility** to make a success of your own life. (*It is ...... you etc.*)

26 Anyone who was offered a chance like that would **accept** it **with enthusiasm**.

27 **Don't walk on** the grass.

28 He dictated so quickly that his poor secretary couldn't **go as fast as he did**. (*couldn't .... him*)

29 I hit him **so hard that he fell unconscious**.

30 If I **don't punish** you this time, will you promise never to do it again?

31 She was very upset over her failure but now she is **recovering from** it.

32 You mustn't **omit** the difficult sentences; do them all.

33 She kept asking me all the difficult words instead of **searching for** them in a dictionary.

34 I took the children to the zoo today to **compensate** for the party they missed yesterday.

35 Students of English often **confuse** the words 'lie' and 'lay'.

36 He swore to **revenge himself on** me for the wrong I had done him.

184 Substituting phrasal verbs for other expressions

■ PEG chapter 38

Replace the words or phrases in bold type by phrasal verbs. Some of the sentences may sound awkward as they stand.

1 If you don't **allow** me **to enter** I'll break down the door.
2 He **regarded** her for a moment and then said, 'She is too tall.'
3 The line was so bad when I **telephoned** him that I couldn't understand what he said.
4 Will you **take care of** the garden while I am in hospital?
5 I don't believe a word of his excuse; I'm sure he **invented** it.
6 He's had the best doctors available but he won't **recover** unless he has the will to live.
7 **Be careful!** The tree's going to fall!
8 Never **postpone** till tomorrow what you can do today.
9 I **regard** him as the greatest living novelist.
10 He **dressed himself in** uniform for the occasion.
11 He keeps hearing strange footsteps in the house, so he has hired a private detective to **investigate** the matter.
12 She was sitting opposite me in the bus but she **pretended not to see** me.
13 Whenever you are in Paris, do **go and visit** my sister.
14 Why was she looking so **annoyed**?
15 The Albert Hall was **erected** in memory of Queen Victoria's husband.
16 I can't **offer hospitality** to you all because my flat is too small.
17 Suppose you **telephone** the station and ask them.
18 He **disparages** his own garden but he likes other people to praise it.
19 She is **in poor health** after working for three years without a break.
20 The village is so small that we are always **meeting** our friends **accidentally**.
21 It is the first time that he has **encountered** any opposition.
22 Peter's leaving. Why don't you **apply for** his job?
23 There is something wrong with the television set; we'd better **summon** an electrician.
24 A man who has always led an open-air life would find it difficult to be **contented** in an office job.
25 I am feeling rather tired today because I **stayed out of bed later than usual** last night.
26 You are not allowed **to offer yourself for election to** Parliament if you are under eighteen, a lunatic, or a bankrupt.
27 He lost his reputation and all his money but he had good friends and they **continued to support and help** him.
28 The father was thoroughly dishonest and the son **resembles** him. He has already been in the courts for stealing.
29 He **started playing** golf as he thought it would help him socially.

Phrasal verbs

30 I used to believe his tall stories; now he rarely succeeds in **deceiving** me.
31 It is silly to **abandon** a good job like yours, just because you don't like the coffee in the canteen.
32 They **rejected** her application because they preferred a man for the job.
33 The factory normally makes clocks and watches but during the last war it **produced** precision instruments for aeroplanes.
34 The chairman **brought his speech to an end** by thanking the staff for their hard work.
35 Take a pencil and paper and **calculate** how long it will take us to reach London from here.
36 He **undertook** evening work to make some extra money but at the end of the year he was completely **exhausted**, and had to **abandon** it.

185 Combinations with off and on

☑ PEG chapter 38

Put in the appropriate verb.

1 The fireworks . . . off with such a noise that we were nearly deafened.
2 The trade talks which had begun between the two countries were . . . off when the fishery dispute began.
3 He . . . off on his journey.
4 I can't hear you. Do . . . off that vacuum cleaner.
5 The astronaut found the experience of weightlessness strange at first but the feeling . . . off after a time.
6 The candidate . . . on everyone in his constituency and asked them to vote for him in the impending by-election.
7 Well-off people used to have servants to . . . on them.
8 If we can't decide on a play we all want to see we'd better . . . off the theatre party tomorrow.
9 Don't be . . . off by her odd appearance; she is really very nice.
10 I said to the shop assistant, 'I like this coat; could I . . . it on?'
11 You won't . . . on very fast with your work if you try to watch television at the same time.
12 Those chalk marks will easily . . . off your jacket if you brush it.
13 Almost all workers like to . . . off (*leave work*) at six. It's hard to get anyone to stay on after that.
14 I was practising the bagpipes but I had to . . . off because my mother complained about the noise.
15 I think you have enough to do as it is. Don't . . . on any more work.
16 They won't be able to have their letters . . . on when they are away as they will be on safari.

17 Many of our men are off sick just now. We have been . . . on with a skeleton staff.

18 It's really your turn to wash up, Mary, but we'll . . . you off this time. You look very tired.

19 When I played in his team he kept shouting advice at me, and this . . . me off.

20 I heard two men planning to break into a house. What should I do? You should . . . on the information to the police.

21 I don't see why we should do all the work while he just . . . on (*watches*) and does nothing.

22 Someone is following us!
Never mind; . . . on walking and pay no attention.

23 Now that we have lost all the money, it's no use . . . on me and saying that it's all my fault.

24 The policeman told the crowd standing round the scene of the accident to . . . on because they were blocking the road.

25 I don't want to . . . on the light in case I waken her.

26 My house was damaged by floods so I had to . . . off the guests I had invited for the following week-end.

27 She doesn't usually wear a hat; she only . . . one on when she goes to a wedding.

28 . . . on. It could do you good to come out for a change.

29 The wedding was planned for the 16th but the bride fell ill so it had to be . . . off.

30 My train leaves at eight tomorrow morning. Will you come and . . . me off?

31 The Scout . . . on his bicycle and hurried away to get help.

32 He doesn't . . . on with his family. That's why he doesn't live at home.

33 That new factory is doing very well; the manager has just . . . on fifty new workers.

34 The plane . . . off at seven and climbed rapidly into the stormy sky.

35 He . . . off his jacket and hung it up.

36 He flew his plane under the bridges of the Thames.
Why did he do that?
I suppose he was just . . . off. (*attracting attention to/displaying his skill*)

186 Combinations with **up**

☑ PEG chapter 38

Fill up the spaces in each of the following sentences by inserting a verb + **up**, or a verb + **up** + preposition combination.

1 It is . . . . . . factory owners to provide fire-fighting equipment in their factories. (*No verb is required here.*)

155

2 Unfortunately he was . . . . . . by his parents to believe that money was the only thing that mattered.

3 The party didn't . . . . . . till 3 a.m. and the guests left very noisily.

4 I ran after him and soon . . . . him. Then we went on together.

5 Mother to child: 'Your clothes are covered with mud; what have you . . . . ?'

6 If you buy the paint I'll . . . . . . this room for you.

7 He . . . . . . a list of conditions and we all agreed to them.

8 If you want a new passport you must . . . . . . this form.

9 He . . . . . . at 8 a.m. and went to bed at 11 p.m.

10 I tried three times to start the car and then . . . it . . . and went by bus.

11 If I . . . . . . alcohol I'd be much healthier, but life wouldn't be so much fun.

12 I saw a policeman so I . . . . him and asked him the way.

13 Most girls expect to get married when they . . . .

14 Cashiers carrying money to the bank are sometimes . . . . . . by gunmen.

15 He couldn't . . . . me as I ran much faster than he did and soon left him behind.

16 I . . . . . . a 20p piece that I saw lying on the ground.

17 He wasted two weeks and tried to . . . . it by working madly the last day.

18 She said that she was going to educate her children herself, for if they went to school they'd only . . . . . . bad habits.

19 Before you go on holiday you should . . . . . . the house and ask the police to keep an eye on it.

20 The car . . . . . . suddenly with screaming brakes.

21 English people have to . . . . English weather.

22 The thieves . . . . . . (*bound*) the housekeeper and ransacked the house.

23 I've stupidly . . . . . . your books and mine and now I don't know which is which.

24 He is a dangerous criminal. He ought to be . . . . . .

25 I want to . . . him . . . . Would you please . . . . . . his telephone number?

26 I . . . . . . at the meeting-place but the others didn't come.

27 He wanted something to do in his spare time so he . . . . . . carpentry.

28 The police . . . . . . a notice saying, 'No Parking'.

29 'Tell me at the end of the week how many hours you have worked and I'll . . . . . . with you then', his employer said.

30 It's probably true. No one would . . . . . . such a stupid story.

31 She sat down in front of the mirror and began to . . . . . . her face.

32 If only we had a dish-washer, we wouldn't need to . . . . . . after every meal.

33 My father said it was all my fault but my mother . . . .
(*defended*) me and said that it wasn't.
34 He . . . . . . his speech by calling for a vote of thanks for last year's
president.
35 Children hate going to bed. They always want to . . . . . . a little
longer.
36 He was lying on his bed but when he saw me he . . . . . . and said,
'I'm not asleep.'

187 Combinations with out

◪ PEG chapter 38

Fill the spaces in the following sentences by inserting a verb + **out**
combination.

1 There were three of us in the original partnership, but Charles
. . . . . . so there are only two of us now.
2 You are not paid to criticize. All you need do is to . . . . . . my
orders.
3 When war . . . . . . prices usually go up.
4 There's an advertisement in today's paper that might interest
Robert. I'll . . . it . . . and send it to him.
5 The fog is so thick that I don't know where we are. I'll have to try
and . . . . . . by asking someone.
6 In a bus: 'Have my seat. I'm . . . . . . at the next stop.'
7 The arrangement of marriages by parents is a custom that has
. . . . . . nearly everywhere.
8 The article is too long. Could you . . . . . . the last two paragraphs?
9 I can't . . . . . . who it is. He is too far away.
10 He volunteered to march in the demonstration but when the day
came he . . . . . . and said that he was not well enough to go.
11 Don't . . . . . . (*get rid of/discard*) that old chair. We could repair it.
12 Which picture do you think is the best? ~
It is hard to . . . . . . the best. They are all so good.
13 Why do you think they have such a high fence round this nuclear
power station? ~
I think they want to . . . people . . . .
14 He was . . . . . . of the windows and didn't see me coming into the
room.
15 . . . . . .! Here's the boss!
16 There was a threat of a gas and electricity strike and in no time the
shops selling candles were . . . .
17 We . . . . . . of milk on Sunday and I had to get some from the milk
machine.
18 Write in pencil. Then if you make a mistake you can easily . . . it
. . . .

19 As we passed Marble Arch he . . . . . . the place where the gallows used to stand.

20 'I'll . . . you . . .,' said my host, and he accompanied me to the front door.

21 We thought that he was an expert on Proust but it . . . . . . that he had never even heard of him.

22 They . . . . . . at nine and arrived at twelve.

23 He was quite . . . . . . when he got no marks at all for his essay and he hasn't forgiven the lecturer yet.

24 I'm leaving this flat. I am . . . . . . tomorrow and the new tenants are moving in the next day.

25 Nothing can ever . . . . . . the memory of that terrible experience.

26 I'll give you the general plan and you can . . . . . . the details,' the director said to his assistant.

27 We haven't invited them to the party. If they . . . . . . about it they will be furious.

28 . . . . . . the light when you leave the room.

29 Children usually grow out of their clothes before they . . . them . . .

30 The wind . . . . . . the first match and he had to strike another.

31 Can I speak to Mr Pitt? ~
I'm afraid he has just . . . .

32 My clothes are all getting too tight. I'll have to . . . them . . . .

33 There are only two of us on this desert island. We mustn't . . . . . .
(*quarrel*)

34 This bottle has been very tightly corked. The cork won't . . . .

35 . . . . . . for pickpockets!

36 He . . . . . . in any crowd because he is so much taller than the average man.

188 Combinations with **down**, **away** and **over**

☑ PEG chapter 38

Fill the spaces in the following sentences by inserting a verb + **down**, **away** or **over** combinations.

1 I offered him part-time work but he . . . it . . ., saying that he'd rather wait for a full-time job.

2 He doesn't think much of contemporary authors; he is always . . . . . . their work.

3 He dictated it and I . . . it . . . in shorthand.

4 The child picked up the knife and his mother shouted, '. . . it . . . !'

5 Some English boys go to boarding school at the age of seven. They usually . . . . . . quickly and are very happy.

6 I am in charge while Smith is away; I . . . . . . from him on June 1.

7 I can't decide now. I'll . . . it . . . with my colleagues and let you know later.

8 He insisted on riding a young excitable horse which . . . . . . with him and threw him into a ditch.

9 He agreed to take my classes while I was away; but he . . . me . . . . He never turned up for any of them.

10 I . . . . . . the accounts several times but couldn't find the mistake.

11 Suddenly there was a rustling in the straw. Everyone . . . . . . and stood watching from a safe distance.

12 This shop is . . . . It will be reopening shortly under new management.

13 He had stage fright at first but he . . . . . . it very quickly.

14 The townsman has always been inclined to . . . . . . on the countryman.

15 The filing system worked splendidly till the secretary went on holiday; then it . . . . . . and no one knew where anything was.

16 Here is my letter; would you just . . . it . . . to see if there are any mistakes?

17 Two men started to fight with knives. The crowd . . . . . . so as to be out of danger, and stood watching.

18 After the blizzard, it took a long time to . . . . . . the snow from the main streets.

19 He hated boarding school and . . . . . . from it, turning up two days later at his own home.

20 Jones tried to make a suggestion but the crowd was too excited to listen and he was . . . .

21 When the first act . . . . . . we had a drink in the theatre bar.

22 They should . . . . . . with licensing laws and let us drink when we like.

23 There was tremendous excitement in the streets and the shouting didn't . . . . . . till after midnight.

24 The embassy was . . . . . . in the recent riots. The ruins are still smoking.

25 When she heard the news of the crash she . . . . . . and cried.

26 The theatre filled up very early and people who came later and who hadn't reserved seats were . . . .

27 I wonder why there's such a smell of gas. ~
Perhaps something on the gas stove has . . . . . . and put out the flame.

28 That old chair would be useful to somebody. If you don't want it, sell it or . . . it . . . .

29 This ring I wear isn't very valuable but it's been . . . . . . in my family for over 200 years.

30 He . . . . . . a little money every week so as to have something for a rainy day.

31 The police caught one thief but the other . . . .

32 The new idea is that young delinquents should gather together in groups and . . . . . . their problems with social workers.

33 We are spending too much; we'll have to . . . . . . our expenses.

34 I'm waiting till prices . . . . . . before buying my new carpet.

35 When the floods . . . . . . we were able to use the road again.
36 The expression 'To . . . . . . a new leaf' means to make a fresh start with the intention of doing better.

189 Mixed combinations used in a connected passage

■ PEG chapter 38

Fill the spaces in the following passage by inserting suitable combinations.

During Bill's last term at school, Mr White offered him a job in a hardware shop. 'It would be in the tool section,' he said, 'helping old Mr Hammer, and if you [1] . . . . . . (*made good progress*) you could [2] . . . . . . (*become responsible for*) the section when Mr Hammer retires.'

Mr White expected Bill to [3] . . . . . . at the offer (*accept it eagerly*) and was rather [4] . . . . . . (*surprised and disappointed*) when the boy looked doubtful.

'You needn't [5] . . . . . . your mind (*decide*) at once,' he said. 'Mr Hammer can [6] . . . . . . (*continue/manage*) without an assistant for another fortnight. But [7] . . . it . . . (*consider it*) and let me know. Your school [8] . . . . . . (*closes for the holidays*) this Friday, doesn't it?' Bill nodded. 'Well, if you decide to accept the job, [9] . . . . . . (*call at the shop*) next weekend. I'll show you round and we'll [10] . . . you . . . (*arrange this matter*) with an insurance card.'

Bill's father urged him to accept. 'If you [11] . . . it . . . (*refuse it*) you'll just be on the dole,' he said. 'It's no use [12] . . . . . . (*loitering*) at home waiting for something better to [13] . . . . . . (*appear*). Very few employers are [14] . . . . . . (*engaging*) more men at present and a lot of places are [15] . . . . . . (*shutting permanently*).'

So Bill took the job and soon [16] . . . . . . in his new environment (*became used to it*). He [17] . . . . . . (*learnt*) to work quickly and when Mr Hammer retired and [18] . . . . . . (*transferred*) the tool section to him, he felt very proud of himself.

Unfortunately, after two years Mr White was transferred to a bigger branch and a new manager, Mr Black, was appointed. He and Bill didn't [19] . . . . . . one another at all (*neither liked the other*). He began, tactlessly enough, by [20] . . . Bill . . . and . . . (*examining*) and saying, 'I don't [21] . . . . . . (*like*) the way you dress. If you want to [22] . . . . . . (*continue*) working here you must smarten up. [23] . . . . . . (*get dressed in*) a tie and [24] . . . . . . (*remove*) those rings. I don't approve of young men wearing rings.'

'Some of our customers wear them,' Bill [25] . . . . . . (*remarked*).

'Don't [26] . . . me . . . (*reply impudently*)!' snapped Mr Black.

Soon afterwards, Bill and the manager [27] . . . . . . (*quarrelled*) again.

'You spend too much time talking to customers,' Mr Black complained.

'But they like a chat,' said another assistant, trying to . . . . (*defend*) Bill. 'People who want silent service go to supermarkets.'

'You ²⁹. . . . . . of this (*remain outside*)!' snarled Mr Black. 'If business doesn't ³⁰. . . . . . (*improve*) you may both be . . . . . . (*seeking*) other jobs.'

'He ³². . . customers . . . (*repels them*) by his bad manner,' muttered Bill to his friends. 'But if profits ³³. . . . . . (*decrease*) he'll . . . . . . (*state falsely*) that it's all our fault. Anyway I'm sick of being ³⁵. . . . . . (*given too many orders*) and I'm not going to ³⁶. . . . . it (*endure it*).'

Fortunately, before rebellion ³⁷. . . . . . (*started*) in the tool department, Mr Black, who had ³⁸. . . . . . for (*applied for*) a more important post, was told that he had got it. He became overnight a much happier man and tried to ³⁹. . . . . (*compensate for*) his previous harshness by being very polite to everyone, even Bill. The staff weren't ⁴⁰. . . . . . (*deceived*) by his sudden affability, but it made a nice change.

190 Mixed combinations used in a connected passage

■ PEG chapter 38

Complete the passage, using suitable combinations.

We ¹. . . . . . early and had breakfast at 7.30. After breakfast my sister Alice ². . . . . . (*washed the dishes*) while I got out the car. We ³. . . . . . (*began our journey*) at 8.30 and drove first to Mr Pitt's house to ⁴. . . . . . (*collect*) his son Tom who was coming with us. Tom had never met my niece Ann and I wasn't sure how the two children would ⁵. . . . . . . But I needn't have worried, for it ⁶. . . . . . (*was revealed*) that they had a lot of interests in common and seemed quite pleased with each other. Even my sister, who doesn't usually ⁷. . . . . . (*like*) small boys, ⁸. . . . . . (*was attracted by/liked at first meeting*) him from the first. She whispered to me that he had very good manners and had obviously been well ⁹. . . . . . . Tom also pleased her very much by ¹⁰. . . . . . (*indicating*) various interesting buildings as we drove through the town. Ann, however, was not much impressed by this and clearly thought that Tom was just ¹¹. . . . . . (*displaying his knowledge*).

Suddenly Alice said, 'Good heavens! I forgot to ¹². . . . . . the iron. We'll have to go back or it will start a fire and ¹³. . . . . . (*destroy by fire*) the house.'

I said, 'Let's try to ¹⁴. . . . . . (*telephone*) our neighbour, Mr Smith, first and see if he can get into the house and [15]. . . . . . the iron.'

'But he won't be able to [16]. . . . . . (*enter*), said Alice. 'The house is
[17]. . . . . . .'

'Then he'll have to [18]. . . . . . (*enter by force*),' I said. 'Better to
have a window broken than let the house [19]. . . . . . in flames.'

So I [20]. . . . . . (*telephoned*) Mr Smith, who said that he'd [21]. . . . . .
the matter. I [22]. . . . . . (*waited, holding the receiver*) while he went to
do this, and very soon I heard his voice saying, 'It's all right. I
[23]. . . . . . (*entered*) through a window you'd left open and [24]. . . . . .
the iron. No damage was done.'

I thanked him warmly and we [25]. . . . . . (*continued*) with our
journey, much relieved.

We stopped at 1.00, [26]. . . . . . of (*left*) the car and picnicked by the
side of the road. Alice was just [27]. . . . . . (*offering to each of us*) the
sandwiches when a police car [28]. . . . . . (*stopped*) beside us.

'You mustn't park here,' said the policeman. 'It's a clearway.' I
explained that I was a foreigner, so he said, 'Well, I'll [29]. . . you . . .
(*overlook the offence*) this time, but don't do it again. You mightn't
[30]. . . . . (*escape unpunished*) it another time.'

My sister was rather [31]. . . . . . (*annoyed*) by this incident but I
explained that these regulations were necessary and we must
[32]. . . . . (*endure/bear patiently*) them.

Tom was very impressed by the police car. He [33]. . . . .
(*respects*) all policemen and hopes to be one when he [34]. . . . . .
(*becomes an adult*). He is already [35]. . . . . (*anticipating with
pleasure*) driving round in a fast car [36]. . . . . . (*seeking*) lawbreakers.

Poor Tom likes fast cars and was rather [37]. . . . . . (*bored/disgusted*)
because so many cars [38]. . . . . (*drew level with*) us and passed
us. As we listened to the sound of their engines [39]. . . . . .
(*diminishing*) in the distance he said, 'Next time I go out with you
I'll come on my bicycle. I'm sure I'll be able to [40]. . . . .
(*remain abreast of*) you, you go so slowly.'

However we did [41]. . . . . . (*arrive at*) Stratford in the end and
went to the house of a friend, who had promised to [42]. . . us . . . (*give
us accommodation*) for the night. We tried to get seats for the
Memorial Theatre but they were [43]. . . . . . (*all sold*) so we spent the
evening sitting by the fire and [44]. . . . . . (*discussing*) our day.

Key

11 some, any etc. and relatives

Exercise 101 1 some 2 some, any 3 any, some 4 any 5 some, any
6 some, any 7 any, some 8 Some, some 9 any 10 any, any 11 Any
12 some/any 13 any, any 14 Some, some 15 any 16 some
17 any/some 18 any 19 any 20 Any 21 some 22 some, some
23 some 24 any 25 any, some/any 26 Any 27 any 28 some
29 some 30 some 31 any 32 some 33 any 34 some, some 35 any
36 some/any, some

Exercise 102 (In some of the answers the relative pronoun is enclosed in brackets; this means that it can be omitted. The answers given are not necessarily the only possible answers to the questions. Notice carefully the presence or absence of commas.)

1 (a) The 8.10 is the train (which/that) Mr Black usually catches. (b) The 8.40 is the train (which/that) he caught today. (c) Mr White is a man who usually travels up with Mr Black. (d) Mr Brown is the man whose paper Mr White borrowed. (e) Mr Black usually catches the 8.10, which is a fast train. (f) Today he missed the 8.10, which annoyed him very much. (g) He caught the 8.40, which doesn't get in till 9.40.

2 (a) The brown umbrella was the one (which/that) Mr Penn left at home today *or* the one (which/that) he didn't take today. (b) The black umbrella was the one (which/that) he took *or* the one (which/that) he left on the bus. (c) The blue umbrella was the one (which/that) Mr Penn took by mistake. (d) Mr Count was the man whose umbrella Mr Penn took.

3 (a) Malta is the place Tom and Jack wanted to go to/went to *or* Malta is the place to which Tom and Jack wanted to go. (b) The Blue Skies Agency is the agency Tom went to *or* the agency to which Tom went. (c) The Blue Seas Agency is the agency Jack went to *or* the agency to which Jack went. (d) the MS Banana is the ship Jack travelled on/in *or* the ship on/in which Jack travelled. (e) Julia is the girl (who(m)/that) Jack met on board. (f) Tom liked flying, so he went to the Blue Skies Agency, who booked *or* Tom, who liked flying, went etc. (g) Jack, who hated flying, went to the Blue Seas Agency, who booked

4 (a) George and Paul were (the) two men who were working on Mr Jones's roof. (b) Bill was a/the burglar who saw them going away *or* who stole the jewellery etc. (c) Tom was a student who lodged with Mr Jones. (d) Mrs Jones was the lady whose jewellery was stolen. (e) Mr and Mrs Smith were the people the Joneses were playing cards with *or* the people with whom the Joneses were playing cards. (f) the ladder Bill

163

climbed up *or* up which he climbed.   (g) the window he climbed through *or* through which he climbed.   (h) the screwdriver he used *or* the screwdriver he opened the drawer with *or* with which he opened etc.
(i) George and Paul, who were working on the roof, left the ladder   (j) Mr and Mrs Jones, who were out playing cards, knew nothing   (k) Bill, whose fingerprints were on the screwdriver, was later caught

5 (a) The Greens are the people Ann works for *or* for whom Ann works. (b) The 12.10 was the train (which/that) Ann caught *or* the train (that/which) Ann came up on.   (c) The 12.30 was the train (which/that) Tom met.   (d) Peter was a boy (who(m)/that) Ann met on the train. (e) Paul was the boy (who(m)/that) Mary had come to meet *or* the boy (who(m)/that) Mary was waiting for.   (f) The Intrepid Fox is the bar where Tom usually goes for lunch *or* the bar Tom usually goes to for lunch *or* the bar where Tom usually has his lunch.   (g) Mrs Green, who thought Ann looked tired, gave her   (h) Peter, who hated eating by himself, hoped   (i) Tom, who had only an hour for lunch, couldn't wait (j) Mary, whose boyfriend didn't turn up, ended by   (k) Tom and Ann wasted half an hour at the station, which meant   (l) Tom and Ann very nearly missed one another, which shows

Exercise 103   (Relatives in brackets may be omitted.)
1 for the present (which/that) you sent.   2 She was dancing with a student who had *or* The student with whom she was dancing   3 I'm looking after some children who are *or* The children I'm looking after are   4 The bed I sleep on has   5 Romeo and Juliet were two lovers whose parents
6 There wasn't any directory in the box (which/that) I was phoning from. 7 This is Mrs Jones, whose son   8 The chair (which/that) I was sitting on collapsed *or* The chair on which I was sitting collapsed.   9 Mr Smith, whom I had come especially to see, was too busy   10 The man (who(m)/that) I had come to see was   11 I missed the train (which/that) I usually catch and had to travel on the next, which was   12 His girlfriend, whom he trusted absolutely, turned out   13 The car (which/that) we were in had bad brakes and the man who was driving didn't know   14 This is the story of a man whose wife suddenly loses   15 the frontier, which will be   16 a small girl whose hand had been cut   17 into a queue of people, four of whom   18 refugees, many of whom   19 The man (who(m)/that) I was waiting for didn't *or* the man for whom I was   20 in patched jeans, which surprised the guests, most of whom were   21 The firm (which/that) I work for is sending   22 The Smiths, whose house had been destroyed, were given   23 I saw several houses, most of which were   24 at 2 a.m., which didn't suit me   25 a group of boys whose plane   26 The string (that/which) they tie the parcels up with   27 his students, most of whom were   28 for 12 eggs, four of which were   29 The people (who(m)/that) he was speaking to didn't know *or* The people to whom he was speaking 30 The boy (who(m)/that) Peter shared a flat with was *or* Peter shared a

flat with a boy who   31 four very bad tyres, one of which burst   32 the
wonderful view (which/that) she had been told about   33 by a man
(who(m)/that) I met on a train.   34 The bar (which/that) I was telephoning
from was *or* the bar from which I was telephoning was   35 The man who
answered the phone said   36 The horse (which/that) I was on kept
stopping to eat grass, which annoyed

Exercise 104   1 Tom, who had been driving all day, was tired   2 Ann,
who had been sleeping, felt   3 Paul, whose tyres were new, wanted
4 Jack, whose tyres were old, wanted   5 Mary, who didn't know about
mountains, thought   6 to his manager, who passed   7 were thieves, which
turned out   8 the Chief of Police, who ordered   9 dry bread, most of
which was   10 a prisoner, whose handcuffs rattled   11 a fire, which soon
dried   12 across the Atlantic, which had never   13 a bus-load of children,
six of whom were   14 refuses to use machines, which makes   15 I met
Mary, who asked   16 prayed aloud all night, which kept   17 and in deep
water the next, which makes it unsafe   18 Mary, whose children couldn't
swim, said   19 Ann, whose children could swim well, said   20 cleaning
ten windows, most of which   21 Jack, whose injuries were very slight, is
being allowed to play, which is a good thing   22 Tom, whose leg is still in
bandages, will have to   23 didn't get a seat, which put him in a temper
and caused him to be rude to his junior partner, who in turn   24 Tom,
who had a hangover, felt   25 His boss, who didn't drink, saw   26 The
report, which should have been on his desk by 2.00, still hadn't arrived.
27 Tom, whose headache was now much worse, put down the receiver
without answering, which   28 Ann, who liked Tom, came   29 the report,
which should have taken an hour and a half, took   30 to Munich, which
31 The headwaiter, whose name was Tom, said . . . recognition, which
disappointed Mr Jones, who liked   32 with Lucy, whom he was
particularly anxious to

Exercise 105   1 what, which   2 which   3 what, what   4 which   5 which
6 what, which   7 which   8 what   9 which   10 which   11 which
12 which   13 what   14 what   15 which   16 which, what   17 which
18 what   19 what   20 which   21 which   22 what   23 which   24 which
25 which   26 which   27 what   28 which   29 what, which   30 which,
which   31 which   32 which   33 what, which   34 which   35 what
36 what

Exercise 106   1 whatever   2 wherever   3 whatever   4 wherever
5 whichever   6 whoever   7 whenever   8 however   9 whoever
10 whichever   11 whoever   12 however   13 whatever   14 however
15 whenever   16 whoever   17 whoever   18 however   19 whatever
20 whenever   21 whoever   22 whichever, whoever   23 whatever,
whichever   24 whoever

Exercise 107 Part I 1 a river to swim in 2 someone to play with
3 a family to cook for 4 accounts for you to check 5 anything to open it
with 6 letters to write 7 anyone to go with 8 a garden for him to play
in 9 anything to sit on 10 a brush to sweep it with 11 a box to keep
them in 12 anyone to send cards to

Part 2 13 the first man to leave 14 the last person to see 15 the only
one to realize 16 the only man to survive 17 the first to come and the
last to go 18 the largest ship to be built 19 the last person to leave
20 the only person to see 21 the second man to be killed 22 the first
man to walk on 23 the first woman to take 24 the fifth man to be
interviewed

12 Prepositions

Exercise 108 1 to; at; in; to 2 to; at, in 3 to, at; at; at 4 to; at, in
5 in; to 6 at, in 7 in; at 8 in, at; at 9 to; at 10 to, at; to 11 at, to, to
12 to, to, in 13 At, in, to 14 at, at; to, in 15 In, at 16 At, to, in
17 At, at 18 to, at, at; at, in 19 at, to, in, at, at 20 in 21 at, to; in; to,
to 22 in; at 23 in, at, in 24 in, at 25 at; to, in 26 in, at 27 to, in
28 to, at, to; to 29 in, at 30 in, at 31 in, at 32 at, to, in 33 in, to
34 To, in; to 35 at, to, to 36 in; in; at

Exercise 109 1 on, with; with; by; in 2 in, on/into 3 to; on; On, by, in,
on 4 at, out, to, of 5 at; on, off 6 to, in; on 7 to, in, on 8 on; with, of
9 of, into, in/with 10 at, on 11 out of, on 12 in, at, on; in 13 with, to,
of 14 to; to, of, at, to/on; to, on 15 at/from, off/out 16 with, in; out of
17 into/out of, of, off; in, on 18 on; on, into 19 with, of, in 20 in; in;
into, on 21 at, with, in; on 22 By; of; with, on 23 on, to, in/on; to, of
24 with, under, of 25 on, to, of 26 of, to 27 in, of; in; in, at/by, of, at,
in 28 into, in, by, of 29 in/at; of, at, on; with, in 30 by, on 31 off; on,
in 32 into, into, with 33 by, by, on, of 34 of, at, of 35 of, in, to
36 off; on; to

Exercise 110 1 in, for 2 at, since 3 At, of, for 4 in, for; During, in
5 for, on, in; from; for/on 6 under, with; in, during/in 7 by, of, in, in
8 by, for, in, of 9 from, since; on; of, to 10 for, during 11 with; for;
for; in 12 for; of, for 13 under, with, for 14 in, for, in, till/until, of
15 for, on/for 16 In, of, off 17 in, by, from 18 on, to, by 19 for/to,
from; in 20 at, during, for 21 by; on, for 22 by, in, on, in, in, over
23 of; in, for 24 in, for, of 25 of, from, to *or* to, from; for, to, by, for
26 at/by; for 27 from, at, with, for 28 for, till; with, for 29 on/into,
off/out of, at, at 30 from, with/at; in, in, in, of 31 of; in, with 32 for,
in 33 with, into/to, with 34 from, with, for; under/of, till 35 of, on;
from 36 on; for

Exercise 111 1 on   2 in, from   3 in, in   4 of; In, of, in   5 on; on, in/at; at, at, at/on   6 to, with; on with; on   7 in; on with; of   8 in, by   9 of, at   10 to, for, of   11 At, to   12 about, to   13 in/by, in, up   14 for; for, for, over   15 for/about, on; about   16 of, for, from   17 for; in   18 in, with, for   19 on; for   20 with, into, with   21 for, in, on   22 In, to, to   23 by/with, out, in, of   24 of, after, in; with   25 at, away/off   26 to, of, to, away/off   27 to; on   28 In, with, of, from   29 to; under   30 on, to   31 of, to   32 about, off, at/by   33 to, of   34 for, with   35 of, of, of   36 under, for, for

Exercise 112 1 –, for   2 –, for   3 –, to   4 –, for   5 –, of   6 for; In, for, for   7 to, –   8 in/at, –; of, for   9 for/to, in   10 –; for   11 to, for   12 –, of/in   13 for, for; of, –, for   14 for; –   15 on; –   16 to/past, –, of   17 –, at/in; –, on   18 –; –, –; to, for   19 for, for, in/at; for, –   20 to, in   21 to, –, –   22 –, in; –, with   23 –, for, at/by/on   24 to, to, in   25 –; to   26 –, –; with, of   27 –, in, in   28 to; –, of   29 –, of   30 on, –, for, for/–   31 –, in, for   32 –, till, in/–   33 –, –, to; –, –, with   34 –; to, in/with   35 –, –, in   36 to, –, in

Exercise 113 Part 1   (till is always replaceable by **until.)** 1 to   2 till   3 to/till   4 till   5 till   6 till   7 to/till   8 to   9 to/till; till   10 to, till   11 to; till   12 to; till

Part 2 1 since; for   2 since   3 since   4 since   5 for   6 Since   7 for   8 since; for   9 since; for   10 for   11 for   12 Since

Part 3 1 then/afterwards; after   2 after   3 After; Afterwards   4 then/afterwards   5 then, then   6 then   7 after   8 then   9 after/afterwards   10 then   11 then   12 then; Then   13 afterwards   14 afterwards   15 then   16 then

13 Auxiliaries + perfect infinitives

Exercise 114   (should used for obligation is replaceable by **ought to. may/might** in the affirmative is replaceable by **could.)**

1 must have worked/been working   2 needn't have translated   3 may/might have forgotten, should have telephoned   4 may/might have got lost, should have given, may/might have had, wouldn't/couldn't have delayed   5 may/might have stopped and got, may/might have run   6 shouldn't have fed   7 must have been   8 should have gone   9 couldn't have been attacked, must have seen . . . and thought   10 must have waited/been waiting (**could/may/might** could replace **must.**)   11 may/might have fallen . . . and been eaten . . . or been kidnapped . . . or caught . . . and died   12 were to have started   13 needn't have walked, could have come   14 must have been stolen, may/might have driven   15 couldn't have got, must have drunk   16 shouldn't have been riding   17 may/might have taken, may/might have been   18 might/should have

told, could have got   19 would have won   20 needn't have written
21 were to have built   22 wouldn't/shouldn't have noticed, would/might
have spread   23 should/might/could have waited   24 may/might have
come, couldn't/can't have come, may/might have come   25 needn't have
done   26 should have been   27 needn't have cooked   28 would/should
have brought, wouldn't/shouldn't have come   29 shouldn't have thrown,
might/could have killed   30 could have painted, could have painted
31 may/might have dropped, may/might have been   32 could have been
started, could have been   33 must have carried, couldn't have done,
would have been, must have waited   34 needn't have done
35 couldn't/can't have been, must have been walking   36 Couldn't it have
been, must have been

Exercise 115   (See notes to Exercise 114 above.)

1 wouldn't/shouldn't have had   2 should have asked   3 should have been
4 may/might have gone; would have told   5 may/might have kept;
wouldn't have kept   6 may/might have gone; may/might have been; would
have rung; couldn't have rung   7 must have had; would have been
8 couldn't have bought   9 should have waited   10 couldn't have carried;
must have helped   11 couldn't have been; must have been   12 must have
crashed; would have reported   13 may/might have blown up; may/might
have planted, may/might have had   14 may/might have tried; may/might
have been   15 may/might have gone, may/might have been; couldn't have
been   16 may/might have collapsed; would have taken over   17 shouldn't
have done, should have said   18 must have been   19 needn't have done;
should have told; shouldn't/wouldn't have wasted   20 could have passed;
should/could have worked   21 couldn't possibly have opened; couldn't
have got   22 must have let; must have followed . . . slipped   23 needn't
have bought   24 must have drugged . . . dumped; might/would have been
run; may/might have been   25 must have bribed; may/might have
followed; couldn't have done; would/should have seen   26 needn't have
stamped   27 couldn't have done; must have given   28 must have been
29 could have taken; may/might have been; may/might have hopped in . . .
snatched   30 should have told; would/could have lent   31 needn't have
taken; could have walked   32 must have been watching/must have
watched   33 needn't have rung/shouldn't have rung; could have
dialled/should have dialled   34 must have had   35 could have had/might
have had; couldn't have had   36 could have married; must have loved;
must have been

Exercise 116   (**may/might** in the affirmative is replaceable by **could**.
In 1, 7, 10, 20, 23 **should** is replaceable by **ought to**.)

1 should have been   2 may/might have written, couldn't have written
3 must have fallen   4 may/might have liked   5 must have been   6 needn't
have sent   7 might/should have left   8 may/might have been
9 can't/couldn't have been, may/might have been   10 shouldn't have
gone   11 may/might have been   12 were to have been   13 should/would

have been   14 needn't have carried   15 may/might have been
16 can't/couldn't have been, must have been   17 must have been   18 was
to have been   19 would have reached   20 could/should have crossed
21 should have brought   22 may/might have been   23 must have been
24 can't/couldn't have been, must have been   25 may/might not have
heard   26 could have put you up   27 would have fallen   28 should have
checked   29 needn't have apologized   30 may/might not have realized
31 might/should have thanked   32 was to have gone   33 should have
warned   34 would have known   35 needn't have bought   36 must have
been

14 Present, past and perfect tenses

Exercise 117 (Negatives are given in their contracted form, affirmatives
are not given in their contracted form, but in speech present continuous
tenses are normally contracted in the affirmative.)

1 are you going; am going, do you want   2 do you smoke; I don't smoke,
smokes, I do; spends   3 sees; are you waiting; am waiting   4 you usually
go; belongs, wants; is using   5 go; takes, passes; is working, am
queueing   6 Are you coming, are you waiting; think, wait, are, looks
7 are waiting; is dialling; Do you know; phones   8 does he come; comes;
speaks   9 wonder, is speaking; comes, suppose, is speaking   10 are
having; are opening; writes; get; have you (got)   11 says, is coming,
wants   12 Do you have/Have you got; don't think; don't see; does a traffic
warden do   13 walks, stays, parks, sticks   14 is putting; sees; hates
15 want; are just closing; we always close, doesn't want   16 is listening, is
reading, is doing, is writing   17 reads; knits, isn't knitting   18 goes,
doesn't go; likes; prefers   19 are watching; are enjoying, don't
understand   20 happens; Does the teacher give; gives, shows, discusses
21 gets; sits, stands, walks, runs   22 is that man standing; is trying, is
waiting; doesn't he use/isn't he using; don't bother; prefer   23 are
wearing; Do you like; suits, doesn't fit   24 speak, come   25 is taking, is
coming   26 talk; prefer; are talking; aren't talking   27 are having; am
meeting; Do you go   28 go, am going; takes, costs   29 Are you doing; am
packing, am catching; are you staying   30 Are you going; I am staying;
are coming; Do you invite; invite   31 am just going; is pouring; don't you
wait; stops   32 gets, washes, shaves, gets, don't hear; hear, makes
33 gets; makes, wakes; sings, bangs, drops, plays   34 don't you ask;
mention, doesn't do; says, doesn't make, think, believes   35 Do you see;
keeps; Do you think, is asking; expect, is making; do you make; stop, ask,
write   36 starts, stays; moves; takes, does, wishes

Key

Exercise 118 1 writes, know, is doing; Does your son write; hear;
seems 2 cost; Do you think; depends 3 am seeing; am changing; are
always changing; don't you leave 4 look/are looking, are you thinking,
am thinking; are only just starting; know, am reading, says, starts
5 is always knocking on my door and asking; does she do; puts; don't
mind, annoys, knows, needs, takes 6 does she do, runs out; borrows,
takes, wants, finds 7 does she owe; don't know, don't keep; is leaving, is
getting; am trying 8 don't you offer; sounds; doesn't realize, owes
9 says, owe, seem, owes, remember 10 don't think, is enjoying; keeps, is
enjoying; enjoys; know, wants, is expecting/expects 11 are you staying;
am leaving; am going 12 are you coming, are you going; depends; agrees;
expect 13 is seeing; don't you come 14 Do you see; is watching; do you
know, is watching; comes, goes, makes 15 are all these people doing, are
they wearing; they are making; are working 16 sounds; Do you think;
don't know, see, finish, are still taking on 17 Is Ann acting; doesn't act;
imagine, knows 18 lives, come, see; doesn't bother, climbs, knocks
19 are moving; are you leaving; suits; know, does, is/are pulling down; are
widening; say 20 ask, likes, says, don't know, thinks, suits, is merely
being 21 want; tells, says, thinks 22 Does your sister's frankness annoy;
does; doesn't want; wants 23 hear; am not living; are still working, is
taking 24 think, take, expects; are they doing; are putting; seem, smoke,
slows 25 are always hammering; keeps, begins, hear; shakes 26 is
stirring, is standing; says, are boiling; don't think, matters, cook, don't
know, isn't getting; thickens 27 is being painted, isn't looking; Do they
stop; are having 28 does the word 'Establishment' mean; doesn't give;
means, have 29 say, belongs, imply, accepts; isn't trying/doesn't try
30 Do all rich men belong; do, are always jeering/always jeer; is used
31 is being pulled; are using; go, get 32 smell; do; think, is coming; is
probably ironing; irons, watches, gets, forgets, is pressing; is thinking
33 are you looking; am looking; am always looking, puts; put; don't you
try 34 are travelling; is reading, is doing, is looking out; stops, falls
35 spends; amuses; is watching, sees 36 does; checks; doesn't need;
happens, makes; makes

Exercise 119 1 decided 2 chose 3 looked, were getting, was mixing,
was washing 4 were, asked, was doing 5 replied, was going, went,
knew, were looking 6 began, found, were 7 were waiting/waited,
remembered, had 8 started, was telephoning, did, came 9 grumbled,
was always telephoning 10 retorted, was always complaining
11 worked 12 started/were starting, rang 13 was, wanted, was playing
14 stayed, went 15 left 16 returned, came, wasted 17 said
18 thought 19 was just climbing, rang 20 said, was getting, went,
opened 21 was, was coming, arriving

170

Exercise 120 1 was walking, realized, was following 2 walked, turned, stopped 3 appeared, stopped 4 went 5 stopped, stopped, looked, was 6 looked, was wearing/wore, wondered 7 decided 8 was standing 9 came, rang, moved off/was moving off, jumped 10 missed, got, was following/followed 11 crawled 12 pulled, looked, was getting/got 13 changed, got 14 left, bought 15 was standing, came 16 was carrying, got, sat, read 17 looked, was getting/got 18 was becoming/became, went, sat, asked, was following 19 said, wasn't following, threatened, admitted 20 told, was, was trying 21 told, advised, didn't want, was being followed

Exercise 121 1 was sitting, saw; seemed 2 was snowing, woke; remembered, was coming, decided, lost 3 reached, realized, did not know; was wondering, tapped 4 was running/ran, struck 5 looked; was going; was drawing 6 were listening, were whispering, was reading; hated, read 7 was reading, burst, rushed 8 went, didn't find; said, didn't know, was doing, thought, was probably playing 9 stopped/used to stop; closed, gave 10 promised, saw, was telling 11 picked, dialled; found; were planning 12 met; were; was studying, wasn't, spent 13 was just starting, opened, leapt 14 were you doing, said; was cleaning 15 looked, said, was leaving the district and (was) going; said, was, was going, told, was getting/got on 16 were building, was 17 were reading, were just turning over; was knitting, was playing; opened, said 18 was; were they doing; heard, were looking; Did they find; discovered 19 told, made; was just pulling 20 was just sticking, came; tried, refused 21 took; Was she actually working 22 said, was coming, wondered 23 was wondering, came, bought 24 was always borrowing, asked, said, hadn't, knew, wanted 25 went, had, was being; turned, saw 26 bumped, asked, said, was having 27 attacked, was putting; thrust, tore; contained; patched 28 did you break; fell, was putting, was, was, was going 29 didn't go; cancelled, spent 30 was just rising, shouted; looked 31 was raining, played/were playing; was trying, didn't get/wasn't getting on, kept 32 were you doing, rang; was making; did you do, heard, went; opened, was 33 rang, found, said, was making 34 Was, rang; answered, was talking, saw; went 35 didn't get, were having/had; rang up, said, were making; pointed out, was, had; said, were always having 36 were you doing/did you do, got; was working/worked; did you stay, stayed; left, were always going; became/was becoming

Exercise 122 Part 1 1 I haven't played for ten years. 2 I haven't sung since I came 3 I haven't milked one since 4 I haven't put one up since 5 I haven't made one for 6 I haven't read any since 7 I haven't bathed a baby for 8 I haven't repaired one since 9 I haven't skiied since 10 I haven't read one for 11 I haven't made one since 12 I haven't sewn any on since 13 I haven't driven (one) for 14 I haven't taken a temperature for 15 I haven't ridden one since 16 I haven't rowed since 17 I haven't painted/done any painting for 18 I haven't typed for

Part 2 19 I haven't had a puncture for 20 He hasn't earned any money
for 21 He hasn't shaved since 22 I haven't drunk champagne since
23 I haven't been in Rome for 24 I haven't seen Tom since 25 I haven't
eaten raw fish since 26 Mary hasn't spoken French for years
27 I haven't had a good night's sleep for 28 He hasn't paid taxes since
29 I haven't eaten meat for 30 The windows haven't been cleaned for
31 I haven't taken any photographs for years. 32 I haven't watched TV
since 33 He hasn't written to me for 34 I haven't been paid for
35 I haven't been abroad since 36 That house hasn't been lived in for

Exercise 123 1 have played/have been playing; Have you played, came;
have played; joined, arrived 2 Have you played; have played; have had,
have won, didn't really deserve 3 played, was, left, dropped, took
4 haven't seen; have you been; I've been; meant, hadn't/didn't have; Did
you have/Had you, were; was; have only just got; enjoyed; skiied, danced
5 skiied, was, broke, haven't done 6 came, was; has been built, has
become 7 hasn't started; has he been, has been, spent 8 have just
heard; didn't you know; flew; Have you heard; got; told; didn't say, liked;
has only been 9 didn't know, were; exploded, burnt 10 has been; used,
rode, have had 11 made; has he been; we have only had; resigned, was
12 has left; left; Has anybody been appointed; have applied/applied, has
been decided 13 Did you have/Have you had; was, have ever had, took;
thought, was, searched, announced, was; took off 14 did you spend; took,
fed, walked, bought, didn't need; passed 15 Have you booked; wrote,
haven't answered 16 didn't know you were; have been; arrived 17 met,
said; made, found, needed, seemed 18 Did you know, arrived; didn't
know 19 have you learnt/been learning; have been learning 20 began,
did; dropped, forgot; spent, studied, have been studying/have studied
21 rang, said; spent, couldn't/wasn't able to, rang; haven't seen, said;
went, haven't come; went 22 have just had; did it go; did you enjoy;
didn't actually hit, made 23 sold, bought, left; arrived; wasn't, said;
hasn't been taken 24 saw; thought, worked, said; worked, explained,
went, told; gave; have worked 25 Have you been; went; were; Did you
go; went; hired 26 have you been, came; have been 27 have seen; did
you go; went; took 28 Did you see, were; saw; walked, asked, had, said,
has just returned 29 Have you been; have been; haven't been 30 Have
you seen; went, saw; Did you like; loved, didn't understand 31 has just
died; knew; worked; didn't see, left, kept 32 thought, was, turned;
shouted; said, didn't know, were 33 Hasn't Tom come; came; went;
didn't hear 34 has just given; have just touched, didn't feel 35 came;
went; looked; coughed, spun; exclaimed, didn't see 36 you have just
agreed; didn't realize, wanted

Exercise 124 1 bought, haven't sold 2 was, began; ran, made 3 caught, didn't get in, arrived 4 looked up, came; have been, growled 5 rang, said; said, haven't had; didn't you tell 6 met, said, didn't see; Did you miss; didn't miss, replied; haven't missed; gave 7 went; worked, went 8 has been; did she go; went 9 bought, asked; told, have waited/been waiting, hasn't come 10 met, offered; said; have just had 11 arrived, landed, climbed out; recognized; exclaimed; didn't know, knew; have only just learnt, said; went 12 tried, heard, called out; have you been; has been 13 Have you been; went; Did you like; didn't see; was 14 have just bought; Have you read; haven't read; haven't even seen 15 Have you been; was; did you get; took 16 Have you seen; rang, got; has been; flew, decided; Have you heard; got, arrived 17 have you been; have been; did you do/were you doing; worked/was working 18 did you work; worked; Did you like; didn't like; did you stay 19 was, stayed, played; did you play; played; lost 20 did you begin; began, was; went; stayed, went 21 was, started; did you get; haven't got; have only been 22 left; rang; answered; said; has just gone, said 23 Have you been; was; Did you go; hitch-hiked 24 haven't seen; has been ill; collapsed, was taken; sent, hasn't come 25 was; Did you see; took, was, said, needed; haven't been able, haven't watched 26 Have you ever been; spent; went, met, wanted, didn't get 27 said; said; hasn't come; rang, were; said; got; didn't come 28 dictated, told; rang; Have you finished, asked; said, have done, haven't started 29 Have you found out; rang, answered, didn't seem; said; has been 30 said, Has Jack moved; said, didn't see; wasn't 31 have you been; have been; bought/have bought; found, got 32 have played, came; has been, inherited; Did you ever play; played, died, arrived 33 Have you seen; left; put 34 Have you met; met; did you talk; talked 35 did, bought, has made; have always done, have always found 36 had; have had, got; told, were; has been, have changed

Exercise 125 1 have been telephoning; Haven't you nearly finished; haven't got; have been trying, has been 2 has failed; has been practising, has got 3 have often wondered; have just found out 4 has been playing; has only just stopped 5 haven't you brought; Haven't you typed 6 Have you been sunbathing; has been raining/ has rained 7 have been building; have been watching/have watched 8 haven't found, has been; has been helping 9 have pulled down, haven't touched 10 have searched/have been searching, haven't seen 11 have been waiting, have waited 12 has been; has been looking, hasn't found 13 have been doing, haven't finished; have done 14 have just picked; have grown/have been growing, have never had 15 have you been doing; have been using 16 has just sold; have been painting, haven't sold 17 has this happened; have had, have thrown 18 have you done; has just gone; has finished 19 has worked/has been working, has never once been; have/has just presented 20 have been mending/have mended, have only done, has broken down 21 has collected/has been collecting; has collected 22 have been looking, have completely forgotten; has happened 23 has been getting/has got, has been rising/has risen; has come 24 has eaten, has lost count, has

Key

attended; Has he put on   25 have been ringing up; has gone; has been working; has found out   26 has been using; haven't been   27 have been standing; hasn't moved; has just shut . . . and gone off   28 has/have been considering; have just given, have decided   29 have been playing, haven't played   30 have been, haven't got   31 has been standing; has already gone   32 has happened; have been waiting/have waited; has often kept, has never been   33 has been living/has lived, has never said   34 have just remembered, haven't paid; hasn't rung; have been; have paid; has lost   35 have been shopping/have shopped; has been losing/has lost, have made, have been told, have known   36 have you been doing; have been looking; have been building

Exercise 126   1 gave, thanked, said, had enjoyed, knew, hadn't read, were   2 had seen, returned, didn't have/hadn't   3 didn't have, had already done, was   4 didn't have, did, left   5 had, was; decided   6 picked, went, slammed   7 felt, had reminded   8 had searched and found, remembered, was   9 had left   10 remembered, were   11 arrived; had been told, was, was   12 asked, said, hadn't been   13 wanted, had come   14 told   15 admitted, never bought/had never bought, assured, sold, wasn't   16 returned, saw, had broken in, was, was   17 were, had only just left   18 Probably they (had) heard/They (had) probably heard, had run/ran   19 had helped, was, poured   20 wondered, had found, hoped   21 had been given, had died   22 hadn't had, hadn't liked   23 seemed, had tak n   24 put, took, had forgotten/forgot, had put   25 came, said, had just swallowed   26 thought, left, was, arrived, learnt, had just left   27 found, had been using/had used   28 parked, rushed; came, was   29 wondered, had stolen, had driven   30 was, was, had been working/had worked   31 was, had had   32 brought, hadn't come   33 kept, had seen   34 looked, went, saw   35 got up, was, wondered, had stayed, had gone away and come back   36 opened, saw   37 had clearly been listening, wondered, had heard   38 asked, had been doing/was doing, said, had dropped, had been looking for/was looking for   39 didn't see, found, had probably dropped, opened   40 had been taking   41 were, turned, asked   42 pulled, ran off   43 (had) recovered, had disappeared   44 moved, found, had been standing   45 had been telling/was telling

Exercise 127   1 Where did they go?   2   How long does it take to get there?   3 What did you think of it?   4 How much does he earn?   5 How much was Tom fined?   6 How big is your room? *or* What size is your room?   7 When did they leave?/How long ago did they leave?   8 How did they come?   9 How long have you been here?   10 Where did the students go?   11 How many miles to the gallon does the car do/What does it do to the gallon?   12 Where did he meet her?   13 What did the neighbours complain about?   14 What did the clerk make him do?   15 Who ate the apples?   16 How did he get in?   17 Who bought the tickets?   18 What were the roads like?   19 How many cigarettes do you smoke a day?   20 What was the hotel like?   21 How far away is the market?   22 How

174

long have you had that cough? 23 What did Guy Fawkes try to do?
24 Who would you like to speak to? 25 Whose is this? 26 How did he
stop the train? 27 How long have you been waiting? 28 Where did Mary
put it? 29 Why did you throw it away? 30 How many hotels are there in
the town? 31 Where did they leave the lawnmower? 32 How did you
find her address? 33 What did Ann give you for lunch? 34 How deep is
the lake? 35 Whose car did you borrow? 36 What did he do with it?

Exercise 128 1 What did he tell you? 2 What is the bridge built of?
3 Where are you all going to? *or* What are you all going to do? 4 How did
he break his leg? 5 How *or* Why did Tom lose his job? 6 Which did you
buy? 7 What is the new theatre like? *or* What does it look like? 8 How
many would you like? 9 When did the concert begin? 10 Who did she go
to the dance with? 11 Why did he buy a car? 12 When is he coming?
13 Which (one) is longer? 14 Who taught you to play poker? 15 What
has she broken? 16 What are you looking for? 17 Whose typewriter has
he borrowed? 18 What was she asking him for? 19 Who is he ringing
up? 20 What does the word 'boss' mean? 21 How did he escape?
22 Who were you talking about? 23 Whose idea did they like best?
24 Who did he complain to? 25 How big was it? 26 What do the
students intend to do? 27 Where do you come from? 28 How much does
the best kind cost? 29 Why did he give it away? 30 What is his sister
like? 31 What's this knife for? 32 What do you have to do in the
mornings? 33 Which one do you like best? 34 How often does he come
to London? 35 Who told you about it? 36 What is he like?

Exercise 129 Part 1 1 have just heard, would/should like 2 Do you
think, could *or* would be able to 3 had, remember, said, was *or* had been,
(had) got 4 can/could, can/could, suits/would suit 5 has, will/would
bring 6 isn't, do not hesitate 7 are, will take him if I ask/would take him
if I asked 8 has been/was, seemed

Part 2 9 am/was, am, are going 10 will be 11 will look 12 enjoyed,
missed, left/had left, looked 13 will be 14 Will you/Would you/Could
you bring, doesn't suit 15 Don't bother, have 16 you'll have, bring,
you'll have/you'll have had

Part 3 17 Do you by any chance know 18 should/would like, have just
heard, would exactly suit, doesn't apply, won't get 19 saw, was just
leaving/had just left 20 said, was going, promised, (had) found 21 have
heard, don't even know, went 22 know, should/would be, would phone
23 have tried, doesn't seem

Part 4 24 am, advertised, are coming/shall be coming, (shall) require
25 Would you please/Could you please tell me 26 should/would like
27 Would I be able/Could I 28 hopes/is hoping, don't drive, won't
be/wouldn't be, need/shall need/should need 29 Do the local shops still
deliver; know, did 30 should/would be, would tell, calls 31 ask/are

asking, sounds; would you like/do you like   32 have been, lived, want
33 is also writing, would like, painted   34 has known, lived, am,
would/will recommend   35 should/would of course be *or* am of course
willing   36 should/would be, enclose

Exercise 130   Part 1   1 wrote, asking *or* to ask *or* and asked   **2** replied,
enclosing, filled up, returned   **3** have heard, am beginning/begin, has
gone   **4** Would/Could you please check, have received   **5** have
received/did receive/received, haven't decided, should/would be, would
tell   **6** has already been, should/would like, don't get, shall/will have to,
do, shall/will have or have

Part 2   7 have suffered/have been suffering, leave/are leaving   **8** stand,
laughing, calling   **9** get, bang/banging, reverse   **10** sounds, finds, has had,
is still learning, don't know, (do) know, takes, roaring, shouting   **11** have
gone, have all been, find   **12** should/would be, would ask, could

Part 3   13 Are you/Would you be   **14** is coming, is bringing *or* is coming
and bringing, *or* will be coming and bringing   **15** haven't met, think,
would/will like   **16** will be able   **17** receives, doesn't get, has asked
18 will probably ring, would be   **19** know, don't usually eat, hope, won't
be; can   **20** passes, remember/will probably remember, will give

Exercise 131   Part 1 (Affirmative auxiliary verbs would usually be
contracted in speech.)   **1** Could   **2** does   **3** does, came, was, did, is,
will/would do   **4** do you want   **5** should/would like   **6** Would Thursday at
4.00 suit   **7** wouldn't; is coming   **8** would be able to/could do
9 would/will be   **10** will/shall expect

Part 2   11 Could   **12** Speaking   **13** have you been; have been trying;
Don't you leave   **14** do, went, have only just got in; is; didn't know, were
15 arrived; would have rung, have been; has only just ended; Are you
doing   **16** am going   **17** is; am   **18** am; had told, would have kept
19 didn't know, dashed, told   **20** did   **21** does, was driving, had, was
taken; am doing; are you really going; can't/couldn't you
22 can't/couldn't; suppose, will/would be   **23** will stay; will get over;
would you like   **24** I'd love; are you, will be, should/would hate   **25** will
be; will ring, am staying; stayed, didn't seem   **26** did you stay; will tell

15 Future forms

Exercise 132   1 are you going; we'll probably go   **2** are having; is
leaving/leaves   **3** shall/will see; will probably look   **4** am seeing; will
refuse   **5** shall/will know; will tell   **6** will be; shall/will miss; will walk,
will probably catch   **7** shall/will probably come; will give, am coming
8 will get; are staying, will have to; will move   **9** will he say; won't mind;
will just buy   **10** won't know; will leave   **11** will never get; will meet, will
fall   **12** am going; Are you coming; shall/will probably have   **13** Are you

walking; will get; will bring   14 am having, are starting; will make
15 Are you taking; am taking; will pass; will/shall take   16 are you
meeting; are meeting; is taking   17 are you doing; will go; will probably
stay   18 is Jack arriving; is he getting; will come   19 are they doing; are
going; is happening; are taking; will enjoy   20 will wake, won't get
21 are spending; shall/will manage; will turn; will be able   22 is catching,
will be   23 is George coming; are moving, shall/will have to   24 am
ringing; Shall I ask; shall/will be; will write   25 are having, are lunching,
is standing; are giving   26 will let, shall/will find   27 are getting; Are you
going; Are they having   28 Shall I wait, will take   29 will you have; will
have; will have; are having, am having; will have   30 will give; am
collecting   31 is getting; will happen; will ring, will sleep, will come
32 am being; is leaving, am taking; will soon be, will spend, will lose *or*
will spend . . . and lose   33 am flying; are you taking; will spend
34 are going; are having . . . and going; will come; is coming; will ask
35 is coming; Shall we go; will get, shall/will be able; won't pay   36 are
opening, are having; will look; will come; are you having; are missing; are
going

Exercise 133   1 are you going; am going; are you going to do; am going
to fish   2 are you going; am not going; am staying/going to stay; am going
to write   3 is going to rain   4 are you staying; am going; are you going to
do; am going to try   5 am going to dye; Are you going to do, are you
going to have it done; am going to have   6 am going to read   7 are you
doing; are coming, am going to show/am showing; are you taking; am
going to take/am taking   8 are starting; are going; Are you going to climb;
is going to climb; am going to sit . . . and do   9 are going; Are you going
to sail; are taking/are going to take; are going to try   10 Aren't you going
to ask; am leaving; are you going to do; Are you going to have; am
starting   11 Are you going to use; am going to live; am going to start; are
you going to do/are you doing, am selling/am going to sell; is getting
12 is going, is having; is going to look; is coming   13 am going to send;
am seeing   14 is arriving; Is he spending; is he catching; is spending; is
giving . . . and attending   15 Is he bringing; is going to do, is giving
16 am starting; are you going to do; am going to study   17 Are you going;
am going to get; am going; am going to ask; is joining/is going to join,
they are all going to pick   18 am going to buy; is going to be   19 are you
going to do; Are you going to sell; am going to learn; am having   20 am
moving in; Are you going to have; am going to paint   21 Are you having;
am going to do/am doing; am going to use; are you going to help; am
hiring/am going to hire   22 am going to do; am going to plant . . . and
make; Are you going to give/are you giving   23 am getting; are starting,
is coming   24 are meeting; Are they just going to repeat; are they going
to climb; are going to offer

Exercise 134 1 am going to have 2 are going to assemble; will come
3 am going to shampoo 4 am going to make; will burn 5 am going to
paint 6 am going to make 7 will look 8 will see 9 will wait 10 are
going to camp . . . and cook 11 am going to put 12 Are you going to
wear; am going to sit . . . and watch; am not going to get 13 will take
14 will have 15 will start; will get, will bake 16 is going to bake; will
soon get 17 Are you going to try; am going to try; will confiscate
18 shall/will have; will come 19 am not going to take; am going to mend;
is going to help 20 Are you going to paint; am going to take 21 will add;
won't be able to read; am going to type; shall/will have 22 will type
23 will ring 24 am going to ring 25 Aren't you going to climb; are going
to climb; are going to try; will cook, will buy 26 am going to wash; will
come 27 are going to pick; will probably come, will start 28 will have to
go, will be; will get; Will you let 29 will stay; will try 30 am going to
start; Are you going to do; is going to help 31 is going to write; will buy;
will buy 32 is going to dig 33 is the new owner going to make; is going
to concentrate 34 are going to bottle 35 will go 36 are going to buy;
will stay

Exercise 135 1 will/shall both be coming 2 will meet, will forget 3 will
be watching; will ring 4 will/shall be doing; will still be working 5 will
get, will do 6 will be coming 7 will/shall be working 8 will/shall be
taking off 9 will come 10 will be playing 11 will get; will still be; will
be going, will ask 12 will be, will be wondering/will wonder 13 will/shall
never be able; will be helping; won't be helping; will/shall be helping
14 will write, will try; will type 15 will/shall be typing; will type 16 will
tell 17 will just be coming 18 will be melting 19 will be talking . . . and
showing, will/shall feel 20 will tell, won't believe 21 will just be getting
up 22 will be wearing; will wrap . . . and go 23 will be; will be
speaking, will be addressing 24 will be reading, will be ringing 25 will
still be standing 26 Will you please forward; will/shall be staying 27 will
be coming 28 will be leaving 29 won't start; will give 30 will be
coming 31 will be looking 32 will you be arriving; will/shall be
travelling; Will there be; will send 33 Will you be using; will put
34 will/shall be having; will be hobbling 35 will enjoy; won't/shan't have;
will/shall be map-reading, will/shall be 36 will write

Exercise 136 1 won't do 2 won't come; won't be driving 3 won't/shan't
be coming 4 won't have; won't come 5 won't/shan't be teaching
6 will/shall be doing; won't/shan't be eating 7 won't eat 8 won't bite
9 won't be coming 10 will be fishing 11 won't clean 12 won't/shan't be
showing 13 won't/shan't be washing; will/shall be having
14 won't/shan't be wearing; won't recognize 15 won't be, won't believe
16 won't/shan't be delivering 17 won't be wearing 18 won't tell
19 won't be using; won't do 20 will/shall have; won't/shan't be paying
21 won't pay; will have 22 won't work 23 will get on; won't be
working 24 won't even show; won't come

Exercise 137 1 will have repaired 2 will have done 3 will/shall have made 4 will have finished 5 will have planted 6 will/shall have passed 7 will/shall have done 8 will have walked 9 will have lost 10 will have spent 11 will/shall have worked 12 will have been driven 13 will/shall have sent 14 will/shall have given 15 will have died 16 will have driven 17 will/shall have picked 18 will have sunk

Exercise 138 Part 1 1 is looking; sees, rings; answers 2 am ringing 3 says; use 4 uses; eats; don't think, likes 5 would suit/suits; like; would we arrange/do we arrange, use 6 includes; doesn't include 7 see; does the room face 8 faces; looks, gets 9 sounds 10 Would 7 p.m. suit *or* Will 7 p.m. suit; can't/couldn't/wouldn't be able to, don't get 11 will/would be; don't think, will have; passes, stops 12 I'll find; I'll see 13 comes, asks 14 is coming 15 She'll probably come, are sitting; get; don't think, give 16 do; listens; will be 17 rings; looks, smiles 18 says, goes

Part 2 19 am speaking; am spending; would you like 20 I'd love; do I get 21 I'll meet 22 I'll do 23 comes 24 sounds 25 see 26 are you doing 27 am spending 28 you'll freeze, doesn't kill; are you getting 29 am catching, is meeting 30 I'll lend; I'll tell 31 likes 32 I'll give, fall, goes; are having, is going, is catching 33 is always going; go 34 comes, hear, will be

16 Conditionals

Exercise 139 1 find, will give 2 smoke, will/may object 3 put, will crack 4 see 5 wins, will get, comes, will get 6 feel 7 wants, will have 8 have finished 9 stands, will capsize 10 isn't working, will have 11 doesn't go 12 hear 13 will get 14 leaves, will be 15 freezes, will be 16 don't take, will have 17 takes, will have 18 don't feel/aren't feeling 19 brakes, will/may skid 20 like, will get 21 would like 22 growls 23 isn't working 24 don't know 25 refuses 26 won't/doesn't help 27 are going 28 do you employ 29 will be 30 hate, don't you change 31 don't want 32 hear 33 will see 34 rings/should ring 35 reach/should reach 36 would care, will send

Exercise 140 Part 1 Drill ('What'll happen if . . .' is normally replaceable by 'What'll you do if' and vice versa. These are possible answers only.) 1 What'll you do if he doesn't pay you tonight? 2 What'll you do if you don't get a permit? 3 What'll you do if you don't pass? 4 What'll you do if he refuses? 5 What'll happen if he chooses Smith? 6 What'll you do if you can't find a cheap room? 7 What'll happen if it doesn't open? 8 What'll happen if I forget it? 9 What'll happen if they don't believe me? 10 What'll you call it if it's a boy? 11 What'll happen if we don't get a lift? 12 What'll happen if it isn't clear of fog? 13 What'll happen/How long will it take if he doesn't help us? 14 What'll

Key

happen if he isn't at home?/What'll we do if . . .? 15 What'll we do if the ice isn't thick enough? 16 What'll happen/What happens if you walk on them when the tide is coming in? 17 What'll we do if it's wet? 18 What'll we do if we (do) have another puncture?

Part 2 1 If you like I can get 2 If you like I'll ask 3 If you like I'll bring the photographs 4 If you like I'll give 5 If you like you can watch 6 If you like I'll arrange a helicopter trip 7 If you like I'll knit you one 8 If you like you can borrow 9 If you like I'll come 10 If you like I'll ask Ann 11 If you like I'll get you an application form 12 If you like I'll go with you 13 If you like I'll paint 14 If you like you can leave 15 If you like we'll postpone 16 If you like I'll ask him 17 If you like I'll arrange for you to meet the President 18 If you like we'll go sailing

Exercise 141 (First person **would** is normally replaceable by **should** except in sentences 8, 9, 22.)

1 gave, would sell 2 woke, would have 3 went, would pine 4 went, would lose 5 said, would you do 6 worked, would finish 7 would happen, blew 8 saw, would climb; would not be, would climb 9 came, would call 10 threw, would have 11 asked, would he say 12 would be; would probably start 13 rang, would be 14 saw, would assume 15 would have, were/was 16 rushed, would get 17 bought, would lose 18 had, would bring 19 did, would not be 20 were/was, would still be 21 were/was, wouldn't be staying/wouldn't stay 22 had, would drink 23 drank, would soon get 24 were/was, would not be playing 25 would you go, did 26 kept, would not be running/would not run 27 was/were, would not be sitting 28 heard, didn't you answer 29 typed, would be 30 had 31 had, would now be sitting 32 would be, would kindly sign 33 stopped, would all fly 34 would still be 35 was, didn't you change 36 won, would be writing/would write

Exercise 142 (The following are possible answers but not the *only* possible answers.)

1 If she wasn't/weren't so shy she would enjoy 2 If he took more exercise he would be healthier 3 If I had the right change we could 4 If they spoke English to her, her English would/might improve 5 If he worked overtime he would 6 If my number was/were in the directory people would ring 7 If the police were armed we would/might have gun battles 8 If the shops delivered, life would be easier/less difficult 9 If he wasn't/weren't so thin he mightn't feel/If he was/were fatter, etc. 10 If we had matches we could light 11 If we had a steak we could cook it 12 If I wasn't/weren't so fat I could/would be able to 13 If I asked him he might help 14 If I could drive we could/would be able to take the car 15 If we had a ladder we could 16 If I were you I should/would sell it 17 If I had more time I'd read more 18 If they cleaned the windows the rooms would look brighter 19 If he polished his shoes he'd look smarter 20 If he paid his staff properly they might work better 21 If we had

180

central heating the house would be warmer   22 If I had a dog I wouldn't
mind being alone   23 If he didn't spend hours watching television he
would have time   24 If I had a vacuum cleaner I'd be quicker   25 If I
knew his address I could write   26 If he shaved he'd look more
attractive   27 If you worked more slowly you wouldn't make   28 If I
could park near my office I'd come by car   29 If I lived nearer the centre
I wouldn't always be late   30 If I had a map I could direct   31 If people
drove more slowly there wouldn't be   32 If English people spoke more
slowly I might/might be able to understand   33 If my house
wasn't/weren't guarded by two Alsatian dogs it would be broken into
34 If the flats were clearly numbered it would be easier to find people
35 If you wiped your feet you wouldn't make muddy marks   36 If I didn't
live near my office I'd spend a lot of time

Exercise 143   (Sometimes **would** below is replaceable by **might** or **could**.)

1 had not taken, wouldn't have got   2 had paid, wouldn't have been
3 had told, would have cooked   4 had had, would have been   5 had
known, would have lent   6 hadn't had, would have fallen   7 had realized,
wouldn't have accepted   8 hadn't taken   9 had been lit   10 hadn't rung
11 had waited, would have seen   12 wouldn't have been, hadn't knocked
13 had patented, would have made   14 had had, would have been   15 had
told, would have agreed   16 had been, would have been able   17 had
been, would have been launched   18 had known, wouldn't have thrown
19 had known, would have brought; would have enjoyed   20 would have
attended   21 would have refused, had offered   22 wouldn't have known,
hadn't told   23 had read, would have refused   24 had been playing, would
certainly have heard   25 would you have done   26 hadn't rained, would
have been   27 had been waiting   28 had used, would have lit   29 hadn't
been wearing, should/would have recognized   30 had known, would have
backed   31 had been, would have phoned   32 had turned   33 had played,
would have had   34 had booked, would have had   35 had been, would not
have been   36 had held, would not have been

Exercise 144   (These are possible answers but not the *only* possible
answers.)

1 If I had seen the signal I would have stopped   2 If I'd known your
number I would have rung   3 If she had known you were in hospital she
would have visited   4 If there had been taxis we would have taken one
5 If she hadn't been so shy she might have spoken   6 If she hadn't
threatened to set fire to her flat I wouldn't have asked   7 If we'd had time
we'd have visited   8 If the lift had been working I wouldn't have come up
the stairs   9 If we had listened carefully we mightn't have made   10 If we
hadn't got a lift we shouldn't/wouldn't have reached   11 If you hadn't
washed it in boiling water it wouldn't have shrunk   12 If we hadn't been
using an out-of-date timetable we shouldn't/wouldn't have missed   13 If
his own men hadn't deserted him he wouldn't have failed   14 If they
hadn't been driving so quickly the accident wouldn't have been   15 If it

hadn't been raining I would have taken 16 If I'd known that in summer
etc. I wouldn't have bought 17 If Tom's father hadn't been on the Board
he wouldn't have got 18 If he'd been looking where he was going he
wouldn't have been run over 19 If I'd been brought up in the country I
might like country life 20 If I'd known he was so quarrelsome I
wouldn't/shouldn't have invited him 21 If it hadn't rained all the time he
might have enjoyed his visit 22 If I'd worked hard at school I
would/should/might have got a good job 23 If they hadn't used closed-
circuit television they wouldn't/mightn't have spotted 24 If he'd been
wearing a shirt they wouldn't have asked him to leave 25 If the streets
had been clearly marked it wouldn't have taken us so long 26 If we'd had
enough money we would/should have gone by air 27 If you'd put your
hand up the bus would have stopped 28 If he hadn't turned up looking so
disreputable they would have given him 29 If I'd known how thin the ice
was I wouldn't/shouldn't have been walking 30 If he had taken the fight
seriously from the beginning he might have won 31 If they hadn't paid
the ransom at once they wouldn't have got 32 If he had read the passage
more slowly the candidates would have understood 33 If they'd been
wearing life-jackets they mightn't have been drowned 34 If his wife had
encouraged him he might have got 35 If the exit doors hadn't been
blocked people would have been able to escape/could have escaped
36 They would have walked further if they hadn't been hampered by *or*
But for the thick dust they would have walked further

Exercise 145   (First person **would** is normally replaceable by **should**.)

1 stays, will be/should be 2 didn't know, wouldn't/couldn't understand
3 hadn't got, would/might have come; wouldn't have been 4 knew, did
you take 5 were not 6 had not been, would not have cheered 7 had not
cheered, would not have run 8 had not run, would not have crashed,
would not have been 9 returns/should return 10 why don't you sell/why
not sell; had, would sell 11 didn't know, did you offer; would refuse
12 leaves, will/may steal 13 wore, would see 14 hadn't loved, would not
have waited 15 had looked, would have been 16 start, will the village
people resist 17 would you like 18 won't be able; can't, can't 19 would
have been, had become 20 had gone, would be 21 had, would make
22 had known, would have brought 23 bathed, would be 24 stood,
would all see, would be 25 were, would get 26 do, please remind/would
you please remind 27 would have realized 28 had admitted, would not
have been 29 had, would grow; would be 30 had known, would have
stayed 31 had, would make 32 had told, would/could have gone
33 spend, won't have 34 hadn't been, mightn't have been 35 had, would
get 36 would happen, had; would play, (would) miss, would fail, (would)
have; would not feed, would get; would catch, (would) die, would have,
would keep.

Exercise 146 Answers are not provided for these open-ended sentences, as the responses by individual students are likely to be varied.

Exercise 147

1 shall/will; will   2 will   3 Shall; will   4 will   5 Will   6 shan't/won't; shan't/won't; will; shall/will   7 will   8 shall   9 shall; won't   10 will   11 Shall; shall/will, won't   12 will   13 shan't   14 won't   15 shall, shall not   16 will; shall/will   17 Shall; will; will, won't   18 shall/will; will   19 shan't; will   20 shall; will   21 shan't/won't; will   22 Will; won't   23 shan't; will   24 shall

Exercise 148   1 should   2 should   3 would   4 Would   5 should   6 would   7 would   8 should/would   9 would   10 should   11 would   12 Would   13 should   14 should; would   15 Would; should   16 should   17 should   18 would   19 should   20 would   21 should   22 should   23 should   24 would   25 Would   26 should   27 should   28 should, should   29 should   30 would   31 would   32 would   33 should   34 would   35 should   36 should

17 Gerund, infinitive and present participle

Exercise 149   1 living, to like   2 to travel; to take, to go   3 to buy; selling   4 to catch; getting, getting   5 to complain; losing   6 going, being, putting; telling, to take   7 to lock; go, do   8 to touch, being   9 house-hunting, to ask; looking   10 go; swimming; going   11 to be paid; taking, measuring; to expect, to do, to be, to die   12 spending, arguing, not to go   13 giving, going to live   14 to leave; to call   15 keep you waiting; apologizing   16 telling, to talk   17 earning, to show   18 to start; filling   19 to carry; to move, carry   20 to take; take; cutting; to get, taking; to saw, escape   21 to ask, to leave; asking Tom to do; asking, to travel   22 to cut; sharpening   23 to buy, to ask   24 cheating, buying, dealing/to deal   25 dining, have; to go; having   26 cutting/to be cut; have, to have   27 to convince, managing, helping   28 travelling, standing; queuing, waiting; to go   29 following, criticizing, to hit   30 to stay; wait; to go   31 to rebel, not to adopt   32 arriving; to wait, waiting; to be   33 to come, going; to climb, making   34 to work, getting   35 start; to risk getting   36 calling, letting, decide

Exercise 150   1 sleeping, to camp   2 to come; listening, listening, talking   3 to leave, to put   4 to park   5 smoking, to risk setting, smoke   6 writing, to receive, go   7 buying; shopping   8 to see, to find, buy; trying to travel   9 to turn; working   10 taking, dropping, pretending   11 to grow, buying; to prevent, playing   12 keeping; to fill; asking, to keep; making   13 going; to come; to go, go; travelling   14 go fishing; coming; to cut, wasting, sitting, watching, fishing   15 being, to wait; to see   16 to prevent, rushing, dashing   17 tossing, crashing   18 to eat, trying

19 walking, take; go; to get   20 to start; raining, walking   21 counting, thinking; moving, being robbed; to get, to make   22 letting, keeping, to sell   23 to lean, watching, going, coming; shouting, talking   24 to know, to learn; to greet/greeting, to talk   25 untying, climbing, crawling   26 finding; getting; to know   27 to see/seeing, sitting; relaxing, reading, produce, to be; performing, keeping   28 spending, living, to think, selling, returning   29 arguing; argue; seeing   30 to hear; seeing; to bring   31 receiving, selling; receiving, selling, to sell   32 hovering, being, climbing; run/running; coming/come, leading   33 to be passing, to give, to pick, to drop   34 having; to have; sitting, swirling, taking   35 writing, showing   36 swim; swimming; going

18 Unreal pasts and subjunctives

Exercise 151   1 left   2 had   3 had   4 had   5 had done   6 began   7 knew   8 had   9 had asked   10 did   11 had nibbled/had been nibbling   12 mended   13 were addressing   14 were   15 stayed, looked   16 had tied   17 hadn't given   18 had known   19 didn't know   20 were   21 drove   22 had been   23 had not taken   24 had never been   25 had kept   26 paid   27 stopped, started   28 had not said   29 had taken   30 had been standing   31 had never set   32 took   33 had/had had   34 had not tried   35 had not had   36 got

Exercise 152   (The following are possible answers, but not the *only* possible answers. All the answers will begin: **I'd rather you**. We are therefore only giving the other half of each sentence.)

1 went by train   2 went with someone/took someone with you   3 started today   4 rang on your own phone/used your own phone   5 slept in the house   6 cooked it under the grill   7 cut it with a knife/with your own scissors   8 stayed on a bit longer   9 came in in time   10 waited till morning   11 cleaned it in the garage   12 said nothing   13 wore shoes   14 didn't   15 painted it blue, and without any decorations   16 rang at 7 a.m.   17 didn't threaten him at all   18 bathed during the day/in daylight   19 parked it in the playing field   20 put them in the goldfish bowl   21 went by train   22 borrowed the other one   23 typed it   24 did it today

Exercise 153   (All the answers begin **I wish**; the words **I wish** will therefore not be given.)

1 I had a washing machine   2 I lived nearer my work   3 our garden got some sun   4 I hadn't called him a liar   5 I knew Finnish   6 I had booked a seat   7 I had a car   8 I could drive   9 Tom would drive more slowly/Tom drove   10 you would keep quiet   11 we hadn't accepted   12 theatre tickets didn't cost   13 shops here didn't shut   14 he had worked   15 you had seen it   16 you weren't going   17 I had a permit   18 it would stop   19 you would wait   20 I had brought a map   21 I had

never come 22 I hadn't left 23 I had stayed 24 he would cut 25 he
would stop 26 he went to bed earlier/didn't go so late 27 we knew
where we were 28 we had 29 I had known 30 you hadn't told
31 I had asked 32 I could swim 33 you were coming 34 you were
going to a job 35 you had asked him 36 every country would stop

19 The passive

Exercise 154 1 The milk is brought, the letters are left 2 letters won't
be brought, they'll have to be collected from 3 Things are stolen from,
twenty bottles were stolen 4 this street is swept, it wasn't swept 5 This
box is cleared, It was last cleared 6 A light was turned on and the door
(was) opened 7 This office is cleaned, the upstairs offices are cleaned
8 He was never seen, all his meals were taken up 9 This purse was left
. . . it was found by the cleaner 10 1,000 new houses are built, last year
1,500 were built 11 Hot meals are served, coffee and sandwiches can be
ordered 12 All sorts of things are left in buses. They are collected by the
conductors and (are) sent 13 He was taken to hospital by ambulance
14 Many people are killed and injured . . . can't something be done
15 The warehouse is guarded by dogs. A thief who tried to get in was
seen by a dog and chased 16 The police were called and the man (was)
arrested 17 Tom, who had only a slight injury, was helped off, but Jack,
who was seriously injured, was carried off 18 This dress can't be
washed, it must be dry-cleaned 19 The entire block is being demolished
20 He recommends that new tyres should be fitted 21 He suggested that
council tenants should be allowed 22 These calculations used to be done
by men; now they are done by a computer 23 The man was tried, found
guilty and sent to prison 24 The knockers of all the flats are polished . . .
mine hasn't been polished 25 My piano is being repaired 26 Tickets
shouldn't be thrown away . . . they may be checked 27 Jack was invited
but Tom wasn't (invited) 28 All the sandwiches were eaten . . . and all
the beer (was) drunk. Nothing was left 29 Has my parcel been posted
30 Why wasn't I informed of 31 The book was written by Tom Smith
and published by Brown and Co. 32 The car will have to be towed 33 all
our copies have been sold but more have been ordered 34 Trespassers
will be prosecuted 35 My car was stolen and abandoned . . . The radio
had been removed but no other damage had been done 36 Dogs must be
kept on leads

Exercise 155 1 The letter hasn't been stamped 2 I wasn't paid for the
work; I was expected to do 3 he was being moved 4 I wasn't
introduced 5 I was awakened by a frightful crash 6 When this street has
been widened the residents will be kept awake all night by the roar
7 The rubbish was thrown away 8 These TV sets are made by a
Japanese firm 9 The town was destroyed by an earthquake 10 This
could be done much more easily by (a) machine 11 Umbrellas and sticks
must be left 12 Tenants are asked not to play 13 Your clock can't be

repaired   14 Articles (which have been) bought during the sale cannot be exchanged   15 Fruit has to be picked very early otherwise it can't be got to the market   16 People shouldn't be allowed to park   17 My house is being watched   18 The passage will be read three times   19 Dictionaries may not be used   20 This letter need not be typed   21 '13' has been crossed out and '12A' has been written   22 This man mustn't be moved; he is too ill/he is too ill to be moved. He will have to be left   23 His house was searched and stolen articles were found   24 This room hasn't been used   25 He was taken for   26 These books should have been taken back   27 The children were brought up   28 The For Sale notice has been taken down . . . the house has been sold   29 His house was broken into . . . a lot of his things (were) stolen   30 You have been warned   31 He was knocked down by a lorry   32 My keys were returned to me; they had been picked up   33 The books had to be given back; we were not allowed to take   34 These documents shouldn't be left . . . They should be locked up   35 Coffee and biscuits were handed round   36 Other people's schemes have been tried. Why has my scheme never been tried?

Exercise 156   1 troops have been called out   2 trains were held up by fog   3 this is to be left here. It will be called for   4 police were called in 5 children were not properly looked after   6 reinforcements are being flown in   7 men of 28 were called up   8 he was looked up to by everyone 9 he will be seen off at the airport by all the ministers   10 bed hasn't been slept in   11 more rooms can be built on   12 he was thrown out 13 different attitude will have to be adopted   14 he ought to be locked up   15 they weren't taken in by her story   16 house was broken into 17 small plastic toys are being given away   18 notice was taken down 19 smoking is frowned on   20 after a million pounds had been spent . . . the scheme was given up   21 my car had been towed away. I asked why this had been done and was told that . . . it had been parked   22 weapons must be handed in   23 he was shouted down   24 he is often taken for his brother   25 the cork hasn't been taken out   26 pool was to have been used . . . it is being filled in   27 students are being turned away   28 sky-scraper will have to be pulled down as the town planning regulations have not been complied with

Exercise 157   1 money was added up and found to be correct   2 I am having the bathroom tiled   3 a terrible mistake seems to have been made 4 you are supposed to make tea   5 he is known to be armed   6 he was seen to pick up   7 you are known to have been   8 he is believed to have 9 this needn't have been done   10 you had better have it taken in   11 he likes to be called 'sir'   12 this switch isn't to be/mustn't be touched 13 you will have to have/get it seen to *or* it will have to be seen to   14 this can't be done   15 we are being followed   16 boys used to be made to climb   17 it has to be seen to be believed   18 I am tired of being ordered about   19 he doesn't like being laughed at   20 this watch needn't be wound/doesn't need to be wound   21 he shouldn't have been told   22 they decided that the money should be divided   23 he is believed to have been

killed   24 letters are to be sent   25 she is considered to have been
26 smoking is not allowed   27 the expedition is known to have reached
28 before printing was invented everything had to be written   29 the
government was urged to create/they urged that more jobs should be
created   30 they suggested that the sale of alcohol should be banned

20 Indirect speech

Exercise 158   (In the exercises on reported speech we often use nouns as
subjects: e.g. the policeman, the children, Paul etc. In the answers, to
save space, we have often used pronouns.)

1 he said he was going out but he'd be in   2 she said she was working . . .
and didn't much care   3 Peter said he couldn't live on his basic salary and
he'd have to   4 Mary said her young brother wanted to be . . . she
couldn't think why because none of her family had ever been   5 they said
they were waiting . . . and it was late   6 he said he had made . . . I said he
was always making . . . and should be used to it   7 he said they made . . .
and sent . . . to their wives   8 he said it was lonely being away from their
. . . but they earned . . . in that/the factory as they would in their own
9 he said they had been there . . . and were going to stay   10 he said he'd
got . . . I said that would be . . . he replied he knew it would be hard but
he didn't mind . . . and it would be   11 he said the ice would soon be . . .
she said she would look for her skates when she got   12 she said she was
living with her parents at the moment but she hoped to have a flat of her
own soon   13 she said she was leaving the following day . . . we said we'd
come and see her off   14 he said he'd just bought . . . but it wasn't
insured yet so he couldn't take me   15 she said she would like to speak
. . . but she was bathing . . . and they would drown if she left . . . she
went   16 Ann says she is coming . . . next week. She hopes we will meet
her   17 She said nothing ever happened . . . it was like . . . people had
drifted   18 he said he had missed his train; he'd be late . . . and his boss
would be   19 they said they would wait for me if I was late/for us if we
were late   20 I said they were supposed . . . but if the fog got . . . the
plane might be   21 she said if I lent her . . . she'd bring . . . in two days'
time   22 he grumbled he hated getting up on dark mornings; his wife
agreed it was horrible but said the mornings would be lighter soon and
then it wouldn't be   23 she said the sales were starting the following day
and as soon as they finished work the whole . . . pool was going . . . I (said
I) hoped they would all get what they wanted   24 he (said he) wished he
had something . . . said he had only just had lunch and she didn't know
how he could be   25 my aunt said if I was short . . . she could lend me . . .
and I could take my time   26 he said he usually took his dog . . . when he
came   27 I said I had . . . for her brother. Ann said he wasn't at home; he
had left two days before   28 I said I had bought the bag . . . he said I
shouldn't have bought . . . it didn't go with my coat   29 she said she must
hurry as her father was always . . . if any of them were   30 he said if I

wanted to smoke I would have to   31 he said he was building himself . . .
he wouldn't show it to me just yet but when the roof was on I could
come   32 he said the lake would probably freeze that night; it was much
colder than the previous night. Mary said she would go . . . and if it was
frozen she would make . . . ducks could   33 He said . . . the strikers went
back the following day it would be . . . things returned   34 She said
someone was trying to murder her. She kept getting   35 she said she was
taking her children . . . the following day   36 she said all she could hear
was . . . she wondered if it was

Exercise 159   (See the note to Exercise 158.)

1 he said there had been . . . road was blocked . . . it wouldn't be clear . . .
he advised us to go/he said we'd better go   2 they suggested lighting . . .
cooking their sausages   3 he said he was thinking . . . aunt advised him
not to go . . . as it was a bad   4 he warned us to take . . . as we might
have to   5 he said he had left some books on my table. He thought I'd
find them useful and said I could keep them as long as I needed them but
that he'd like . . . when I had finished with them. I thanked him and said
I'd take/promised to take   6 he said that if the children could . . . were
. . . should be able . . . he was teaching   7 he said the puppy could sleep
on their bed . . . she said she'd rather he slept . . . would soon be . . . there
wouldn't be . . . all three of them   8 she said she'd try by herself . . . and
if she found that she couldn't . . . she'd ask Tom to help her   9 Mary
suggested camping by the stream as, *or* pointing out that if they went on,
it might be dark before they found   10 they wished they'd brought their
. . . as then they could have offered . . . and perhaps they (the restaurant)
would have given them   11 Jones said he'd booked . . . The receptionist
said she (was afraid that they) hadn't got his letter . . . all rooms had been
taken . . . but they could give him . . . Jones said that wouldn't do him
12 he said he'd had gypsies on his land and they'd given . . . Council had
asked him . . . . He didn't see why . . . and was writing to his MP
13 he grumbled that the letter was . . . . She admitted she had done it . . .
and said she supposed she'd better   14 he said if they'd like to go on any
of the tours the hotel would arrange it. They said they'd like   15 he said
they'd try to find my passport but it would be . . . slept . . . might have
robbed me   16 she suggested going . . . and said they might make their
. . . . She'd been given . . . . He said he had had . . . from her . . . they had
been   17 he said he didn't know why she wasted . . . the neighbours all
polished . . . she didn't want their Mini . . . . If he were any good . . . he'd
help her   18 he apologized for not having a tie on. He said he didn't know
it was going   19 he said he would have enjoyed . . . if the man next to him
hadn't snored   20 I said I was thinking . . . he advised me to take
someone with me. It was safer as one could . . . slept   21 Paul says that
the plans have been changed; we're going tomorrow now not the next day.
He wants us to meet him at Victoria tonight   22 He said that if he wanted
. . . he had to . . . it wasn't hot. I said that was ridiculous and that it was
high time he left   23 he said he knew the umbrella belonged to me but he

thought it would be all right if he borrowed it because I wasn't going out the following day and he was   24 he suggested putting my . . . and making . . . It would be . . . what they were planning. I said/objected that my recorder made . . . and they'd be sure . . . and then they'd find . . . and ask   25 she said whenever her father was unhappy he would go out and buy . . . their rooms were full . . . they couldn't use. Tom said that he was sorry for her father; he must have been   26 he said I could leave my . . . in his garage if I liked . . . he would keep . . . while I was away   27 he told Ann that if she wanted a job she should read . . . it was no use . . . outside her door   28 he said it used to be . . . but that now it was impossible. When summer came I'd have to   29 he said I must leave a note for my . . . otherwise she'd be . . . when I wasn't in at my   30 she said . . . had just arrived . . . and he was . . . She wondered if she should ring . . . wait till he came

Exercise 160   (See note to Exercise 158.)

1 she asked who had been using her   2 he asked if I wanted   3 he asked if I minded   4 they asked if I would like to come with them/they invited me to come with them   5 she asked who I had given   6 he asked how long it took   7 he asked how much I thought it would cost   8 she asked him what he had missed most when he was/had been   9 he asked if the seat was taken   10 He asked how I got on with my   11 they asked him how he had got   12 he asked what I was/had been doing with the skeleton . . . and if I was/had been trying   13 she asked me if I had slept   14 they asked him if he had been there   15 she asked if I could tell her why Paul (had) left   16 he asked how many . . . knew   17 she asked if there were . . . for her   18 he asked how long I had been   19 he asked why I wasn't   20 the customer asked if they were   21 I asked where they were going for their   22 she asked if it would be . . . if she came . . . that night   23 he asked if I had ever seen   24 she asked him where she could park her   25 she asked if I would like . . . I asked which way she was going   26 she asked who I wanted   27 he asked if anyone wanted   28 I asked what he was going to do with his   29 I asked if she grew her own   30 he asked what train I was going   31 she asked him if he could change . . . and said she was afraid she hadn't got/and apologized for not having   32 she asked how many . . . he had taken. He said he had no idea   33 they asked if they could see the manager/they asked to see the manager. The secretary asked if they had   34 he asked if I thought I could live . . . on my own . . . or if I would get   35 he asked if any of us had actually seen   36 she asked if she could see/she asked to see/she asked for Commander Smith. I said I was afraid he was in orbit and asked if she would like

Exercise 161   1 he suggested having . . . Ann agreed and suggested going . . . Jack was always   2 she said Jack's parents had asked her . . . the following night and asked what she should wear. Her mother advised her to wear . . . as it was   3 he said he was broke. Peter offered to lend him   4 the clerk said it would take . . . to look up her file. Ann asked if it was worth waiting or if she should   5 he asked if he would have to do . . . if he

failed . . . The teacher said that he would   6 I asked where he would be
the next day in case I had to ring him. He said that he would be in his . . .
at his flat. He wouldn't be going   7 Mary asked what she should do with
the cracked cup and her mother advised her to throw   8 she wondered if
she would ever see   9 he asked me to get out . . . and he had to change
. . . I offered to help   10 he said he'd run . . . and asked me to give
him/asked for a lift   11 he suggested going . . . She said she liked . . . but
that her only . . . shoes were being . . . She suggested going   12 he said I
had a lot . . . and offered to carry some of them for me   13 he wondered if
they would be   14 he asked what he should do with all the money. Mary
advised him to take . . . and get/Mary suggested taking . . . and getting
15 Peter offered jack a cigarette. Jack thanked him and said he didn't
smoke   16 They asked if she'd like to go/invited her to go with them,
saying that there was . . . Ann said she'd love to/Ann accepted   17 she
asked Mr Jones if he could do without her that day as she had . . . and
thought it might . . . if she stayed. Mr Jones advised her to stay . . . and to
take the next day off too if she wasn't better   18 Mary told Paul that
she'd just come back to her flat . . . in her chair. He was still there . . .
and she asked/wanted to know what she should do. Paul advised her to
wake him and ask him who he was, adding that there was   19 he said he
wasn't quite . . . and asked Jack to wait/if he could wait . . . Jack said he
couldn't wait long because the train went   20 I asked her to take off her
hat/if she would mind taking . . . She pointed out that the theatre was . . .
and suggested my/me moving   21 he said he often saw . . . and asked if I
thought he should   22 I asked what changes he would make if the house
was his. He said he'd pull . . . The site was all right   23 he asked for my
name   24 he offered to send it round to his hotel/asked if he should send
. . . The tourist said he wasn't staying . . . and he'd take it with him
25 I asked (him) how long they would go on looking . . . He said they'd
stop when it got . . . and start . . . the following day   26 I said we couldn't
discuss it over the phone . . . and suggested meeting in my flat the
following day. He said he'd rather I came to his . . . and asked if I could
get there   27 he asked for 40p to buy an ice-cream/as he wanted to buy an
ice-cream   28 he asked (us) if we would like . . . of his flat, or if we would
rather   29 she asked me to help her with her luggage, and said that if I
took . . . she'd take . . . I said it was ridiculous . . . and asked if she
couldn't manage . . . but she said she couldn't   30 Ann said she couldn't
come . . . (so) Peter suggested Tuesday . . . Ann agreed (to this)

Exercise 162 (The verb of command given below is not necessarily the
only possible one. See also the note to Exercise 158.)

1 she told him not to put . . . in his   2 she begged him not to do 3 he
urged me to apply . . . as it would just suit me   4 he advised me to say
nothing 5 she asked them to wait in the lounge till their flight number
was called 6 I advised her not to lend . . . as he never paid 7 she asked
him to ring 8 he asked me to move my case/asked if I'd mind moving my
case as it was blocking 9 she reminded him to book 10 he told/warned

me to get 11 he warned me to avoid Marble Arch as there was going
12 he told me to hold the ladder as it was . . . I suggested tying/advised
him to tie it . . . as it was much safer 13 he told them to read . . . and not
to write 14 he warned me not to leave my money 15 he advised me to
open 16 he invited her to lunch that day. She said she was afraid she
couldn't as she couldn't leave/She refused, explaining that she couldn't
leave 17 he warned me not to take more than two of them 18 I asked to
speak to Albert/asked if I could speak . . . She said he was . . . I asked her
to wake him as I had 19 he advised me to buy 20 they said I was being
exploited and that I ought to leave my job/and advised me to leave
21 she told them to fasten their . . . as there might be 22 he warned me
not to drive . . . or oncoming drivers might take me 23 he asked to see
my licence 24 I advised him to sweep up 25 she said the bathroom was
empty and asked me to put . . . when I had 26 he reminded me to insure
my 27 she begged him not to . . . and reminded him that they had to
28 I urged Tom to go . . . before his toothache got 29 he advised me to cut
my hair, saying that I would find . . . if I looked 30 he asked for some more

Exercise 163 (See the note to Exercise 158.)

1 the clerk asked me to fill up the form 2 he asked me to read 3 she
asked for a new cheque book. He asked her to show him her 4 Tom says
that we are to be ready/should be ready 5 he begged me not to tell his
mother 6 he ordered/warned us not to fire 7 he advised me to take
8 she asked me to help her 9 he warned me not to drive 10 he
warned/told/advised me not to smoke 11 she said that when I'd chosen a
book I was to bring it to her and she would 12 he told me to show 13 a
notice warned/ordered us to reduce speed at once 14 he asked to see my
ticket 15 he warned me to keep an eye on my luggage as the place was
16 he said that when I'd read it I was to pass it on *or* he told me to pass it
on . . . when I'd read it 17 he suggested lighting . . . and cooking 18 he
told me to press the button whenever I saw . . ./he said that whenever I
saw . . . I was to press 19 he told her to sit down and tell him what was
worrying her 20 he told me to walk . . . and just to nod if I recognized
my attacker but not to say/and said that if I recognized my attacker I was
just to nod but not to say 21 he said that even if I felt hungry I wasn't to
eat/shouldn't eat . . ./he advised me not to eat . . . even if I felt 22 he
asked Ann to ring and order a taxi for him. She suggested (his)
going/advised him to go by tube as it was 23 she suggested buying some
yeast and making their own bread as the bread they were getting was
24 he advised them to boil the water (first) if they had to use it, and
warned them not to drink it unboiled 25 he suggested not telling
anyone/that they shouldn't tell anyone till they were . . . report was
26 Tom says he's got the tickets and (that) we're to meet him 27 he
urged the strikers to show that they were . . . 28 A notice advised
customer to count their . . . as mistakes could not 29 he warned me not
to clap yet, as she hadn't finished. He added (that) singers loathed people
who clapped 30 he reminded me to put my name

Exercise 164 1 Paul wants me to get him 2 Mr White would like you to meet him 3 Ann offered to get . . . Mr Jones said he'd rather she got . . . Ann said there weren't any and (that) the shops were 4 he told me not to worry . . . as he made . . . I asked if he learnt from his . . . or if he kept 5 I said I was looking for . . . who drank in that bar. The barman advised me to keep away from Albert as he didn't like strangers 6 He asked to have a look at my paper/asked if he could have . . . I said I hadn't . . . and asked him to wait . . . He said he couldn't wait long as he was getting 7 she said we had woken *or* woke . . . the previous night and that we must try . . . that night. I promised we would 8 he complained that the soup was cold . . . and asked why he never had . . . She explained it was because the kitchen was . . . If he insisted on . . . he must/would have to put up . . . He suggested getting . . . She said (that) she wouldn't 9 he said my licence was . . . I admitted that it was but said I had applied . . . He warned me next time to apply . . . before my current one had expired 10 I said I'd have the money for him the following . . . and asked if I should post it to him. Tom asked me to keep it in my safe till he could come . . . a lot of his mail had been going astray lately and he would hate to lose one of my 11 he asked to borrow my map/asked if he could borrow my map. I said he was always borrowing it and advised him to get/suggested his getting/asked why he didn't get one of his own 12 he said that when we heard . . . we were to shut . . . and go *or* he told us to shut the windows and go downstairs when we heard . . . I asked what we were to do/should do if the stairs were blazing 13 she asked if I could hear the noise and what I thought it was. I (said I) thought it was . . . but she (said she) thought it was . . . and advised me to go/said I'd better go 14 they told Ann it was her turn . . . that night. She protested that it couldn't be as she (had) babysat the previous night and the night before that, and she was only supposed . . . They begged her to do it just that once and promised not to ask her to do any the following week 15 he said it was the best . . . problem was that they expected . . . The tourists asked why he had brought them there. He told them not to get excited as he kept ties . . . in their predicament, and he asked what colour they would like, adding that the ties were 16 I suggested starting/offered to start/asked if I should start the next day. Tom said he'd rather I started that day 17 I advised her to go and see the film as it might help her . . . Ann pointed out that the film was 18 he said he saw/had seen . . . and one of them (had) sat up and waved to him. I asked which of them (had) waved. He said he didn't know; he wasn't/hadn't been near enough 19 I asked what (had) caused . . . He said she must . . . but he couldn't understand . . . the wreck was 20 she said her car wouldn't start. The battery was flat. She asked them to give her a push just to start her . . . Bill advised her to sell the car. Peter said nobody would buy it and suggested putting 21 he said he'd been given . . . that he'd have to . . . I suggested (his) throwing . . . and saving himself . . . *or* I advised him to throw . . . and save himself 22 he told me to press . . . I said that last time he (had) told me to press . . . He said that that had been 23 Tom told me not to brake if I found myself skidding as that only made . . . He

advised me to try . . . I said I knew what I should do but that when I
started . . . I got . . . that I did. Tom told me to stop and let him . . . as we
were just coming . . . and he didn't want 24 he said he'd run out . . . and
asked if I'd got any. I said I hadn't but offered to go out and get some/but
said I'd go out . . . if he liked. He told me not to bother as he'd missed
25 he said that repairs to cars rented from them must be arranged through
their office. So if anything went wrong with the car I'd hired I was to ring
. . . on my card. The office was open . . . I asked what I should do if
something went 26 asked why he hadn't . . . He said that they had
signalled but that she had come *or* came on in and had run *or* ran aground.
I asked what was going . . . He said they were going . . . but that if they
didn't get . . . that night . . . she would be there till she broke up, and
there'd be 27 I asked why he was spending . . . on the accounts. He said
he couldn't . . . he seemed to be . . . and that meant he'd have to . . . of his
own money . . . I asked if he'd like me to go through them and see if I
could . . . He said he wouldn't, but he'd like me to lend him 28 I asked
(Jack) why he was looking so . . . He said he'd just asked Ann to marry
him and she'd refused. I said I thought she preferred . . . and advised him
to cut his hair and shave off his beard 29 she asked how he (had) got up
the tree. He said he (had) used . . . but that someone went/had gone off
. . . he was sawing. He told her to go . . . and not just stand 30 he asked
if I was ill and I said that I wasn't. He asked if I'd slept well the previous
night and I said that I had. Then he asked/wanted to know why I was
sitting . . . were working, and told me to go out . . . and give 31 he
asked/told passengers . . . to go . . . Peter advised Mary to go . . . but said
that he'd have to . . . He said he'd take . . . than she would and asked her
to wait for him 32 Tom says that we aren't to worry about him. He
wasn't badly . . . and is being . . . He says he's coming back next
Wednesday . . . and wants us to meet the plane 33 he asked what he was
to do with his . . . She advised him to stuff . . . but warned him not to put
. . . or they'd go hard 34 he suggested driving on . . . and trying . . . I
asked what we would do if that was . . . He said we'd just . . . as it would
be 35 she said they had . . . but that he was . . . wouldn't hear me . . . I
asked what I was to do/should do if he woke up. Ann told me to give him
some of the biscuits if he started growling. I asked how she knew he liked
those . . . She assured me that all dogs liked them. It said so 36 he
warned me that if I even touched . . . alarm bells would ring . . . and I
would be . . . I asked if he was . . . He told me to try it and see

Exercise 165 1 suggested going . . . and I agreed 2 urged his colleagues
to show the nation that they were worthy of their 3 begged his mother to
let him stay . . . that night 4 suggested eating . . . Tom objected that it
was/would be . . . and suggested going to her flat . . . and having
5 suggested leaving/that they should leave the wrecked car there . . . and
said it might remind 6 She said the neighbours would object and Tom
said he didn't care 7 suggested going . . . Mary agreed reluctantly
8 said that Tom had made the mess and that he was to clear 9 said that
the next day was . . . and suggested buying their mother 10 suggested

193

taking . . . and camping out. Mary suggested going . . . and being
11 suggested giving a party but her husband was against the idea/opposed
the idea 12 advised them not to jump . . . and suggested waiting until
they heard . . . of the rumour *or* suggested that they shouldn't jump . . .
but wait 13 warned him that . . . would say it was . . . he said they could
say what they liked/he expressed complete indifference
14 urged/exhorted the nations to forget . . . and to work 15 begged him
to let her explain and asked him not to be 16 told the gardener to let the
children play . . . if they wanted to adding that she was sure they wouldn't
do 17 suggested staying there/that we should stay there till the storm
had passed 18 grumbled that it was . . . and said that they should do

Exercise 166 1 said that if what she said was true he would have to
go/must go 2 said that he had to/would have to/must be . . . the following
day 3 asked if he had to make 4 told us that we mustn't come 5 told
my nephew that his ticket would cost . . . he said . . . he would have to go
. . . the next day 6 The park notice said that dogs must be kept 7 said
that Tom must/would have to work 8 said that I needn't come in the
following day and told me to take 9 said he had to/must go . . . the
following day as he had 10 The notice said that passengers must not
lean 11 said that there must be . . . because there was smoke 12 told
him that when he was . . . he would have to tie his 13 said that port wine
must never be shaken 14 said he hadn't had . . . and that he must be
15 said that the passport photo wasn't like her and that she must
have/would have to have 16 told the children that they must not 17 said
that I needn't/wouldn't have to/didn't have to get up till nine the next
day 18 The railway regulations said passengers must be 19 asked
(Tom) how he had got his dog . . . He/Tom said that he had carried him. I
said that he must be 20 said that I mustn't/wasn't to tell anyone what she
had just told me 21 asked (his mother) if he had to/need eat it all and she
said that he must/had to 22 said that she had had to drive his pigs out of
her garden 23 The notice said that sticks . . . must be left 24 asked her
if she had to do it all that night or if she couldn't leave some for the
following day 25 told me that when I went through Bayeux I must see
26 said that I must walk faster, I was far too slow 27 told me that I
mustn't forget . . . or my friend would have to pay 28 said that he
needn't tell me how grateful he was

Exercise 167 1 'Would he like to go to the concert?' she asked, 'I'm sure
he would,' I said. 2 'Look where you are going,' she said to me; 'the road
is full of holes and very badly lit.' 3 'While we were bathing,' they said,
'we saw someone examining our clothes.' 4 'Have you looked
everywhere?' I asked. 'Yes,' she said. 5 'Let's give her/what about giving
her a bottle of wine?' he said. 6 'The new carpet has arrived. Where am I
to put/shall I put it?' he asked. 7 'An enormous load of firewood was
dumped at my front gate two days ago. Since then I haven't been able to
get my car out,' he said. 8 'Have some more wine?' they said. 'Yes,
please,' I replied. 9 'If you find the front door locked, go round the back,'

he said to me. 10 'Who are you?' she asked the burglars, 'And who let
you in?' 'Sit down and keep quiet,' they replied, 'unless you want to get
hurt.' 11 'What was the weather like during your holiday?' he asked. 'It
was awful,' I answered. 12 'Let's go down to the harbour and see/What
about going down . . . and seeing if we can hire a boat?' he suggested.
13 'If you don't like escalators, you can go up the emergency staircase,'
he told me. 'Thank you, I'll do that,' I said. 14 'What about Tom and you
going ahead and getting the tickets?' or 'Suppose you and Tom go ahead
and get the tickets?' he said to me. 15 'I think your electric iron is
unsafe. I advise you to have it seen to' or 'I should have it seen to' or
'Why don't you have it seen to?' he said to me. 16 'If war breaks/broke
out, I shall/should have to leave the country at once,' he said. 17 'Did
you enjoy house hunting?' I asked him. 'No,' he said. 18 'I am surprised
to see that the grandfather clock has stopped. Has anyone been fiddling
with it?' she asked. 19 'I tried to ring up my mother several times
yesterday, but I didn't succeed in getting through,' she said. 20 'Would
you like to borrow this book?' I asked her. 'I have read it already, thank
you, and didn't like it very much.' 21 'Are you going to the dance? Let's
make up a party and go together' or 'What about making up a party and
going together?' he said. 22 'Stop making a fuss about nothing! You are
lucky to have got a seat at all,' I told her. 23 'Do you want a single or a
return ticket?' asked the clerk in the booking office. 'Is a return any
cheaper?' I asked. 'It makes no difference,' he said. 24 'I hope you won't
be offended,' my employer said, 'if I tell you that in my opinion you would
do better in some other kind of job.' 25 'If your wheels had gone a couple
of inches nearer the edge, madam,' said the AA man, 'the car would have
plunged into the ravine.' 26 'You mustn't mind if the first one isn't any
good,' he said to me. 27 'Do you think I am a liar?' he asked the crowd.
'Yes!' they shouted. 28 Stopping a man in the street, I asked,
'Would/could you help me with my car?' 'Would/will it take long?' asked
the man. 'I'm on my way to catch a train.'

21 Time clauses

Exercise 168 1 begins 2 gets 3 open 4 are 5 start 6 receive/have
received 7 like 8 are 9 slows 10 stops 11 will explain, are
12 read/have read 13 have been 14 have cleaned . . . and painted or
clean . . . and paint 15 have settled/settle 16 see 17 have seen
18 have finished/finish 19 have reached/reach 20 have done 21 lifts/has
lifted 22 arrives 23 know, will give 24 has cooled/cools 25 have
finished/finish 26 have given 27 will tell, are 28 have been, will let
29 have flown 30 has been 31 come 32 shall/will have finished, see,
finish/have finished, start 33 have seen 34 have driven 35 will give,
wakes 36 arrived

Exercise 169 1 gets 2 come 3 stops 4 have done 5 saw 6 comes
7 go/are going 8 get; see 9 come, cross 10 arrive; gets 11 am sitting;
am walking 12 has finished/finishes 13 starts 14 have paid/pay
15 arrives 16 have worked 17 do/are doing 18 have done 19 have
finished 20 have had 21 have been 22 have read 23 reached 24 has
saved 25 are queueing 26 shall/will be cruising 27 am 28 have seen
29 retires/has retired 30 has saved 31 stopped 32 arrived 33 had
finished/finished 34 am waiting 35 was cleaning, or pretending
36 needed

Exercise 170 1 As 2 As 3 When 4 As 5 When 6 As 7 As
8 When 9 When/Whenever 10 when 11 As 12 As 13 When 14 as
15 When 16 When/Whenever 17 As 18 as 19 as 20 as 21 As
22 When/Whenever 23 as 24 When 25 as 26 as 27 as 28 As
29 When 30 When 31 As 32 As 33 When 34 When 35 As
36 When

22 Phrasal verbs

Exercise 171 1 out, in/back 2 for 3 on with 4 out of 5 up to 6 away
with 7 up 8 out/about 9 off/away 10 up to 11 out 12 on with
13 over 14 over 15 up 16 away 17 through 18 off 19 up to
20 through 21 away 22 over 23 off 24 up to 25 in 26 over 27 out
28 for 29 off/into/on 30 on 31 up to 32 back 33 on/along
34 away with 35 back/in 36 out of

Exercise 172 1 on 2 back 3 down 4 after 5 in 6 ahead
7 off/away/back 8 at/for 9 out of/away from 10 back 11 up 12 back
13 up with 14 round/back 15 out 16 for 17 out for 18 out 19 back
20 forward to 21 in 22 into/at 23 on 24 out on/on to
25 through/over 26 through 27 up 28 up 29 up, down 30 foward to
31 up to 32 at 33 down on 34 up 35 on 36 through

Exercise 173 1 to/round 2 ahead/on 3 round 4 for 5 on 6 out
7 into/over 8 off 9 up 10 out 11 in for 12 out 13 down 14 round
15 up to/over to 16 through 17 back on 18 through with 19 up
20 into 21 down 22 back 23 over/through 24 off 25 along/on
26 off/away 27 away/off 28 in for 29 across/upon 30 up 31 without
32 down 33 round 34 on with 35 out 36 down

Exercise 174 1 in 2 away with 3 aback 4 through 5 up 6 up
7 down 8 after 9 after 10 over 11 up 12 back 13 up against 14 to
15 away with 16 up 17 down 18 off 19 over/through 20 to 21 over
22 for 23 into 24 in 25 for 26 out of 27 out 28 on 29 away 30 in
31 down 32 down 33 on/over 34 into 35 in 36 over

Exercise 175 1 down 2 away 3 at 4 into 5 down 6 in 7 down
8 off 9 out 10 on 11 down 12 on 13 for 14 off 15 out 16 in
17 down 18 at 19 for 20 off 21 up 22 out 23 down 24 off 25 in
26 up 27 out 28 off 29 back 30 up 31 out 32 into 33 over 34 up
35 out of 36 out/up

Exercise 176 1 away 2 back 3 up 4 off 5 for 6 back 7 off 8 out
9 off/out 10 up 11 down 12 up 13 away 14 out 15 up 16 away
17 on 18 in 19 up 20 off 21 down to 22 up 23 out 24 out/off
25 up with 26 up 27 on 28 up for 29 up 30 out 31 up 32 down
33 up 34 forward/on 35 out 36 down

Exercise 177 1 away 2 back 3 down 4 in 5 through 6 off 7 off
8 out of 9 off 10 in 11 away 12 up 13 down 14 out 15 out 16 on
17 in with 18 down/on 19 down 20 up/away 21 off 22 off 23 over
24 off 25 in 26 up 27 up 28 off 29 up 30 down 31 off 32 out
33 back on 34 out/on 35 round 36 out

Exercise 178 1 about 2 for 3 away with 4 for 5 out/off
6 over/about 7 for 8 up 9 away 10 off/out 11 through 12 for
13 up 14 round/to 15 out 16 up 17 up 18 over 19 up 20 up
21 round 22 in 23 about/around 24 out 25 out 26 away 27 down
28 out 29 up 30 on 31 up 32 down 33 up 34 up 35 on to 36 up

Exercise 179 1 out 2 out of 3 up 4 about 5 back 6 in 7 out
8 back 9 up 10 up to 11 for 12 out 13 up 14 out 15 up 16 up
17 up to 18 in 19 up 20 up 21 in 22 out 23 back 24 on 25 for
26 away 27 into 28 out 29 out 30 on 31 by 32 up 33 off
34 up for 35 down 36 off

Exercise 180 1 over 2 out 3 for 4 off 5 up 6 out 7 to/about 8 out
9 up 10 in/out/round 11 away 12 through 13 back 14 up 15 up
16 out 17 up 18 out 19 out of 20 out 21 away 22 after 23 up with
24 up 25 to/about 26 up with 27 in/up 28 out 29 down 30 out
31 up/in 32 back 33 off 34 away 35 up 36 out

Exercise 181 1 down 2 up 3 off 4 up 5 up 6 down 7 in 8 up
9 out 10 up 11 in 12 at 13 up 14 up 15 up 16 with 17 out 18 on
19 off 20 up 21 out 22 out 23 on 24 up 25 down 26 for
27 out for 28 up 29 off, off 30 on 31 without 32 out 33 down
34 up 35 out 36 up to

Exercise 182 1 out of 2 out for 3 up to 4 up to 5 up with
6 up against 7 up for 8 away with 9 back on 10 out of 11 up for
12 away with 13 in with 14 up with/in 15 on with 16 on to
17 away with 18 up to 19 back on 20 out for 21 round to 22 over to
23 up to 24 out of 25 up with 26 up with 27 up to 28 down on
29 forward to 30 out to 31 on with 32 out of 33 out on/on to 34 up
with 35 up, down 36 in for

Exercise 183   1 account for   2 blew it up   3 broke off   4 called off
5 carry out my orders/carry my orders out   6 catch up with them/catch
them up   7 clear up a mystery/clear a mystery up   8 came across   9 come
off   10 came round/to   11 cutting road deaths down/cutting down road
deaths   12 enter for/go in for   13 get off/out of   14 get out of it   15 gave
out the names/gave the names out   16 give up smoking   17 go up, come
down   18 went into/looked into   19 set off/out   20 take up   21 bring up
children/bring children up   22 held up   23 turn up   24 picked Spanish
up/picked up Spanish   25 up to you   26 jump at it   27 keep off · 28 keep
up with him   29 knocked him out   30 let you off   31 getting over it
32 leave/miss out *or* leave/miss . . . out   33 looking them up   34 make up
for   35 mix up   36 pay me back/out

Exercise 184   1 Let me in   2 looked at her   3 rang him up   4 look after
5 made it up   6 pull through   7 look out   8 put off   9 look on him   10 put
on uniform   11 look into   12 looked through me   13 look up my
sister/look my sister up   14 put out   15 put up   16 put you all up   17 ring
up   18 runs down his own garden   19 run down   20 running into   21 run
up against   22 put in for   23 call in/send for   24 settle down
25 sat/stayed up   26 stand for   27 stood by him   28 takes after him
29 took up golf   30 taking me in   31 throw/give up a good job   32 turned
down her application/turned her application down   33 turned out
34 wound up   35 work out   36 took on, worn out, give it up

Exercise 185   1 went   2 broken   3 set   4 turn   5 wore   6 called   7 wait
8 call/put   9 put   10 try   11 get   12 come   13 knock   14 leave   15 take
16 sent   17 carrying   18 let   19 put   20 hand/pass   21 looks
22 go/keep   23 turning   24 move   25 put/switch/turn   26 put   27 puts
28 Come   29 put   30 see   31 got/jumped   32 get   33 taken   34 took
35 took   36 showing

Exercise 186   1 up to   2 brought up   3 break up   4 caught up with
5 been up to   6 do up   7 drew up   8 fill in   9 got up   10 gave it up
11 gave up   12 went up to   13 grow up   14 held up   15 keep up with
16 picked up   17 make up for   18 pick up   19 lock up
20 pulled up/drew up   21 put up with   22 tied up   23 mixed up
24 locked up   25 ring him up, look up   26 turned up   27 took up   28 put
up   29 settle up   30 make up   31 make up   32 wash up   33 stood up for
34 wound up   35 stay up/sit up   36 sat up

Exercise 187   1 dropped out   2 carry out   3 breaks out   4 cut it out
5 find out   6 getting out   7 died out   8 cut/leave out   9 make out
10 backed out   11 throw out   12 pick out   13 keep out   14 looking out
15 Look/Watch out   16 sold out   17 ran out   18 rub it out   19 pointed
out   20 see/show you out   21 turned out   22 set out   23 put out
24 moving out   25 wipe out   26 work/find out   27 find out   28 put out
29 wear them out   30 blew out   31 gone out   32 let them out   33 fall
out   34 come out   35 look out/watch out   36 stands out

Exercise 188 1 turned it down   2 running down   3 took it down   4 Put it down   5 settle down   6 took over   7 talk it over   8 ran away   9 let me down   10 went over/through   11 backed away   12 closing down   13 got over   14 look down   15 broke down   16 look it over   17 backed away   18 clear away   19 ran away   20 shouted down   21 was over   22 do away   23 die down   24 burnt down   25 broke down   26 turned away   27 boiled over   28 give it away   29 handed down   30 puts away   31 got/ran away   32 talk over   33 cut down   34 come/go down   35 went down/were over   36 turn over

Exercise 189 1 get on   2 take over   3 jump at   4 taken aback   5 make up   6 carry on   7 think it over   8 breaks up   9 look in   10 fix you up   11 turn it down   12 hanging about   13 turn up   14 taking on   15 closing down   16 settled down   17 picked up   18 handed over   19 take to   20 looking Bill up and down   21 care for   22 go on   23 put on   24 take off   25 pointed out   26 answer me back   27 fell out   28 stand up for   29 keep out   30 look up   31 looking for   32 puts customers off   33 fall off   34 make out   35 ordered about   36 put up with   37 broke out   38 put in   39 make up for   40 taken in

Exercise 190 1 got up   2 washed up   3 set out/off   4 pick up   5 get on   6 turned out   7 care for   8 took to   9 brought up   10 pointing out   11 showing off   12 turn/switch off   13 burn down   14 ring up   15 switch/turn off   16 get in   17 locked up   18 break in   19 go up   20 rang up   21 see to   22 held on   23 got in   24 turned/switched off   25 went on   26 got out   27 handing/passing round   28 pulled/drew up   29 let you off   30 get away with   31 put out   32 put up with   33 looks up to   34 grows up   35 looking foward to   36 looking for   37 fed up   38 caught up with   39 dying away   40 keep up with   41 get to   42 put us up   43 sold out   44 talking over